INTRODU
OLDER LANGUAGES

W. P. LEHMANN
Founding Editor

1. AN INTRODUCTION TO OLD IRISH
   R. P. M. and W. P. Lehmann

2. AN INTRODUCTION TO THE GOTHIC LANGUAGE
   William H. Bennett

3. AN INTRODUCTION TO OLD FRENCH
   William W. Kibler

4. AN INTRODUCTION TO OLD OCCITAN
   William D. Paden

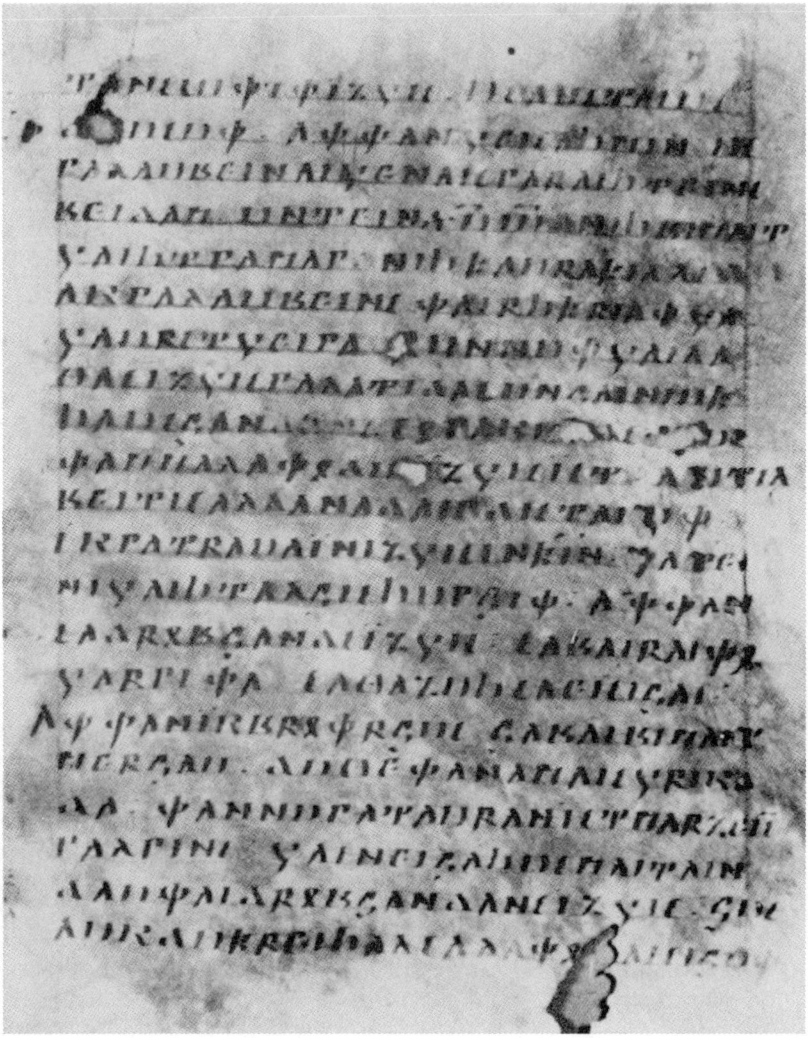

I. Cod. Ambrosianus B sup., fol. 112r: Galatians 5.4–13 (photograph by courtesy of the Biblioteca Ambrosiana).

c d

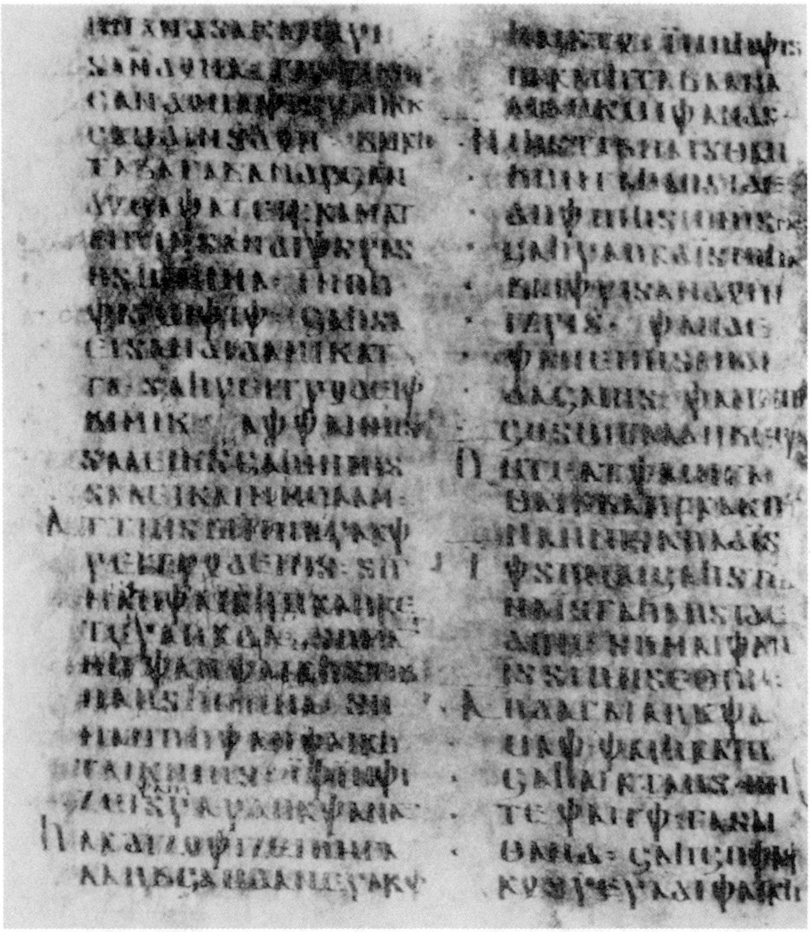

II. Cod. Ambrosianus E 147 sup., p. 310: Skeireins VIcd (photograph by courtesy of the Biblioteca Ambrosiana).

AN INTRODUCTION TO THE GOTHIC LANGUAGE

WILLIAM H. BENNETT

The MLA gratefully acknowledges the generous help of Paul Roberge, Frederick W. Schwink, and Christopher M. Stevens, who provided numerous corrections to *Introduction to the Gothic Language*, making the paperback a more accurate and reliable text for its student and scholar readers.

Printed in the United States of America
Third paperback printing 2006

Library of Congress Cataloging-in-Publication Data

Bennett, William Holmes.
An introduction to the Gothic language / William H. Bennett.
p. cm. — (Introductions to older languages ; 2)
Includes bibliographical references and index.
ISBN-10: 0-87352-295-8 (paper)
ISBN-13: 978-0-87352-295-3 (paper)
1. Gothic language—Grammar. I. Title. II. Series.
PD1123.B4 1999
439'.9—dc21 99-26535
ISSN 1099-0313

Published by The Modern Language Association of America
26 Broadway, New York, New York, 10004-1789
www.mla.org

FOREWORD

William Bennett's *An Introduction to the Gothic Language* is the second in the series of introductory texts on older languages authorized by the Committee on Research Activities. Gothic has traditionally been the Indo-European dialect through which Germanists made their way into Indo-European linguistics as well as comparative Germanic linguistics and philology. Bennett's *Introduction* reflects this position for the language, providing a thorough treatment of the basic problems, especially in phonology and morphology.

Since the Gothic texts are literal translations of the Greek original, they give only meager information on syntax. For this reason a basic principle of the series has been modified, in including materials which are not originals. If any contemporary scholar could produce materials in accordance with those handed down, this distinction must go to William Bennett. Moreover, this edition is based on three previous editions which have been widely used. Bennett's thoroughly tested handbook may therefore provide further generations of students with thorough and well-planned guidance to the Gothic language and important topics associated with its study.

I would like to thank Helen-Jo Jakusz Hewitt for preparation of the glossary with references to each occurrence of a form; support for the preparation was provided by the Research Institute of the University of Texas at Austin.

W. P. Lehmann

PREFACE

An Introduction to the Gothic Language has been written specifically for beginning students. It presents twenty-seven graded readings, each accompanied by a vocabulary and an explanation of grammatical details; the final chapter provides a sample of the Codex Argenteus. Among the readings, the first seven are in effect preliminary exercises; the text on page 8, for example, contains thirty-seven case and number forms of masculine *o*-declension nouns and fifteen of *sa*. The remaining twenty readings represent the Gothic Bible and the *Skeireins*. The external history of the language is outlined in Chapters 2 to 7, the elements of phonetics in Chapters 8 to 10, and the essentials of phonologic and analogic change in Chapter 11. The phonologic history of Gothic extends through Chapters 12 to 27. The terminology used in designating inflectional categories reflects an Indo-European rather than a purely Germanic point of view.

After long consideration I have canceled earlier plans for adding a reference grammar, which would greatly lengthen the present volume and yet would not differ very markedly from the grammars that are already available.

This book has profited from suggestions offered by students and colleagues alike. Within the Modern Language Association, I am greatly indebted to the Committee on Research Activities, to the Director of Research Programs, Walter S. Achtert, and to the founder and general editor of this MLA series, Winfred P. Lehmann, who has generously provided a number of useful suggestions. Dr. Helen-Jo Jakusz Hewitt has prepared the admirable computerized glossary. As a visiting colleague, E. A. Thompson has been very helpful with the external history of Gothic. To all who have aided, and especially to my wife for her unfailing encouragement, my profound thanks.

Decatur, Georgia — William H. Bennett

CONTENTS

CONTENTS

GOTHIC TEXTS

CONTENTS

ABBREVIATIONS & SYMBOLS

Arm.	Armenian	OE	Old English
Av.	Avestan	OFr.	Old French
CL	Classical Latin	OFris.	Old Frisian
Cret.	Cretan	OHG	Old High German
Cz.	Czech	OI	Old Icelandic
Dor.	Doric	OIr.	Old Irish
Fr.	French	OL	Old Latin
Gc.	(Common) Germanic	OS	Old Saxon
Gk.	Greek	Osc.	Oscan
Go.	Gothic	OSw.	Old Swedish
Hit.	Hittite	OW	Old Welsh
IE	Indo-European	PGc.	Proto-Germanic
It.	Italian	pre-Gc.	pre-Germanic
L	Latin	Pre-Go.	Pre-Gothic
Lesb.	Lesbian	Sk.	Sanskrit
Let.	(early) Lettic, Latvian	Sp.	Spanish
Lith.	(early) Lithuanian	Umbr.	Umbrian
LL	Late Latin	Ved.	Vedic
ME	Middle English	WS	West Saxon
MHG	Middle High German	>	developed to
NE	New (Modern) English	<	developed from
NHG	New (Modern) High German	/	alternating with
OCS	Old Church Slavonic		

An asterisk (*) after a word form indicates that it is not recorded; thus Go. *kniu** 'knee' does not appear in the singular. An asterisk before a form implies that it is hypothetical; since all Indo-European, Proto-Germanic, and Pre-Gothic forms are reconstructed, they will be cited here without this marking. In paradigms, forms not attested within their own inflectional subclasses are enclosed within square brackets [ ]. In texts, editorial insertions are written within angle brackets <>, editorial deletions within square brackets [ ].

Standard abbreviations are used throughout the text for grammatical terms and for other words common in linguistic studies:

for the three genders: m. f. n.
for the five cases: N V G D A
for the three numbers: sg. du. (dual) pl.
for parts of speech: adv. adj. cj.
for verbal forms: imper. infin. opt. p.p. pret.

A list of abbreviations used in the glossary appears on page 137.

Qēnái meinái þizái liubōstōn

THE PLACE OF GOTHIC IN INDO-EUROPEAN AND GERMANIC LINGUISTICS

Indo-European, the common ancestor of most European and some Asiatic languages, has left no written records, nor have its first descendants. At an early period, probably before 2500 B.C., the speech of the Indo-European tribal communities had already become divergent, subsequently developing into parent forms of Indo-Iranian, Greek, Italic, Celtic, Germanic, Baltic, Slavic, Albanian, Armenian, as well as of languages with no modern representatives—Tocharian, Anatolian, etc.; these in turn were to break up in preliterate times, leaving groups and subgroups of descendant Indo-European languages.

Proto-Germanic, the common parent of the Germanic group, had broken up into several dialects before the beginning of our era. Among these was **Pre-Gothic**, the immediate ancestor of the Gothic language. The essential features of Pre-Gothic, like those of Proto-Germanic and Indo-European, can be determined only through reconstruction.

Gothic is known chiefly through extensive portions of a biblical translation ascribed to Wulfila (c. 311–c. 383), the apostle and bishop of the West Goths. Among the older Germanic literary records, which include Scandinavian, English, Frisian, Saxon, Low Franconian, and High German texts, the Gothic are by far the earliest. The first comparable writings in the other Germanic languages are four to nine centuries later. More significant from a linguistic point of view, however, is the fact that Gothic is the most generally archaic representative of the Germanic group to appear in extensive specimens. The only prior records of Germanic are the first few runic inscriptions, which are very brief, and individual loanwords preserved in non-Germanic languages. It is for this reason that the study of Gothic is the foundation of Germanic linguistics and constitutes an important factor in comparative Indo-European grammar.

1
PRONUNCIATION

1.1. The Gothic alphabet (see p. 123) is transcribed with the letters *a b d e f g h ƕ* (labialized *h*) *i j k l m n o p q r s t þ* (the Old English thorn) *u w x z*.

VOWELS

1.2. In comparative grammar the diacritic marks macron (¯) and acute (´) are added to Gothic vowel spellings in order to indicate original distinctions in length and quality:

SPELLING	VALUE	AS IN GERMAN	EXAMPLES
a	[a]	Stadt	ana, faran, salt
ā	[ā]	Staat	fāhan, hāhan
ē	[ē]	geht	mēna, nē, tēkan
i	[i]	Widder	ita, silba, wasti
ei	[ī]	wider	ei, leik, marei
ō	[ō]	Lohn	blōma, namō, ō
u	[u]	Tunnel	munan, ufar, sunu
ū	[ū]	tun	fūls, rūna, ūt

In the time of Wulfila *ai au* represented only open (low-mid) vowels, but etymologically each of the spellings *ai au* may represent a short vowel, a long vowel, or a diphthong. These etymological values are highly important in comparative grammar, and they are regularly assumed in comparing Gothic with other Indo-European languages. Since this *Introduction* is designed to instruct students in Germanic comparative grammar, the etymological values of *ai au* are indicated throughout.

The short vowels are distinguished by means of the spellings *aí aú*, with the acute above the second letter:

aí	[e]	Bett	baíran, taíhun, faíhu
aú	[o]	Dock	daúr, faúra, taúhun

The long vowels are not marked:

ai	[ę̄]	Bett (prolonged)	faian, saian, waian
au	[ǭ]	Dock (prolonged)	bauan, sauil, taui

The diphthongs are distinguished by means of the diacritic spellings *ái áu*, with the acute above the first letter:

ái	[aj]	Kaiser	áins, twái, nimái
áu	[aw]	Kraut	áuk, láun, nimáu

iu was nearly like *ew* in English *few* but was stressed on the first element: [íw], e.g., *diups*, *iup*, *siuks*.

Vocalic *w* in words taken from Greek corresponded to Gk. [y] (like *ü* in German *dünn*), but this vowel was foreign to Gothic. *w* was probably pronounced:

(a) As a close, native *u*-vowel occurring between consonants and finally after a consonant: *Lwstrws*, final *-w* in *waúrstw*

(b) As the vowel-glide [w] in other positions: *waúrstwa, lēw*, *kawtsjōn* (*j* like *y* in English *you*) for L *cautionem*

CONSONANTS

1.3. *k l m n p t* were pronounced approximately as in English: *x* was like *k*: *Xristus*. *q* represented [k^w], i.e., a lip-rounded *k*: *qēns*, *riqis*. For practical purposes, *r* may be pronounced as a tongue-point trill.

1.4. *b* had two values. Medially after a vowel or diphthong, it represented [ƀ], a sound resembling that of *v* in English *have* but formed with both lips (bilabial): *haban*, *ibns*, *láibōs*. Elsewhere, *b* represented [b] as in English *bob*: *baíran*, *arbi*, *lamba*. *bb* denoted a prolonged (double) [b]: *abba* [áb-ba] (see 1.14).

1.5. *d* likewise had two positional values. Medially after a vowel or diphthong, it represented [ð], a sound like that of *th* in English *father*: *fadar*, *hidrē*, *páida*. Elsewhere, *d* represented [d], approximately as in English *did*: *daúr*, *huzd*, *land*. *dd* indicated a prolonged (double) [d]: *Addin* [ád-din], *iddja* [íd-dja]. See 1.14.

1.6. *f* was formed somewhat as in English *fife* but probably was bilabial like *b*, above: *afar*, *filu*, *fimf*.

1.7. As in Greek, *gg* was used to spell [ŋg] as in English *finger*: *figgrs*, *laggei*, *siggwan*. Similarly, *gk* represented [ŋk] as in English *ink*, and *gq* represented [ŋk^w], roughly as in English *inkwell*: *drigkan*, *dragk*, *sigqan* [siŋk^{w}an].

The stems *bliggw-* 'scourge,' *glaggw-* 'accurate, diligent,' *skuggw-* 'mirror,' and *triggw-* 'faithful, true' may have contained [gg] in Pre-Gothic, but by the time of Wulfila [gg] probably had become [ŋg] as in *siggwan*, above.

1.8. In Proto-Germanic, *g*, when not occurring before *g k q* represented [ǥ], a sound like that of *g* in North German *sagen*. [ǥ] may be produced by voicing the sound of *ch* in German *ach*: Go. *dagōs*, *steigan*, *liugan*, *gaf*. When occurring finally or before final *s* or *t*, *g* represented the corresponding voiceless sound [x], as in German *ach*: *dags*, *dag*, *balg*, *magt*.

1.9. In Proto-Germanic, *h* represented [x], as in German *ach*, and *ƕ* represented lip-rounded [x^w]: *hláifs*, *jah*, *mahts*; *aƕa*, *ƕō*, *leiƕan*.

h in the time of Wulfila probably denoted [h] as in English *he*, and it is possible that *ƕ* denoted lip-rounded [h^w] or voiceless [ʍ], but for the purposes of comparative grammar it is convenient to retain the older pronunciations [x x^w].

1.10. *j* was pronounced like *y* in *you*: *arbja*, *jēr*, *juk*.

1.11. *s* was pronounced as in *hiss*, *z* as in *buzz*: *is*, *saísō*, *was*; *huzd*, *izē*.

1.12. *þ* represented voiceless [þ], a sound like that of *th* in *myth*, *thorn*: *miþ*, *þaúrnus*, *þō*.

1.13. *l r m n* may have been syllabic (i.e., may have formed the nucleus of a syllable, as in English *meddle* [medl̥]) when:

(a) Final after consonants: *hunsl*, *tagr*, *bagm*, *sōkn*

(b) Between consonants: *fugls*, *akrs*, *máiþms*, *táikns*

1.14. Prolonged consonants were normally doubled in spelling: *inn* (contrast *in*), *-fill*, *-qiss*. Between vowels, they ended one syllable and began the next: *atta* [át-ta], *allái* [ál-laj]. On *gg* for [ŋg], as in Greek, see 1.7. Consonant clusters had no "silent" letters: *kniwa*, *lamb*, *wlits*, *wraks*.

STRESS

1.15. Root syllables bore primary stress (´) when initial, secondary stress (`) when medial or final, as in English *góing* : *éasygòing*, *áche* : *héadàche*. Compare:

hairtō 'heart'	:	*hráinja-haìrts* 'pure-hearted'
gúlþ 'gold'	:	*fíggra-gùlþ* 'finger gold, ring'

Prefixes were stressed like initial roots, above. Compare:

máhts 'might, power'	:	*ún-màhts* 'unmight, weakness'
slḗpiþ 'is asleep'	:	*saí-slḕp* 'was asleep'

Suffix syllables—not including endings—were almost certainly stressed like medial and final root syllables, above, when directly following weak stress (neither ´ nor `); compare:

sálbōnd 'they anoint'	:	*sálbō-dēdeina* 'they might anoint'
míkils 'great'	:	*míkil-dūþs* 'greatness'
þíudans 'king'	:	*þíudin-àssus* 'kingdom, reign'

1.16. Verbs per se had initial primary stress, but preverbs (except *ga-*) began with secondary stress. Compare:

lḗt 'let thou'	:	*àf-lḗt* 'forgive thou'
saíslēp 'was asleep'	:	*àna-saíslēp* 'fell asleep'
wáit 'I know'	:	*mìþ-wáit* 'am conscious of'

Accordingly, the stress of preverbs plus verbs contrasted sharply with that of compound nouns and adjectives. Contrast:

àf-lḗt 'forgive thou'	:	A *áf-lēt* 'forgiveness'
ànd-nímiþ 'accepts'	:	*ánda-nēms* 'pleasant, acceptable'
mìþ-wáit 'am conscious of'	:	*míþ-wìssei* 'conscience'

1.17. Weak stress occurred on other syllables, namely:

(a) On *ga-* (= German *ge-*), on the interrogative particle *-u*, and on *uh* 'and': *ga-léiks* 'like,' *ga-u-láubjats* 'do ye two believe?' *ní-u* 'not?' *ùb-uh-wṓpi-da* 'and he cried out'

(b) On syllables occurring between other degrees of stress, e.g., the second syllables of *àna-saíslēp* and *sálbō-dēdeina*

(c) On vowels of suffixes directly following primary or secondary stress, e.g., *-ō-* and *-ei-* in *sálbō-dēdeina*, above

(d) On all final syllables except roots and except suffixes directly following weak stress (1.15): *slḗpiþ*, *þíudin-àssus*, *sálbōnd*, *ànd-nímiþ*, *míþ-wìssei*, etc., above

1.18. Pronounce the Gothic words in 1.2–17. Note that the acute mark, when used to distinguish short *aí aú* and originally diphthongal *ái áu* (1.2), has no bearing on stress.

The Lord's Prayer: Matt. vi.9–13

(9) Atta unsar þu in himinam, weihnái namō þein. (10) qimái þiudinassus þeins. waírþái wilja þeins, swē in himina jah ana aírþái. (11) hláif unsarana þana sinteinan gif uns himma daga. (12) jah aflēt uns þatei skulans sijáima, swaswē jah weis aflētam þáim skulam unsaráim. (13) jah ni briggáis uns in fráistubnjái, ak láusei uns af þamma ubilin; untē þeina ist þiudangardi jah mahts jah wulþus in áiwins. amēn.

PRELIMINARY EXERCISES

2
MASCULINE *o*-DECLENSION; THE INDO-EUROPEAN LANGUAGES

Gabaúrans ist Iēsus in Bēþlahaím

(1) In dagam Hērōdis þiudanis qēmun Iōsēf jah Maria in Bēþlahaím. (2) jah jáinar gabar Maria Iēsu. (3) jah haírdjōs wēsun jáinar ana akra. (4) jah sái aggilus qam us himina. (5) jah qaþ sa aggilus du þáim haírdjam ana þamma akra: (6) haírdjōs sái gabaúrans ist himma daga Xristus in Bēþlahaím; (7) sái sa ist þiudans himinis jah þiudans þiudanē. (8) jah þái haírdjōs gasēƕun jáinar hari himinis jah háusidēdun þis harjis liuþarjans in himinam. (9) galiþun þan sa aggilus jah sa harjis faírra þáim haírdjam in himin. (10) iþ þái waírōs qēmun in wig du gasaíƕan þana þiudan þizei háusidēdun. (11) jah in maúrgin dagis bigētun Iōsēf jah Marian jah Iēsu. (12) afar dagans qēmun jah ·g· þiudanōs. (13) jah þiwōs þizē þiudanē bērun máiþmans. (14) jah þái þiudanōs gēbun þans máiþmans Iēsua, untē sa was þiudans himinis jah þiudans þiudanē.

---

afar dagans   after some days
aggilus m.   angel
akrs 2.3   field
ana (+ D/A)   on, upon, in
bērun   carried (3 pl.)
Bēþlahaím   Bethlehem
bigētun   found (3 pl.)
dags 2.3   day
du (+ D)   to, for, as
faírra   far from, afar
·g· (þreis*)   three
gabar   bore (3 sg.)
gabaúrans   born
galiþun   went (3 pl.)
gasaíƕan   see (infin.)
gasēƕun   saw (3 pl.)
gēbun   gave (3 pl.)
haírdeis 2.3   herdsman
harjis 2.3   host, army
háusidēdun   heard (3 pl.)
Hērōdis G   of Herod
himins 2.3   heaven
himma daga   today, this day
Iēsus, A -u, D -ua   Jesus
in (+ A)   in, into, toward
in (+ D)   in, into, among

Iōsēf Joseph
ist is
iþ but
jah and, also
jáinar there, yonder
liuþareis 2.3 singer
máiþms 2.3 gift
Maria, A -an Mary
maúrgins 2.3 morning
qam came (3 sg.)
qaþ said (3 sg.)
qēmun came (3 pl.)
sa m. (see 2.2–3)
sái lo!
þan then
þiudans 2.3 king
þiwōs 2.3 servants
þizei m. G of whom
untē for, because
us (+ D) out of, from
waír 2.3 man
was was
wēsun were (3 pl.)
wigs 2.3 way, road
Xristus Christ

2.1. Gothic has three genders, which are largely independent of sex: masculine, feminine, and neuter. Nouns have two numbers, singular and plural (some forms also have a dual), and five cases: nominative, vocative, genitive, dative, and accusative. The nominative and vocative are identical in the plural, and in the singular also except when the nominative singular ends in *-s*, as below in 2.3. The nominative and accusative are always identical in the neuter and sometimes in the other genders. In order to simplify paradigms, accordingly, the cases will be listed in the order nominative, vocative, accusative, genitive, dative.

2.2. The demonstrative pronoun *sa* m., *sō* f., *þata* n. 'this, that' serves also as a definite article and as a demonstrative personal pronoun meaning literally 'this one, that one.' When modifying a noun, the demonstrative–definite article agrees with it in case and normally in gender and number.

2.3. A great many Gothic nouns belong to the masculine *o*-declension, e.g., *sa dags* 'the day,' *sa hláifs* 'the bread,' *sa harjis* 'the host, army,' and *sa haírdeis* 'the herdsman.' The label "*o*-declension" refers to the stem vowel in Proto-Indo-European. A typical *o*-stem noun is the word for *wolf*, as in Sk. *vr̥kas*, Gk. *lúkos*, L *lupus*, Go. *wulfs*, on the basis of which IE **wl̥k^{w}os* is reconstructed. The root is **wl̥k^{w}-*, to which some scholars ascribe the meaning 'destroy.' To this a suffix is added in its noun declension: *-o-*; such a suffix is known as a stem vowel. Declensions are named after the stem vowels, which besides *o* are *ā*, *i*, *u*, and *n*. Finally, endings after root and suffix indicate each case, such as *-s* for the nominative singular. The same structure of root, suffix, and ending is found in verbs.

sg.	N	sa		dags	hláifs	harjis	haírdeis
	A	þana	A-V	dag	hláif	[hari]	haírdi
	G	þis		dagis	hláibis	harjis	haírdeis
	D	þamma		daga	hláiba	harja	haírdja

pl.	N	þái	dagōs	hláibōs	harjōs	haírdjōs
	A	þans	dagans	hláibans	harjans	haírdjans
	G	þizē	dagē	hláibē	[harjē]	haírdjē
	D	þáim	dagam	hláibam	harjam	haírdjam

N sg. *-s* is lost after a short vowel plus *r*, e.g., *waír* 'man'; in *stiur* 'calf, steer'; and after *s*, e.g., *hals* (A *hals*) 'neck.' *þiwōs* 'servants' occurs only in the plural nominative and genitive. The alternations *f/b* in *hláifs/hláibis, j/i* in *harjis/hari*, *ei/i/j* in *haírdeis/haírdi/haírdja* result from phonological changes that will be considered separately.

2.4. Decline like:

(a) *sa dags*: *sa áiþs* 'the oath,' *sa bagms* 'the tree,' *sa fisks* 'the fish,' *sa fugls* 'the bird,' *sa stáins* 'the stone'
(b) *sa hláifs*: *sa láufs** 'the leaf'
(c) *sa harjis*: *sa andastaþjis* 'the adversary,' *sa niþjis* 'the kinsman'
(d) *sa haírdeis*: *sa asneis* 'the hireling,' *sa bōkareis* 'the scribe,' *sa sipōneis* 'the follower, disciple'

THE INDO-EUROPEAN LANGUAGES

2.5. Common Indo-European words indicating seasons, flora, and fauna, together with ethnic and geographic data, suggest that the home of the Indo-Europeans was a district connecting southeastern Europe with Asia, probably southern Russia. As the tribes expanded over an increasingly wider area, they became separated into numerous smaller groups, which absorbed varying proportions of other populations. Whether the Indo-Europeans were already of mixed origin is a matter for conjecture; their possession of a common language indicates only that they had been affiliated by social and cultural ties. In the course of the expansion and ethnic mixture, extending over many centuries, the speech of the separate Indo-European groups became progressively divergent, though within each community some degree of linguistic reintegration must have taken place as certain dialects became predominant and others became extinct.

By historic times the tribal expansions had covered a vast area. Some tribes had reached India by way of the Iranian plateau, which had been occupied by a closely related group. Among the **Indo-Iranian** languages, the most archaic Indic representatives are Vedic (c. 1200–c. 800 B.C.) and Sanskrit. East Iranian first appears in the Avestan scriptures of the Zoroastrians, West Iranian in the Old Persian cuneiform inscriptions (c. 520–c. 340 B.C.). A **Tocharian** settlement in Eastern Turkistan has left specimens of two dialects, Agnean and Kuchean, in documents of the sixth to the eighth century of our era. An **Armenian** group had reached Lake Van in Asia Minor before 600 B.C. and produced written records with the introduction of Christianity in the fifth century; the related but little-known Thracian and Phrygian may stem from earlier phases of this same migration. The Hittite records of Asia Minor (second millennium B.C.) represent an **Anatolian** group, probably one of the first to become separated from the parent tribal community.

Several waves of Indo-European tribes entered the Balkan Peninsula. They are represented mainly by **Greek**, beginning with Mycenaean inscriptions of about 1450–1200 B.C., and by **Albanian**, texts of which appear about 2,800 years later. Here too are found fragments of such Indo-European dialects as Thracian and Macedonian. To the neighboring Illyrian may be related the similarly little-known Venetic and Messapic of ancient Italy. A separate **Italic** group has left extensive records, chiefly in Latin; Osco-Umbrian, though perhaps forming a separate group, is usually classified as Italic. From the vernacular Latin of Roman Europe have come the Romance languages: Portuguese, Spanish, Catalan, Provençal, French, Italian, Sardinian, Dalmatian (extinct), Rhaeto-Romanic, and Romanian.

In southern and western Germany are traces of early **Celtic** settlements. Before the present era the Celts had expanded over most of western Europe, extending eastward to a Galatian colony in Asia Minor, but their known languages, which form a Britannic and a Gaelic division, appear only in the far west. To Britannic belong Welsh, the extinct Cornish with its offshoot Breton, and fragmentary specimens of Gaulish beginning in the third century B.C. Gaelic, embracing Irish with its Scottish extension Erse and the extinct Manx, first appears in Old Irish inscribed in the fifth century of our era.

The early home of the **Germanic** tribes lay within a district embracing what is now southern Sweden, Denmark with its neighboring islands, and the northern German lowlands between the Elbe and the Oder. To the east of the Germanic homeland appear Baltic and Slavic settlements. **Baltic** includes Lettic, Latvian, and Lithuanian, with records beginning in the sixteenth century, and the extinct Old Prussian. **Slavic**, which is first known through Old Church Slavonic (Old Bulgarian) of the ninth century, now embraces three divisions: western (Polish, Czechoslovakian, Wendish), eastern (Great, White, and Little Russian), and southern (Bulgarian, Serbo-Croatian, Slovenian).

Linguistic changes that occurred between Indo-European and Germanic times are distinguished as **pre-Germanic**, and those that took place within the earliest form of Germanic as **Proto-Germanic**. Where it is necessary to denote a comparatively late stage of the parent Germanic language, it may be designated by the term **Germanic** or **Common Germanic**.

3
NEUTER *o*-DECLENSION; THE GERMANIC LANGUAGES

Hērōdēs jah maúrþr barnē in Bēþlahaím

(1) Jah was Iēsus miþ Mariin jah Iōsēfa. (2) iþ Hērōdēs gatáujands garūni miþ þáim þiudanam jah gaháusjands bi þata barn jah bi þata liuhaþ in himinam, fullnōda agisis jah hatizis; (3) untē bi waúrda bōkarjē wēsi Iudaiē þiudans gabaúrans in Bēþlahaím in gáuja Iudaias. (4) jah wilda Hērōdēs þata barn usqiman. (5) jah filu waldufneis habands bi witōda, insandida andbahtans in þata gawi du usqiman all barnē und twa jērē habandō; (6) untē þaírh þō tōja maúrþris wilda usqiman Iēsu. (7) iþ aggilus gudis qam us himina jah qaþ du Iōsēfa: usstandands þliuh miþ Mariin jah þamma barna! (8) jah þlaúhun faírra us þamma gáuja. (9) iþ wēsun sáir jah tagra jáinar, jah ni habáidēdun bērusjōs barnē ana kniwam; (10) untē blōþ was ana daúram, jah háubida jah leika þizē barnē wēsun in wigam.

---

agis 3.1 fear
all n. A sg. each, each one
andbahts m. officer, servant
barn 3.1 child
bērusjōs m. parents
bi (+ A) about, regarding
bi (+ D) according to, by
blōþ 3.1 blood
bōkareis m. scribe
daúr 3.1 entrance
filu (+ G) much, many, very
fullnōda became full (3 sg.)
gaháusjands hearing
gatáujands garūni 3.1 consulting
gawi, G gáujis 3.1 district
guþ, G ?gudis God
habáidēdun had (3 pl.)
habands having
hatis 3.1 wrath
háubiþ 3.1 head
Hērōdēs Herod
insandida sent (3 sg.)
Iōsēfa D Joseph
Iudaias G of Judea
Iudaiē G of the Jews
jēr 3.1 year

jēre habandō 3.4 years old
kniwa 3.3 knees
leik 3.1 body, flesh
liuhaþ 3.1 light
Mariin D Mary
maúrþr 3.1 murder
miþ (+ D) with, among
ni not
sáir 3.1 sorrow
tagr 3.1 tear
taui, G tōjis 3.3 deed
twa n. N-A two
þaírh (+ A) through, by
þata 3.1 this, that, the
þlaúhun fled (3 pl.)
und (+ A) up to, until
usqiman kill (infin.)
usstandands þliuh rise and flee!
waldufni 3.3 authority
waúrd 3.1 word
wēsi was (opt. 3 sg.)
wilda wished (3 sg.)
witōþ 3.1 law

3.1. The neuter *o*-declension includes many nouns, e.g., *þata waúrd* 'the word,' *þata witōþ* 'the law,' *þata hatis* 'the wrath,' *þata kuni* 'the race,' and *þata gawi* 'the district':

sg.	N-A	þata	waúrd	witōþ	hatis	kuni	gawi
	G	þis	waúrdis	witōdis	hatizis	kunjis	gáujis
	D	þamma	waúrda	witōda	hatiza	kunja	gáuja
pl.	N-A	þō	waúrda	witōda	hatiza	kunja	gáuja
	G	þizē	waúrdē	witōdē	hatizē	kunjē	gáujē
	D	þáim	waúrdam	witōdam	hatizam	kunjam	gáujam

The alternations *þ/d* in *witōþ witōdis*, *s/z* in *hatis hatizis*, *i/j* in *kuni kunjis*, and *awi/áuj* in *gawi gáujis* result from phonologic changes that will be considered separately. *guþ* 'God' may have been declined like *witōþ*: G *gudis*, D *guda*. In the manuscripts, the nominative-vocative-accusative singular is contracted to $\overline{g\text{þ}}$, the genitive singular to $\overline{g\text{þs}}$, and the dative singular to $\overline{g\text{þa}}$; some scholars take the genitive and dative contractions to represent respectively *guþs guþa. guþ* is neuter by origin but is used in the singular to denote the Hebrew-Christian deity and is treated as a masculine; its plural remains neuter and denotes heathen gods (*þō galiugaguda*).

3.2. Decline like:

(a) *þata waúrd*: *þata gulþ* 'the gold,' *þata haúrn* 'the horn,' *þata juk* 'the yoke,' *þata wein* 'the wine'
(b) *þata witōþ*: *þata háubiþ* 'the head,' *þata liuhaþ* 'the light'
(c) *þata hatis*: *þata riqis* 'the darkness'
(d) *þata kuni*: *þata awēþi* 'the sheepfold,' *þata badi* 'the bed'
(e) *þata gawi*: *þata hawi* 'the grass'

3.3. A few neuter *o*-declension nouns in *-i* have G sg. *-jis* or *-eis*, e.g., *waldufni* 'authority,' G. sg. *waldufn-jis, -eis*. *taui* 'deed' has G *tōjis*, etc. *triu* 'tree' has G *triwis*, etc.; *kniu** 'knee' (no singular forms occur) is similarly declined.

3.4. A partitive genitive occurs frequently, e.g., *akranis* 'some fruit' (lit. 'of fruit'), *all bagmē* 'every tree' (lit. 'each of trees'), *ni was im barnē* 'they had no child' (lit. 'not was to them of children'), *mannē sums* 'a certain man' (lit. 'of men a certain one'), *filu jērē* 'many (of) years.'

THE GERMANIC LANGUAGES

3.5. A number of Germanic tribes, including such peoples as the Goths, Vandals, Burgundians, Herulians, and Rugians, emigrated from their homeland in the course of the last two or three centuries B.C. At the beginning of the present era their settlements extended along the Baltic coast in eastern Germany, the Goths inhabiting the region about the lower Vistula. Most of these tribes appear to have come from southern Scandinavia. Öster- and Västergötland in southern Sweden and the island of Gotland still retain the name of the Goths, as Ryfylke in southern Norway and the island of Rügen preserve that of the Rugians. Bornholm (OI Borgundarhōlmr) was the "island of the Burgundians"; the Vandals may have come from the district in northern Jutland now called Vendsyssel. Among the dialects spoken by these tribes, only **Gothic** has left literary records.

3.6. Another series of expansions came from the southern part of the homeland and led mainly to the west and southwest.

A Saxon tribal group, first appearing in an area between the lower Elbe and the Baltic coast, expanded westward as far as the Ems, subsequently spreading to colonies on the north coast of Gaul (the "Litus Saxonicum") and ultimately dominating most of northern Germany. **Old Saxon**, the ancestor of Middle Low German (c. 1100–c. 1500) and modern Plattdeutsch (from about 1500 on), is known from about 800.

A Frisian group appeared at the beginning of our era along the North Sea coast between the Elbe and the Rhine. **Old Frisian** is known from about 1275. Its speakers may have stemmed from an early western extension of Angles from Schleswig, who also spread northward in Jutland after the first emigrations and southward to Thuringia. Modern Frisian begins c. 1600.

In the fifth and sixth centuries several Germanic groups invaded England, Northumbria and most of the midland ("Mercian") area being occupied by Angles, the southwest ("West Saxon") district with an adjoining midland section by Saxo-Frisians and Saxons, and the southeast ("Kentish") corner by so-called Jutes, probably Juto-Frisian descendants of early migrants from Jutland. **Old English** is known from about 700 but is preserved mainly in West Saxon of about 900–1050. The language of c. 1100–c. 1500 is called Middle English. New (or Modern) English dates from about 1500.

A Frankish group first appeared around the lower Rhine about the year 260. By 486 the Franks had spread partway through the Low Countries, had covered a great part of midland Germany, and had become the dominant power in Gaul. **Old Low Franconian**, the ancestor of Middle Low Franconian (c. 1200–c. 1500) and Modern Dutch-Flemish, is known almost exclusively through a late, fragmentary copy of a Psalm translation probably dating from the tenth century.

With the withdrawal of Roman control in the fifth century, southern Germany was occupied by two Suebian tribal groups, the Bavarians and the Alemannians, perhaps originally from the lower Elbe. Bavarian, Alemannic (including Swiss German), and the midland Frankish dialects (East, Rhenish, and Central Franconian) together formed Old High German, which is known from c. 700. The language of c. 1100–1500 is called Middle High German, and that from about 1500 on is New (or Modern) High German.

3.7. The last Germanic tribes to establish colonies remote from the homeland were the Scandinavians (Northmen), whose expeditions were to extend over a wide area. With the great Viking expansions, beginning about 700, settlements were established in the Faroes, the Shetlands, the Orkneys, the Hebrides, Iceland, Greenland, Ireland, England, Normandy, Finland, Estonia, and Russia. Iceland was settled about 874–930, chiefly by Norwegians; here the great part of **Old Scandinavian** literature was written in Old Icelandic, c. 1050–c. 1530. East Scandinavian survives in Swedish, Danish, and Gotlandic, and West Scandinavian in Norwegian, Faroese, and Icelandic.

3.8. Scandinavian is classified as **North Germanic**, and English, Frisian, Dutch-Flemish, Low German, and High German as **South** (or **West**) **Germanic**. Gothic, which shows some marked similarities to Scandinavian, is often included in North Germanic, though some scholars believe that the distinctive characteristics of the language warrant its being classified separately as East Germanic.

4
STRONG VERBS: CLASSES I TO III; THE GOTHS

Iēsus in láisarjam witōdis

(1) Biþē Iēsus twalibwintrus warþ, galáiþ miþ Mariin jah Iōsēfa in Iaírusalēm. (2) jah ustaúhun jáinar biūhti bi witōda gudis. (3) jah biþē dags biūhtjis ustaúhans warþ, aflunnun þái bērusjōs jah galiþun dagis wig inu Iēsu, untē hugidēdun þata barn wisan in ganiþjam. (4) iþ biláif in Iaírusalēm in láisarjam witōdis. (5) jah biþē funþun þái bērusjōs þatei fralusans was, háuf Iōsēf jah wann Maria. (6) jah galiþun miþ ganiþjam in Iaírusalēm, jah warþ afar dagans þrins funþun þatei was in þáim láisarjam. (7) jah qaþ Maria du þamma barna: ƕa þatei biláift hēr? (8) sái wunnum jah hufum dagans þrins. (9) iþ qaþ: ƕa þatei wunnuþ jah hufuþ? (10) skulda in andbahtjam gudis wisan. (11) jah galiþun in Nazaraíþ, jah þáih þata barn fraþja jah kunþja.

---

afar (+ A/D) after
aflinnan IIIa depart
andbahti n. service
bileiban Ia remain
biþē when, afterward
biūhti n. custom, practice
finþan IIIa find out
fraliusan IIa lose
fraþi n. understanding
galeiþan Ia go, travel
ganiþjis m. kinsman
hēr here
hiufan IIa mourn
hugidēdun supposed (3 pl.)
ƕa þatei why
Iaírusalēm Jerusalem
inu (+ A) without
kunþi n. knowledge
láisareis m. teacher
Nazaraíþ Nazareth
skulda had to (1 sg.)
twalibwintrus twelve years old
þatei that
þeihan Ib thrive
þrins A m.-f. three
ustiuhan IIb fulfill
waírþan IIIb become, be, happen
winnan IIIa sorrow

4.1. The Gothic preterit, which is used where English would have the present perfect, past, or past perfect, has three persons; singular, dual, and plural numbers; indicative and optative moods; an active voice; and a past participle, which is used with *wisan* 'be' or *waírþan* 'become' to express the preterit passive. The dual expresses 'we two, ye two.'

4.2. Nonreduplicating strong verbs, which embrace six main classes, form all tense stems solely by means of systematic vowel alternations called **ablaut series.** The following verbs represent Classes I to III, each of which has two subclasses:

		INFINITIVE	PRETERIT INDICATIVE SG. 1	PL. 1	PAST PARTICIPLE
Ia	'ascend'	steigan	stáig	stigum	stigans
Ib	'tell'	ga-teihan	ga-táih	ga-taíhum	ga-taíhans
IIa	'choose'	kiusan	káus	kusum	kusans
	'shut'	ga-lūkan	ga-láuk	ga-lukum	ga-lukans
IIb	'lead'	tiuhan	táuh	taúhum	taúhans
IIIa	'bind'	bindan	band	bundum	bundans
IIIb	'become'	waírþan	warþ	waúrþum	waúrþans

4.3. All classes of strong verbs have the same preterit indicative endings; the dual always has the same stem as the plural, e.g., *kiusan* IIa 'choose':

	SINGULAR	DUAL	PLURAL
1	káus	[kusu]	kusum
2	káust	kusuts	kusuþ
3	káus	—	kusun

(a) After vowels or diphthongs in the first and third persons:

when final, *b* is replaced by *f*: *gadōf*, infin. *gadaban* 'be fitting'
when final, *d* is replaced by *þ*: *baþ*, infin. *bidjan* 'entreat, pray'

But *b* and *d* may be leveled in scribal spelling: *gadōb*, *bad*.

(b) Before the second person singular ending *-t*:

b is replaced by *f*: *gaft*, infin. *giban* 'give'
d is replaced by *s*: *anabáust*, infin. *anabiudan* 'bid, command'
t is replaced by *s*: *bigast*, infin. *bigitan* 'find'
þ is replaced by *s*: *qast*, infin. *qiþan* 'say'

4.4. Form as above the principal parts of the following strong verbs of Class:

Ia: *greipan* 'seize,' *ur-reisan* 'arise,' *sweiban* 'cease' (4.3a)
Ib: *leiƕan* 'lend,' *þreihan* 'crowd, press,' *weihan* 'fight'
IIa: *biugan* 'bend,' *ana-biudan* 'bid' (4.3ab), *us-lūkan* 'open'
IIb: *af-tiuhan* 'draw away,' *at-tiuhan* 'draw to,' *þliuhan* 'flee'
IIIa: *drigkan* 'drink,' *hilpan* 'help,' *spinnan* 'spin'
IIIb: *baírgan* 'hide,' *ga-þaírsan* 'wither,' *ƕaírban* 'walk'

4.5. The accusative may express extent of time or space: *dagans þrins* 'for three days,' *dagis wig* 'a day's journey.'

THE GOTHS

4.6. The archaism of Gothic is ascribable not only to the age of its records but also to the fact that it became separated from the other Germanic dialects at a very early period; Gothic shows no traces of some developments that appear in all the other known Germanic languages. The Gothic historian Jordanes (551) says that his people, led by a King Berig, sailed "ex Scandza insula" to "Gothiscandza," probably the area about the lower Vistula (3.5). Overpopulation was probably a motive for this emigration, but an added factor may have been flooding of the Gothic homeland. Geological considerations suggest that the Baltic was still a lake before the first millennium B.C., and that great floods attacked the Baltic coastline as erosion gradually joined the lake to the North Sea where now are the straits of the Skagerrak and the Kattegat.

Early in the present era a number of Germanic tribes in the eastern Baltic area migrated southward, the Goths appearing at the Black Sea shortly after the beginning of the third century. Within a few years they had begun forays into the Balkans and into Asia Minor, and from about 237 on they engaged in a series of intermittent battles with Roman forces. In a raid (c. 264) into Cappadocia, two Christian ancestors of Wulfila were taken as captives by the Goths. Along the northern shore of the Black Sea, the Goths founded an empire extending from the Don to the mouth of the Danube. Here, with the Dniepr forming a natural division, they constituted two major groups, the Austrogothi to the east and the Visigothi to the west. Austro- (later Ostro-) may well mean 'east' (Lith. *aušrá*, L *aurōra* 'dawn'), but Visi (Vesi) appears to be a Latinized form of a tribal name rather than a word meaning 'west.'

The onslaught of the Huns (375) destroyed the Gothic empire, inducing a series of migrations that were to extend as far as the Atlantic. Many East Goths were taken westward with the forces of Attila, while West Goths sought refuge in Lower Moesia, now eastern Bulgaria, where Wulfila and his followers had settled a few years before. Here the newcomers soon rebelled against Roman despotism, virtually devastated the area, and annihilated Valens' army at Adrianople (378). Several decades later Visigoths moved into Italy, captured Rome (410) under the leadership of Alaric, then entered southern Gaul. From here they penetrated into what is now Spain and Portugal, where they remained dominant until the coming of the Moors (711). In 418 Visigoths established the kingdom of Toulouse in southern Gaul. Farther north, the victory of Clovis and his Franks at Vouillé (507), a village near Poitiers, preserved the great part of Gaul from Visigothic domination. In the ninth century, according to Walafrid Strabo, some West Goths remained in the Balkans, where Gothic was still used in religious services at Tomi (now Constantsa in southeastern Romania).

The East Goths, though long subjugated by the Huns, recovered their independence with the defeat of Attila (Go. 'Little Father') in 451. Under Theodoric in 493 they seized Ravenna, which had come under control of the Herulian leader Odoacer. The ensuing East Gothic rule over Italy and Pannonia lasted until 554, when it was destroyed by the forces of Justinian. In the Crimea a form of Gothic (or a closely related dialect) was still spoken in the sixteenth century, but in the west the language was to disappear much earlier.

The Goths were known to the Lithuanians as Gudaĩ. This name, apparently antedating the Germanic shift of IE /d/ to /t/, became applied to Poles and White Russians, who were enslaved by Goths in the Ukraine. Classical writers first designate the Goths by *n*-stems: L *Gutones Gotones*, Gk. *Goútones Goútōnes*; the stem is sometimes compared with *gutan-*, occurring in a runic inscription on a gold ring found in Pietroassa, near Bucharest. Later references have vowel stems (L *Gothi Gothae*, etc.), and Gothic preserves the form *Gutþiuda* 'Gothic people.' The meaning of *Gut-*, which is related to the name of the Gautar (OE *Gēatas*) of southern Sweden and to that of Gotland (OSw. *Gutland*), is obscure; possibly the Goths were named for their flooded homeland (cf. Go. *giut-/gáut-/gut-* 'pour'). The unetymological *th* in English *Goth* (OE *Gota* but ME *Gothe*) was introduced from LL *Gothi Gothae*, etc.

5
STRONG VERBS: CLASSES IV TO VI; WULFILA

Iōhannēs

(1) In jáináim dagam andnam Iōhannēs waúrd gudis jah snáu mērjands jah dáupjands and all gáujē Iaúrdanáus. (2) jah sipōnjōs qēmun jah gastōþun jáinar du ganisan. (3) jah andnēmun þata waúrd jah dáupidái wēsun. (4) jah bōkarjōs jah mōtarjōs jah Fareisaieis jah Saddukaieis snēwun jáind. (5) iþ ni frōþun þamma waúrda, jah frēhun ƕas wēsi Iōhannēs, niu aúftō sa Xristus. (6) iþ andhōf jah afaíáik, swaswē gadōf, untē was þatáinei praúfētus. (7) jah sōk þáim Iōhannēs jah qaþ: kuni nadrē, þliuhiþ faúra hatiza gudis! (8) naúh ni was Iēsus in þamma gáuja. (9) iþ biþē qam jáindrē jah saíƕans was fram Iōhannēn, qaþ sa praúfētus faginōnds: sái sa ist wiþrus gudis.

---

afaíáik denied (3 sg.)
and (+A) along, among, throughout
andhafjan VI 5.2 answer
andniman IVa receive
dáupidái m. pl. baptized
dáupjands baptizing
faginōnds rejoicing
Fareisaieis m. Pharisees
faúra (+D) before, for
fraíhnan Vb 5.4 ask, question
fram (+D) from, by
fraþjan VI 5.2 (+D/A) understand
gadaban VI be fitting
ganisan Va be saved
gastandan VI 5.4 abide, stay
ƕas m. who
Iaúrdanáus G of the Jordan
Iōhannēs, A-D Iōhannē, -ēn John
jáináim m. D those
jáind, jáindrē thither
kuni n. brood, race, generation
mērjands preaching
mōtareis m. publican
nadrs m. viper, adder
naúh yet, still
niu aúftō (uftō) whether
praúfētus m. prophet
qiman IVa come
qiþan Va say

Saddukaieis m. Sadducees	swaswē as, even as
saíhvan Vb see	þatáinei only (adv.)
sakan VI (+D) rebuke	þliuhiþ flee! (2 pl.)
sipōneis m. disciple	wisan Va be
sniwan Va 5.3 hasten	wiþrus m. lamb

5.1. The following strong verbs represent Classes IV to VI:

		INFINITIVE	PRETERIT INDICATIVE SG. 1	PL. 1	PAST PARTICIPLE
IVa	'come'	qiman	qam	qēmum	qumans
IVb	'bear'	baíran	bar	bērum	baúrans
Va	'say'	qiþan	qaþ	qēþum	qiþans
Vb	'see'	saíhvan	sahv	sēhvum	saíhvans
VI	'rebuke'	sakan	sōk	sōkum	sakans

One verb in Class IVa has *u* in place of *i* in the infinitive: *trudan* 'tread.' *fra-itan* Va 'devour' has pret. sg. 1 *frēt*, pl. *frētum*.

5.2. *bidjan* Va and seven verbs of Class VI, e.g., *hafjan*, have *-j-* only in the infinitive and present:

Va	'pray'	bidjan	baþ	bēdum	bidans
VI	'raise'	hafjan	hōf	hōfum	hafans

5.3. Instead of *aw*, *áu* appears in the preterit singular:

Va	'hasten'	sniwan	snáu	snēwum	—

5.4. *fraíhnan* has an *n*-suffix and *standan* an *n*-infix, but only in the infinitive and present:

Vb	'question'	fraíh-nan	frah	frēhum	fraíhans
VI	'stand'	sta-n-dan	stōþ	stōþum	—

5.5. As a result of phonologic changes that will require separate consideration, each class of Gothic strong verbs from I through V is divided into two subclasses. Where the Gothic ablaut series Ia, IIa, IIIa, IVa, Va have *i u*, the corresponding b series have respectively *aí aú*. This difference depends upon the following consonant.

i is replaced by *aí* before:

h: *stigans* but *þaíhans* (past participles, Class I)
ƕ: *qiþan* but *saíƕan* (infinitives, Class V)
r: *bindan* but *waírþan* (infinitives, Class III)

u is replaced by *aú* before:

h: *drusum* but *taúhum* (preterit plurals, Class II)
r: *qumans* but *baúrans* (past participles, Class IV)

5.6. Form as above the principal parts of the following strong verbs of Class:

IVa: *niman* 'take,' *uf-brikan* 'reject,' *us-qiman* 'kill'
IVb: *at-baíran* 'bring, offer,' *ga-taíran* 'break, destroy'
Va: *bi-gitan* 'find,' *diwan* (5.3) 'die,' *giban* (4.3a) 'give'
Vb: *bi-saíƕan* 'look about,' *ga-fraíhnan* (5.4) 'inquire'
VI : *fraþjan* (5.2) 'understand,' *ga-daban* (4.3a) 'be fitting'

WULFILA

5.7. Our knowledge of the Gothic language is ascribed almost entirely to the missionary zeal and industry of Wulfila. Some details concerning him are recorded by the ecclesiastical historians, particularly the Arians Philostorgius and Auxentius and the Catholics Sokrates and Sozomen, all of the fifth century. According to Philostorgius, a Cappadocian, Wulfila descended from two natives of Sadagolthina, near Parnassus in western Cappadocia, who were among many Christians captured by Gothic raiders under Valerianus and Gallienus (c. 264). Wulfila was born nearly fifty years later, and it is generally believed that the two captives in question (described as *progonoi*) were his grandparents, one of his immediate parents being a Goth. Wulfila's birthplace is not known, and the details of his education are vague, though it is clear that he studied Latin as well as Greek. Sokrates states that the young man was instructed in Christianity by a certain Theophilus, who attended the Council of Nicaea and subscribed to its acts as a bishop of the Crimean Goths, though this account may be erroneous.

When about twenty-one, Wulfila went with an embassy to Constantinople, where he may have remained to study. After serving as a lector, at about the age of thirty he was consecrated as the first bishop of the Goths north of the Danube. Apparently the consecration was administered at Antioch in 341 by the Arian Eusebius of Nicomedia, who died later in the same year. For the next seven years the young missionary devoted himself to his people in Dacia, i.e., Gothia north of the Danube. He and his followers were persecuted, however, perhaps under the heathen leader Athanaric, so that the bishop asked the emperor Constantius for permission to settle in Roman territory. Constantius agreed, and Wulfila with a large number of converts crossed the Danube and proceeded into the Balkans, settling near Nicopolis in Lower Moesia (modern Trnovo in Bulgaria). Here he worked for more than thirty years. He died about the year 383 in Constantinople, where he had come for a meeting summoned by Theodosius the Great.

The dates of these events are largely conjectural. Auxentius, who describes himself as a pupil and protégé of Wulfila, states that his teacher became a bishop at the age of thirty, labored for seven years in Dacia, served in his high office for forty years, and died at the age of seventy. Philostorgius asserts that the consecration of the young bishop was administered by Eusebius, evidently Eusebius of Nicomedia. If the ceremony took place in 341, shortly before the latter's death, Auxentius' figures would indicate that Wulfila was born in 311, became a lector before 341, left Dacia in 348, and died in 381. It is possible, however, that Auxentius' account may have been altered in places, and his figures may be round numbers suggested by biblical and mystical parallels. At present, the greater weight of evidence would suggest that Wulfila died at a meeting summoned in 383 in an attempt to settle the dispute between the Catholics and the Arians.

Wulfila's faith, as professed in a deathbed statement recorded by Auxentius, was Arian, regarding God the Son as subject to the Father, the Holy Spirit as subject to the Son, and the Father and the Son as not having the same nature. This doctrine, rejected at Nicaea in 325 and again at Constantinople in 381, soon died out in the east but was carried westward by the Goths and still constituted an impediment to religious unity in the time of Charlemagne. The influence of Wulfila in the spread of Arianism may have been considerable; Sozomen states that the Goths believed their spiritual father to be incapable of doing or saying anything wrong.

The name of Wulfila ('Little Wolf') variously appears as Oulphílas (Sokrates, Sozomen, Theodoret), Ourphílas (Philostorgius), Ulfila (Auxentius), Vulphilas (Cassiodorus), Gulfila and Gylfila (Isidore of Seville), Ourphḗlas, Ourphēlâs, and Oúrbilas (Passio S. Nicetae), and, most accurately, as Vulfila (Jordanes). A bronze signet with the form OURPHILA has been preserved, but its history is obscure.

6
STRONG VERBS: CLASS VII; *ā*-DECLENSION; GOTHIC TEXTS

Dáupiþs ist Iēsus

(1) Jah was Iōhannēs dáupjands in áuþidái jah mērjands idreiga. (2) jah qēmun sipōnjōs in þō áuþida jah dáupidái wēsun in Iaúrdanē aƕái. (3) untē sa was stibna wōpjandins in áuþidái; jah qaþ sō stibna: raíhtōs waúrkeiþ stáigōs gudis! (4) jah in jáináim dagam qam Iēsus us Nazaraíþ jah dáupiþs was fram Iōhannē in þizái aƕái. (5) jah sái fōr Iēsus in áuþida. (6) jah was in þizái áuþidái dagē fidwōr tiguns miþ diuzam; jah grēdags warþ. (7) jah faífráis diabaúlus Iēsu jah qaþ: qiþ þamma stáina ei waírþái hláifs! (8) jah sakans was fram Iēsua iþ ni laílōt. (9) jah atáugida þan sa diabaúlus all þiudangardjō jah gahaíháit Iēsua þōs þiudangardjōs du fráistubnjōm. (10) iþ ni kara was Iēsu þizō þiudangardjō, untē gastaístald þō þiudangardja himinē. (11) jah afar þata qam us þizái aírþái jah galáiþ in Nazaraíþ.

---

aƕa 6.3 river, water
aírþa 6.3 region, earth
atáugida showed (3 sg.)
áuþida 6.3 desert, waste
dáupiþs m. sg. baptized (p.p.)
diabaúlus m. devil
diuzam n. D pl. wild animals
ei waírþái that it become
faran VI go, fare
fidwōr tiguns A (4.5) forty
fráisan VIIa tempt
fráistubni 6.3 temptation
gaháitan VIIa promise, call, profess
gastaldan VIIa possess
grēdags hungry
hláifs m. bread, loaf
Iaúrdanē D Jordan
idreiga 6.3 repentance
lētan VIIb let, leave, permit, desist
ni kara was Iēsu (+G) Jesus had no concern for
qiþ tell! = command! (2 sg.)
raíhtōs waúrkeiþ make straight! (2 pl.)
sō 6.3 this, that, the, she
stáiga 6.3 path

stáins m.	stone	þiudangardi 6.3	kingdom
stibna 6.3	voice	wōpjandins	of one crying

6.1. Strong verbs of Class VII form the preterit by means of a reduplicating syllable prefixed to the stem (for stress see *saí-slèp* in 1.15).

(a) Class VIIa preterits employ reduplication exclusively. Before vowels, the reduplicating syllable is the vowel *aí* (for the preterit indicative endings of strong verbs see 4.3):

	INFINITIVE	PRETERIT INDICATIVE SG. 1	PAST PARTICIPLE
'increase'	áukan	aíáuk	áukans
'deny'	af-áikan	af-aíáik	af-áikans

Before one or more consonants, the reduplicating syllable usually consists of the first consonant plus *aí*:

'seize'	ga-fāhan	ga-faífāh	ga-fāhans
'tempt'	fráisan	faífráis	fráisans
'sleep'	slēpan	saíslēp (saízlēp)	slēpans

But *skaí-* occurs before *sk*, and *staí-* before *st*:

'sever'	skáidan	skaískáiþ (4.3ab)	skáidans
'possess'	ga-staldan	ga-staístald	ga-staldans

(b) Class VIIb preterits combine reduplication with ablaut:

'let'	lētan	laílōt	lētans
'sow'	saian	saísō, 2 saísōst	saians

Go. medial *ē*, as in *lētan* and p.p. *lētans*, is replaced by *ai* when followed by a vowel, hence *saian* and p.p. *saians*.

6.2. Form as above the principal parts of:

VIIa: *falþan* 'fold,' *hāhan* 'hang,' *háitan* 'call,' *ƕōpan* 'boast'
VIIb: *grētan* 'weep,' *ga-rēdan* (4.3ab) 'reflect upon,' *waian* 'blow'

6.3. *ā*-declension nouns, which are exclusively feminine in Germanic, are numerous in Gothic, e.g., *sō giba* 'the gift,' *sō bandi* 'the band, bond.'

sg.	N	sō	giba	bandi
	A	þō	giba	bandja
	G	þizōs	gibōs	bandjōs
	D	þizái	gibái	bandjái
pl.	N-A	þōs	gibōs	bandjōs
	G	þizō	gibō	bandjō
	D	þáim	gibōm	bandjōm

mawi 'maiden' has A *máuja*, G *máujōs*, etc.; *þiwi* 'handmaid' has A *þiuja*, G *þiujōs*, etc.

6.4. Decline like:

(a) *sō giba*: *sō bida* 'the request,' *sō graba* 'the ditch,' *sō razda* 'the language,' *sō sáiwala* 'the soul, life'

(b) *sō bandi*: *sō frijōndi* 'the friend,' *sō háiþi* 'the field'

GOTHIC TEXTS

6.5. Gothic has been preserved chiefly in a fragmentary but extensive translation of the Gospels and Epistles, forming in all about three-quarters of the New Testament. The books of the Old Law are represented only by fragments of three chapters (5–7) from Nehemiah. It is generally believed that Wulfila translated at least the extant portions of the New Testament, but there is unfortunately no direct evidence on this question, and the assertions of the early historians are of no great assistance. Auxentius says only that his teacher wrote and preached in Greek, Latin, and Gothic and left "plures tractatus et multas interpretationes" in these languages. Philostorgius states that Wulfila translated the entire Bible except for the Books of Kings. Sokrates adds that these books were omitted in order to avoid arousing the warlike spirit of the Goths, though it is more likely that the Books of Joshua and Judges would be deleted for such a reason. In any event, the stylistic character of the Gothic New Testament would appear to reflect the work of a single original translator, and the surviving text of Nehemiah, though brief and given partly to genealogies, shows no marked stylistic divergence from the rest of the Gothic Bible.

The Gothic translation was based on a widely current Greek text used in the diocese of Constantinople, the Antiochene-Byzantine recension of Lucian the Martyr (c. 312). Much study has been devoted to reconstructing this text, but its precise form is still very doubtful in many instances. Occasionally, too, the Gothic version shows evidence of modifications conforming with the Pre-Vulgate Latin. With few exceptions, the order of words in the Gothic text corresponds to that of biblical Greek, but in this respect also Latin influence is sometimes discernible. Considered as a whole, the Gothic version is marked by uniformity of treatment. Perhaps the most outstanding virtue of the translation is its expressive choice of words. The extent to which the Gothic Bible represents idiomatic, everyday Gothic phrasing may well be disputed, but there is no question that this version possesses a stately dignity and expressiveness that make it well worth reading for its literary value alone.

6.6. A separate literary document is known through eight unconnected leaves of a commentary now called the *Skeireins* (for *Skeireins aíwaggēljons þaírh Iōhannēn* 'Explanation of the Gospel according to John,' a name supplied in 1834 by the editor Massmann). Other records of the language appear in a fragment of a calendar of martyrs, in some marginal notes on a Veronese manuscript, in a Latin title deed of about 551 from Ravenna, and in another from Arezzo, which is now lost. A few Gothic phrases with quasi-phonetic transcriptions in Latin, some specimens of Gothic letters with a name given to each, and a few transcriptions of numerals appear in a Salzburg-Vienna manuscript of the ninth and tenth centuries. Latinized and Romance forms of Gothic words, including proper names, are widely scattered. A few runic inscriptions have been supposed to be Gothic. One occurs on a spearhead from Dahmsdorf, Brandenburg (*ranja*), another on a large gold ring from Pietroassa, Romania (*gutaniowihailag*), a third on a spearhead from Kowel, Poland (*tilarids* or *tilarios*?).

Among various reports indicating a late survival of Gothic in the Crimea, the most important is that of the diplomat Ogier Ghislain de Busbecq. At some time within the years 1555 to 1562 he met two envoys from the Crimea and transcribed sixty-eight of their words together with a few phrases and numerals. All but a few of the cited words are Germanic, and (excepting three lines of a song) all are glossed in Latin. Unfortunately, however, the circumstances governing the transcription and its publication were not ideal. One of the informants, though originally a native speaker of Crimean Gothic, had "forgotten" it in favor of Greek; the other was a native speaker of Greek who had learned Gothic through contact with Crimeans. Busbecq, who spoke seven languages, tolerated some inconsistency in his transcription, and his report was published in a pirated printing that may well have introduced further complexities.

The Gothic manuscripts, which require separate attention, are listed in 7.5.

7
WEAK VERBS; THIRD PERSON PRONOUN; MANUSCRIPTS

Dáuþiþs ist Iōhannēs

(1) Warþ þan, athaíháit Hērōdēs andbahtans jah insandida ins du gahaban Iōhannēn in Hērōdiadins. (2) jah eis gahabáidēdun ina jah galagidēdun in karkarái. (3) untē sō Hērōdia qēns brōþrs Hērōdis was, jah Hērōdēs galiugáida ija. (4) biþē ija ba ni idreigōdēdun sik, qaþ Iōhannēs du imma: (5) galiugáidēs qēn brōþrs þeinis; þata ni skuld ist. (6) iþ si mundōda sis þō waúrda izē jah fullnōda hatizis jah wilda Iōhannēn usqiman. (7) jah biþē Hērōdēs nahtamat waúrhta, plinsida sō daúhtar izōs jah galeikáida imma. (8) jah frah ija sa þiudans ƕis wildēdi. (9) iþ si in Hērōdiadins baþ háubidis Iōhannis. (10) jah skamáida sik Hērōdēs faúr ijōs jah ni ufbrak izái. (11) jah in izō insandida spaíkulatur jah anabáuþ imma briggan im háubiþ Iōhannis þis dáupjandins. (12) jah is afmaímáit imma háubiþ jah brāhta þata háubiþ izái. (13) jah sipōnjōs Iōhannis habáidēdun leik is jah galagidēdun in hláiwa.

See 7.3 for the declension of the third person pronoun.

afmáitan (VII) imma háubiþ behead him
anabiudan II command
atháitan VII summon
ba n. 7.4 both
bidjan V (+G/A) ask, beg, pray
brāhta 3 sg. brought
briggan bring
brōþrs m. G of the brother
daúhtar f. daughter
dáupjandins G Baptist
dáuþjan 7.1 put to death
faúr (+A) before
fullnan 7.1 become full
gahaban 7.1 seize
galagjan 7.1 lay, put
galeikan (+D) 7.1 please
galiugan 7.1 marry
haban 7.1 have, take
Hērōdia, G -adins Herodia
hláiw n. tomb, grave
ƕis wildēdi what she wished

idreigōn sik 7.1 repent
in (+G) because of
insandjan 7.1 send
Iōhannis G of John
karkara f. prison
mundōn sis 7.1 note, mark
nahtamat m. A supper
plinsjan 7.1 dance
qēns f., A qēn wife, woman
skaman sik 7.1 be ashamed
skuld n. lawful
spaíkulatur m. executioner
þeinis G of thy
ufbrikan IV (+D) reject
waúrhta 3 sg. arranged

7.1. Weak verbs form the preterit by means of a *d-/þ-* (or *t-*) suffix. All have the same preterit indicative endings:

		WEAK VERB CLASS			
		i	ii	iii	iv
		'save'	'anoint'	'have'	'become full'
infinitive		nas-jan	salb-ōn	hab-an	full-nan
pret. ind. sg.	1	nasida	salbōda	habáida	fullnōda
	2	nasidēs	salbōdēs	habáidēs	fullnōdēs
	3	nasida	salbōda	habáida	fullnōda
du.	1	[nasidēdu]	[salbōdēdu]	[habáidēdu]	[fullnōdēdu]
	2	nasidēduts	salbōdēduts	habáidēduts	fullnōdēduts
pl.	1	nasidēdum	salbōdēdum	habáidēdum	fullnōdēdum
	2	nasidēduþ	salbōdēduþ	habáidēduþ	fullnōdēduþ
	3	nasidēdun	salbōdēdun	habáidēdun	fullnōdēdun
past participle		nasiþs	salbōþs	habáiþs	—

stōjan 'judge' has pret. *stauida*, p.p. *stauiþs*. *táujan* 'do, make' has pret. *tawida*, p.p. *tawiþs*. A few similar verbs occur in isolated forms. Weak preterits with *t*-suffixes, e.g., *brāhta* 'he brought,' will be considered separately (17.2).

7.2. Conjugate in the preterit indicative like:
(a) *nasjan*: *hazjan* 'praise,' *lagjan* 'lay,' *wasjan* 'clothe'
(b) *salbōn*: *faginōn* 'rejoice,' *frijōn* 'love,' *idreigōn* 'repent'
(c) *haban*: *munan* 'consider,' *þahan* 'be silent,' *witan* 'watch'
(d) *fullnan*: *fraqistnan* 'perish,' *usmērnan* 'be proclaimed'

7.3. The third person pronoun is declined as follows:

	MASC.	NEUT.	FEM.	REFLEXIVE (ALL GENDERS)
sg. N	is	ita	si	—
A	ina	ita	ija	sik
G	is	is	izōs	seina*
D	imma	imma	izái	sis

	MASC.	NEUT.	FEM.	REFLEXIVE (ALL GENDERS)
pl. N	eis	ija	ijōs*	—
A	ins	ija*	ijōs	sik
G	izē	izē*	izō	seina
D	im	im	im	sis

The nominative forms serve chiefly for emphasis or contrast.

7.4. Subject pronouns, *bái* 'both' (n. *ba*), and adjectives referring to two persons of different gender are neuter (or, from a historical point of view, dual), e.g., *ija ni frōþun* 'they (= Mary and Joseph) did not understand,' *ba framaldra* (n.) *wēsun* 'both (= Zachary and Elizabeth) were very old.'

MANUSCRIPTS

7.5. The early history of the extant Gothic codices is obscure. All are copies and appear to have been written between 476 and 552, some very probably originating in Italy, others perhaps in southern France or in the Danube area.

(a) The **Codex Argenteus** is represented by 188 of 336 original leaves containing the Gospels in the "Western" order (Matthew, John, Luke, Mark), with each being divided into sections in accordance with the Eusebian canons. Of the surviving leaves, 187 are in the University of Uppsala library (Sig. DG 1); the 188th was discovered in the cathedral of Speyer on the Rhine in October 1970. This codex, an originally purple but now somewhat faded, reddish parchment, is written in silver ink, with gold for the beginning of a gospel, the first lines of sections and the Lord's Prayer, and symbols for the gospels at the bottom of each page.. The Argenteus, long unknown, was discovered in the sixteenth century in the abbey of Werden. From here it was taken to Prague and, with the capture of the city by Swedes in 1648, to Stockholm. After passing to Holland, where it was copied and later published by Franciscus Junius (1665), it was purchased by the Swedish chancellor de la Gardie, who had it bound in silver plates. The text is written in two scribal hands, one appearing in Matthew and John, the other in Luke and Mark. See page 124.

(b) The **Codex Gissensis**, found in Egypt in 1907 but ruined by seepage while stored in a bank vault during World War II, consisted of four pages containing verses from Luke 23–24 in Gothic and Latin. This was the only text on the leaves, though a few strokes and perhaps some Gothic letters had been added on two pages.

The other Gothic manuscripts are palimpsests (codices rescripti).

(c) The **Codex Carolinus**, like the Ambrosian documents listed below, once belonged to the famous monastery library at Bobbio in Liguria. This manuscript, which was found in the abbey of Weissenburg and is now in the Wolfenbüttel library (Sig. 4148), consists of four leaves containing about forty-two verses from the Epistle to the Romans 11–15 in Gothic and Latin.

(d) The five **Codices Ambrosiani**, excepting seven leaves (see below), are now in the Ambrosian library, Milan.

Codex A (Sig. S 36 parte superiore) has 102 leaves, six of them blank and one illegible, containing fragments of the Epistles to the Romans, 1 and 2 Corinthians, Ephesians, Galatians, Philippians, Colossians, 1 and 2 Thessalonians, 1 and 2 Timothy, Titus, and Philemon, together with the one-page remnant of the Calendar. To this manuscript also belong four badly damaged leaves now in Turin (Codex Taurinensis) containing fragments of the Epistles to the Galatians and Colossians.

Codex B (Sig. S 45 parte superiore) has seventy-eight leaves, one of them blank, with 2 Corinthians complete and fragments of 1 Corinthians, Ephesians, Galatians, Philippians, Colossians, 1 and 2 Thessalonians, 1 and 2 Timothy, and Titus; see frontispiece I.

Codex C (Sig. J 61 parte superiore), two leaves, preserves a few verses from Matthew 25–27.

Codex D (Sig. G 82 parte superiore) has on three leaves the fragments of the Book of Nehemiah.

Codex E, which preserves the remnants of the Commentary on John, consists of eight unconnected leaves, five of which are kept in the Ambrosiana (Sig. E 147 parte superiore), the other three in the Vatican library, where they have been incorporated into Cod. lat. 5750. See frontispiece II.

In addition, some marginal notes in Gothic occur in a collection of Latin biblical homilies in Cod. bibl. cap. Veronensis 51, which belongs to the same period as the Gothic manuscripts listed above.

The title deed of Ravenna is now in Naples, but the Arezzo deed, which has been lost, is known only through a facsimile printed at Florence in 1731 (Gori, *Inscriptiones antiquae*). Both documents were written on papyrus. The Salzburg manuscript is now in Vienna (Codex Vindobonensis, Hofbibliothek, 795). Busbecq's Crimean specimens were printed in Paris in 1589, though without authorization, in an account relating his experience as an envoy to the court of Solyman the Magnificent (*Augerii Gislenii Busbeqii D. Legationis Turciae epistolae quatuor*).

8
n-DECLENSION; PRESENT PARTICIPLE; PHONETIC NOTATION

Iēsus in Galeilaia

(1) Jah afar þatei Iōhannēs in karkarái galagiþs was, qam fráuja in Galeilaian rōdjands du manageim in gajukōm jah mērjands aíwaggēljōn. (2) jah faúr marein gasaƕ Seimōnu miþ gasinþjam in skipam; wēsun áuk fiskjans. (3) iþ haíháit þans mans jah gatawida ins waírþan nutans mannē. (4) jah galiþun in Kafarnaum. (5) jah was jáinar manna unhulþōn habands. (6) iþ fráuja gasaíƕands aglōn þis mans qaþ du þizái unhulþōn: usgagg ūt us þamma! (7) jah suns sái usiddja ūt us þamma mann. (8) jah qēþun sō managei: sái miþ waldufnja anabiudiþ þáim ahmam. (9) jah swaíhrō Seimōnáus lag in brinnōn, jah bēdun fráujan bi þō. (10) iþ qimands urráisida þō, jah aflaílōt þō sō brinnō. (11) jah manageins qēmun du fráujin allaþrō. (12) gaháilida áuk usliþan jah uswarp unhulþōns in namin attins jah usnam siukeins áuganē jah tuggōnō jah haírtanē. (13) jah áusōna mannē gaháusidēdun frōdein aíwaggēljōns.

---

aflētan VII leave, forgive
aglō f. 8.1 distress
ahma m. 8.1 spirit
aíwaggēljō f. 8.1 gospel
allaþrō from all sides
anabiudiþ he commands
atta m. 8.1 father, the Father
áugō n. 8.1 eye
áuk cj. for
áusō n. 8.1 ear
brinnō f. 8.1 fever
fiskja m. 8.1 fisherman
fráuja m. 8.1 lord, the Lord
frōdei f. 8.1 wisdom
gaháiljan heal
gaháusjan hear
gajukō f. 8.1 parable
Galeilaia N-D, A -an Galilee
gasaíƕan V see
gasinþja m. 8.1 companion
gatáujan do, make
haírtō n. 8.1 heart
háitan VII call
Kafarnaum Capernaum
ligan V lie, recline
managei f. 8.1 multitude

manna m. 8.3 man
marei f. 8.1 sea, lake
namō n. 8.1 name
nuta m. 8.1 catcher
rōdjan 8.4 speak
Seimōn, A -u, G -is Simon
siukei f. 8.1 sickness
skip n. ship, boat
suns at once, soon
swaíhrō f. 8.1 mother-in-law
tuggō f. 8.1 tongue
unhulþō f. 8.1 evil spirit
urráisjan raise
usgagg 2 sg. go forth!
usiddja 3 sg. went forth
usliþa m. 8.1 paralytic
usniman IV take away
uswaírpan III cast out
ūt adv. out

8.1. *n*-declension nouns include all three genders:

		MASCULINE	NEUTER	FEMININE	
		'cock'	'heart'	'multitude'	'tongue'
sg.	N	hana	haírtō	managei	tuggō
	A	hanan	haírtō	managein	tuggōn
	G	hanins	haírtins	manageins	tuggōns
	D	hanin	haírtin	managein	tuggōn
pl.	N-A	hanans	haírtōna	manageins	tuggōns
	G	hananē	haírtanē	manageinō	tuggōnō
	D	hanam	haírtam	manageim	tuggōm

aba m. 'man, husband' has pl. G *abnē*, D *abnam*. *aúhsa* m. 'ox' has pl. G *aúhsnē*. *namō* n. 'name' has pl. N-A *namna*, G *namnē*, D *namnam*. *watō* n. 'water' has pl. D *watnam*.

8.2. Decline like:
(a) *hana*: *blōma* 'flower,' *skula* 'debtor,' *haúrnja* 'trumpeter'
(b) *haírtō*: *áugadaúrō* 'window,' *kaúrnō* 'grain,' *þaírkō* 'hole'
(c) *managei*: *áiþei* 'mother,' *balþei* 'boldness,' *diupei* 'depth'
(d) *tuggō*: *driusō* 'slope,' *hēþjō* 'chamber,' *mizdō* 'reward'

8.3. *manna* m. 'man' is declined as follows:

sg.	N	manna	pl.	N	mans, mannans
	A	mannan		A	mans, mannans
	G	mans		G	mannē
	D	mann		D	mannam

8.4. The present participle, which has a stem in *-nd-*, is declined like *hana*, *haírto*, *managei*, above, but also has the masculine nominative singular ending *-s*, as in *qimands* 'coming' beside *sa qimanda* 'the coming one, he who is to come':

		MASCULINE	NEUTER	FEMININE
sg.	N	qimanda, qimands	qimandō	qimandei
	A	qimandan	qimandō	qimandein
	G	qimandins	qimandins	qimandeins
	D	qimandin	qimandin	qimandein
pl.	N-A	qimandans	qimandōna	qimandeins
	G	qimandanē	qimandanē	qimandeinō
	D	qimandam	qimandam	qimandeim

8.5. A collective singular subject often has a plural verb, e.g., *andhōf sō managei* (sg.) *jah qēþun* (pl.) 'the multitude answered and (they) said.'

PHONETIC NOTATION

8.6. The brackets [ ] denote phonetic notation. The symbols [a ā ē f i j k l m n ō p r s t þ u ū z] represent the corresponding Gothic spellings as they are used in comparative Gothic grammar. The following symbols require separate attention:

[aj] like *ai* in NE *aisle*, NHG *Kaiser*
[aw] like *au* in NE *kraut*, NHG *Haus*
[æ] like *a* in NE *at*
[b] like *b* in Go. *bandi*, *lamb*
[ƀ] like *b* in Go. *haban* or like NE *v* formed with both lips
[č] like *ch* in NE *church*
[d] like *d* in Go. *driusō*, *land*
[ð] like *d* in Go. *fadar* or like *th* in NE *father*
[e] like *e* in NE *etch*, NHG *Bett*
[ę̄] like *e* in NE *etch*, NHG *Bett* when prolonged
[ə] like *a* in NE *about*, *china*, *sofa*
[g] like *g* in NE *go*, *dog*
[ǥ] like *g* in Go. *dagōs*, North German *sagen* (see 1.9)
[h] like *h* in NE *he*, also like the aspiration accompanying the first [t] in NE *title* [tʰajtl̥]
[ī] like *i* in NE *pique*, NHG *wider*, or like *ei* in Go. *weis*
[iw] like *ew* in NE *few*, but with stress on [i]: [íw]
[ǰ] like *j* in NE *judge*
[ŋ] like *ng* in NE *song*
[o] like *aú* in Go. *daúhtar* or like *o* in NHG *doch*
[ǭ] like *o* in NHG *doch* when prolonged
[š] like *sh* in NE *she*
[w] like *w* in NE *we*; [ʷ] denotes lip-rounded articulation

[x] like *ch* in NHG *ach*
[ž] like *z* in NE *azure*
[$\bar{a}^{n}$ $\bar{\imath}^{n}$ $\bar{u}^{n}$] represent long nasal vowels.
[l̥ r̥ m̥ n̥ ŋ̥] are syllabic, as in NE *little kitten* [n̥d] for [ænd].
[’], as in NE *apt* [æp’t], indicates unreleased breath.
[̥] denotes voiceless articulation.
[+] denotes a clear-cut syllable break, as in NE *night + rate* (with open juncture) beside *nitrate* (with close juncture).
[∅] (“zero”) indicates the absence or loss of a sound.
[̣] below a vowel indicates a high tongue position (10.7). [̣] below a consonant indicates that the point of the tongue is turned upward and curled back (retroflexed).

8.7. The Gothic texts on pages 38 and 42 are shown below in phonetic transcription. For the purposes of comparative grammar, Gothic *ái áu iu g h ƕ* are assumed to retain their archaic values, vowel length is assumed to be distinctive, and long (prolonged) consonants are represented by double symbols.

ðə pærəbəl əv ðə sōər n̥ ðə sīd

(3) . . . saj urrann sa sę̄ands du sę̄an frajwa sīnamma. (4) jax warþ, miþþanī sesō, sum rextis ǥadraws for wix, jax k^{w}ēmun fuǥlōs jax frētun þata. (5) anþaruþ-þan ǥadraws ana stajnaxamma, þarī ni xaƀajða erþa manaǥa, jax suns urrann in þizī ni xaƀajða diwpajzōs erþōs. (6) at sunnin þan urrinnandin ufbrann, jax untē ni xaƀajða wortins ǥaþorsnōða. (7) jax sum ǥadraws in þornuns; jax ufarstiǥun þaj þornjus jax afx^{w}apiðēðun þata, jax akran ni ǥaf. (8) jax sum ǥadraws in erþa ǥōða jax ǥaf akran urrinnandō jax waxsjandō, jah bar ajn þrins tiǥuns jax ajn sexs tiǥuns jax ajn texuntēxund.

ðə sōər n̥ ðə sīd–eksplənēšən

(14) sa sę̄jands word sę̄jiþ. (15) aþþan þaj wiþra wix sind, þarī sę̄aða þata word; jax þan ǥaxawsjand unkarjans, suns k^{w}imiþ satanas jax usnimiþ word þata insę̄anō in xertam izē. (16) jax sind samalīkō þaj ana stajnaxamma sę̄anans, þaj-ī þan xawsjand þata word, suns miþ faxēðaj nimand ita, (17) jax ni xaƀand wortins in sis ak x^{w}īlax^{w}erbaj sind; þaþrōx biþē k^{w}imiþ aǥlō eþþaw wrakja in þis wordis, suns ǥamarzjanda. (18) jax þaj sind þaj in þornuns sę̄anans, þaj word xawsjandans, (19) jah sorǥōs þizōs liƀajnajs jax afmarzīns ǥaƀīns jax þaj bi þata ạnþar lustjus inn atǥaŋǥandans afx^{w}apjand þata word, jax akranalaws werþiþ. (20) jax þaj sind þaj ana erþaj þizaj ǥōðōn sę̄anans þaj-ī xawsjand þata word jax andnimand jax akran berand, ajn þrins tiǥuns jax ajn sexs tiǥuns jax ajn texuntēxund.

GOTHIC TEXTS

9
i- AND *u*-DECLENSIONS; CONSONANTS

The Parable of the Sower and the Seed: Mark iv.3–8

(3) . . . sái urrann sa saiands du saian fráiwa seinamma. (4) jah warþ, miþþanei saísō, sum raíhtis gadráus faúr wig, jah qēmun fuglōs jah frētun þata. (5) anþaruþ-þan gadráus ana stáinahamma, þarei ni habáida aírþa managa, jah suns urrann in þizei ni habáida diupáizōs aírþōs; (6) at sunnin þan urrinnandin ufbrann, jah untē ni habáida waúrtins gaþaúrsnōda. (7) jah sum gadráus in þaúrnuns; jah ufarstigun þái þaúrnjus jah afƕapidēdun þata, jah akran ni gaf. (8) jah sum gadráus in aírþa gōda jah gaf akran urrinnandō jah wahsjandō, jah bar áin ·l· jah áin ·j· jah áin ·r·.

(3) *fráiwa seinamma*] '(with) his seed,' an instrumental dative.

(5) *anþaruþ-þan* for *anþar-uh-þan*. *-h* in *-(u)h* 'and' (also in *jah* 'and,' *nih* 'and not, nor,' *nuh* 'then?') may be assimilated to the initial consonant of a following word.

diupáizōs aírþōs] partitive genitive (3.4).

(6) *at sunnin þan urrinnandin*] see 9.5, below.

---

afƕapjan choke
áin . . . áin n. one . . . another
akran n. fruit
anþar-uh-þan and another
at (+D/A) at, by, from
baíran IV bear
diupáizōs f. G sg. deep
fra-itan V devour
fráiw n. seed
fugls m. bird
gadriusan II fall, fail
gaþaúrsnan be withered
giban V give, yield
gōda f. A sg. good
in þizei because
·j· (A saíhs tiguns) sixty
·l· (A þrins tiguns) thirty
managa f. A sg. much
miþ-þan-ei while, when
·r· (taíhuntēhund) a hundred
raíhtis namely, indeed
saian VII sow
saiands m. sower
seinamma n. D sg. his

stáinahamma D sg. adj. stony (place)	ufarsteigan I mount up
sum n. some, one	ufbrinnan III scorch
sum . . . sum n. one . . . the other	urrinnan III go forth, spring up, rise
sunnō n. (also f.) sun	wahsjan VI grow, increase
þar-ei where	waúrts f. 9.1 root
þaúrnus m. 9.3 thorn	

9.1. Gothic *i*-declension nouns are masculine or feminine:

		MASCULINE			FEMININE	
		'court'	'place'		'grace'	'joy'
sg.	N	gards	staþs		ansts	fahēþs
	A-V	gard	staþ	A-[V]	anst	fahēþ
	G	gardis	stadis		anstáis	fahēdáis
	D	garda	stada		anstái	fahēdái
pl.	N	gardeis	stadeis		ansteis	fahēdeis
	A	gardins	stadins		anstins	fahēdins
	G	gardē	stadē		anstē	fahēdē
	D	gardim	stadim		anstim	fahēdim

Nominative singular *-s* does not occur after short vowel plus *r*, e.g., *baúr* m. 'son,' or after *s*, e.g., *runs* m., A *runs* 'a running.' *náus* m. 'corpse' has pl. N *naweis*, A *nawins*. *háims* f. 'village' follows *ansts*, above, in the singular but *giba* (6.3) in the plural. Feminine abstracts in *-eins*, e.g., *láiseins* 'doctrine,' have pl. N *-ōs*, G *-ō*, as in *giba*, but otherwise follow *ansts*.

9.2. Decline like:

(a) *gards*: *arms* 'arm,' *hups* 'hip,' *muns* 'thought,' *sáiws* 'sea'
(b) *staþs*: *brūþfaþs* 'bridegroom,' *juggaláuþs* 'young man'
(c) *ansts*: *andahafts* 'answer,' *mahts* 'power,' *táikns* 'token'
(d) *fahēþs*: *arbáiþs* 'labor,' *manasēþs* 'man-seed, mankind'

9.3. *u*-declension nouns consist chiefly of masculines and feminines, which are declined alike, e.g., *sunus* m. 'son':

sg.	N	sunus	pl.	N	sunjus
	A-V	sunu		A	sununs
	G	sunáus		G	suniwē
	D	sunáu		D	sunum

u au may interchange in endings: *-us* for *-aus*, *-au* for *-u*, etc. Only vestiges of neuters occur, e.g., *faíhu* 'cattle,' D *-áu*.

9.4. Decline like *sunus*: m. *fōtus* 'foot,' m. *magus* 'boy,' m. *sidus* 'custom,' m. *tunþus* 'tooth,' f. *kinnus* 'cheek.'

9.5. Absolute phrases, denoting time or circumstances, have no syntactic relation to other parts of sentences. A dative absolute contains a participle modifying a dative noun or pronoun: *at sunnin þan urrinnandin* 'when the sun came out,' *þáim swa waúrþanam* (past participle, 10.4) 'these things thus having come to pass,' *at libandin abin* 'while the husband lives.'

MOVABLE ORGANS OF SPEECH

9.6. In addition to the lungs, the following movable organs have speech functions:

(a) In the larynx, which forms the upper part of the windpipe, the breath passage may be opened, narrowed, or closed by two liplike folds of elastic membrane, the **vocal lips.** In ordinary breathing, these lips are separated, and the breath flows between them without modification. If, however, they are drawn lightly together and are set into vibration by breath forcing its way between them, the sound of voice is produced. For "whispering voice" they are pressed firmly together except for a small cleft, and the breath rustles as it flows between them. Complete closure of the opening between the vocal lips, called the glottis, shuts off the breath.

(b) The **velum** (soft palate) with its pendant tip, the **uvula**, forms the rear, movable roof of the mouth. The velum may be raised to meet the back wall of the upper throat passage, thus sealing the adjoining entrance to the nasal cavities, or may be relaxed and lowered so as to permit nasal breathing.

(c) The size and shape of the resonating chamber embracing the mouth and the upper throat cavity (called the pharynx) may be variously altered by the **tongue**, the **lower jaw**, the **lips**, and to some extent the pharyngeal and cheek muscles.

PHONETIC CLASSIFICATION OF CONSONANTS

9.7. For a **voiceless** consonant, the vocal lips neither vibrate nor produce whispering voice; for a **voiced** consonant, they are set into vibration (9.6a). Thus, with the addition of vocal vibration, the voiceless hiss [s] becomes the voiced buzz [z]; the vibration is especially noticeable if the ears are stopped. The same contrast can be heard in pronouncing the pairs [f ƀ], [þ ð], [š ž], [č ǰ], [x ǥ], [p b], [t d], and [k g], provided that each consonant is sounded aloud without an accompanying vowel.

9.8. Consonants are generally characterized by narrowing or closure of the breath passage; for example:

(a) At the lips for **labial** [p b m f ƀ]

(b) At or near the front teeth for **dental** [þ ð t d n l r s z š ž č ǰ]

(c) At the hard palate, the bony roof of the mouth, for **palatal** [j] (and for [k g ŋ x ǥ] when formed as palatals)

(d) At the velum for **velar** [k g ŋ x ǥ]
(e) At both the lips and the velum for **labiovelar** [w k^w x^w]
(f) At the vocal lips for **glottal** [h], though breath friction for [h] can be produced without glottal narrowing

9.9. With respect to the manner in which the breath is modified, the foregoing consonants may be classified into:

(a) **Stops**, viz., [p b t d k k^w g], for which the breath is suddenly pent up and/or released
(b) **Affricates**, viz., [č ǰ], for which stopped breath is released through a narrow opening so as to produce friction
(c) **Fricatives**, viz., [f ƀ þ ð x x^w ǥ h] and the sibilants [s z š ž], for which the breath flow is impeded and frictional
(d) **Liquids**, including the lateral [l], for which the breath flows around one or both sides of the tongue, and [r]
(e) **Nasals**, viz., [m n ŋ], for which the mouth remains stopped while the velum is lowered to permit nasal breathing
(f) **Semivowels**, viz., [j w], for which the breath is modified by frictionless vowel glides, [j] corresponding to the vowel [i] and [w] to the vowel [u]

9.10. The consonants described above, with the exception of [h], are summarized in the following table. Where two consonants are listed together without intervening punctuation, the first is voiceless and the second voiced:

	LABIAL	DENTAL	PALATAL	PALATAL OR VELAR	LABIOVELAR
Stops	p b	t d		k g	k^w
Affricates		č ǰ			
Fricatives	f ƀ	þ ð, s z, š ž		x ǥ	x^w
Liquids		l, r			
Nasals	m	n		ŋ	
Semivowels			j		w

[þ ð] may be further distinguished as interdental, [s z] as postdental, and [š ž č ǰ] as palatodental.

10
PRESENT INDICATIVE; WEAK FORMS OF ADJECTIVES; VOWELS

The Sower and the Seed—Explanation: Mark iv.14–20

(14) Sa saijands waúrd saijiþ. (15) aþþan þái wiþra wig sind, þarei
saiada þata waúrd; jah þan gaháusjand unkarjans, suns qimiþ Satanas jah
usnimiþ waúrd þata insaianō in haírtam izē. (16) jah sind samaleikō þái
ana stáinahamma saianans, þáiei þan háusjand þata waúrd, suns miþ fahēdái nimand ita. (17) jah ni haband waúrtins in sis ak ƕeilaƕaírbái
sind; þaþrōh biþē qimiþ aglō aíþþáu wrakja in þis waúrdis, suns gamarzjanda. (18) jah þái sind þái in þaúrnuns saianans, þái waúrd háusjandans. (19) jah saúrgōs þizōs libáináis jah afmarzeins gabeins jah þái bi
þata anþar lustjus inn atgaggandans afƕapjand þata waúrd, jah akranaláus
waírþiþ. (20) jah þái sind þái ana aírþái þizái gōdōn saianans þáiei háusjand þata waúrd jah andnimand jah akran baírand, áin ·l· jah áin ·j· jah
áin ·r·.

(14) *saijands*] MS for *saiands*   *saijiþ*] MS for *saiiþ*.

(15) *þái* 'these, those' refers to persons except in verse 19.

(19) *þái bi þata anþar lustjus*] lit. 'those desires about the other thing,' i.e., desires concerning other things.

---

afmarzeins f. deceitfulness
aíþþáu or
ak but
akranaláus fruitless
anþar other, second
atgaggan come, go, enter
aþþan but, however
fahēþs f. joy
gabei f. riches, wealth
gamarzjan offend
gōda 10.4 good
háusjan hear, harken
ƕeilaƕaírbái m. N pl. inconstant
inn adv. in, within
insaian VII 10.4 sow in
libáins f. life

lustus m. desire, lust
niman IV take, accept
samaleikō likewise
Satanas Satan
saúrga f. sorrow, care
sind are (3 pl.)
þái-ei those who
þaþrōh afterward
unkarja 10.4 careless (one)
wiþra against, by
wrakja f. persecution

10.1. The Gothic present, which also expresses the future, includes the same persons and numbers as the preterit; an active and a passive voice; indicative, optative, and imperative moods; the infinitive; and the present participle.
10.2. The present indicative active and passive of the strong verb *baíran* 'bear' and the weak verbs *nasjan* 'save,' *sōkjan* 'seek,' *haban* 'have,' and *salbōn* 'anoint' are representative of nearly all Gothic verb classes:

ACTIVE

sg.	1	baíra	nasja	sōkja	haba	salbō
	2	baíris	nasjis	sōkeis	habáis	salbōs
	3	baíriþ	nasjiþ	sōkeiþ	habáiþ	salbōþ
du.	1	baírōs	nasjōs	sōkjōs	habōs	[salbōs]
	2	baírats	nasjats	sōkjats	[habáits]	[salbōts]
pl.	1	baíram	nasjam	sōkjam	habam	salbōm
	2	baíriþ	nasjiþ	sōkeiþ	habáiþ	salbōþ
	3	baírand	nasjand	sōkjand	haband	salbōnd

PASSIVE

sg.	1	baírada	nasjada	sōkjada	habada	salbōda
	2	baíraza	nasjaza	sōkjaza	[habaza]	[salbōza]
	3	baírada	nasjada	sōkjada	habada	salbōda
pl.	1–3	baíranda	nasjanda	sōkjanda	habanda	salbōnda

10.3. Conjugate in the present indicative like:
(a) *baíran*: *niman* 'take,' *steigan* 'ascend,' *skeinan* 'shine'
(b) *nasjan*: *lagjan* 'lay,' *matjan* 'eat'
(c) *sōkjan*: *fōdjan* 'feed,' *mikiljan* 'magnify, glorify'
(d) *haban*: *hatan* 'hate,' *liugan* 'marry,' *witan* 'watch'
(e) *salbōn*: *frijōn* 'love,' *skalkinōn* 'serve'

10.4. Declension of adjectives and past participles may be weak or strong. Whereas the weak declension is based on Indo-European *n*-stems, the strong declension is based on *o*- and *ā*-stems. The strong declension is used when adjectives are undetermined, that is, not preceded by determiners (definite articles or pronouns). The weak declension is used when determiners precede the adjective and when the adjective itself "determines" the nominal phrase. Some adjectives that are inherently definite, such as comparatives, take the weak declension when not preceded by determiners. The weak or *n*-declension of adjectives and past participles has the same endings as *hana, haírto, tuggō* (8.1):

		MASCULINE	NEUTER	FEMININE
sg.	N	blinda 'blind'	blindō	blindō
	A	blindan	blindō	blindōn
	G	blindins	blindins	blindōns
	D	blindin	blindin	blindōn
pl.	N-A	blindans	blindōna	blindōns
	G	blindanē	blindanē	blindōnō
	D	blindam	blindam	blindōm

This declension is used after *sa, þata, sō* (as above in Mark iv.20: *þái ana aírþái þizái gōdōn saianans*) for *sama* 'same' and *silba* 'self,' and for noun-adjectives like *unkarjans* 'careless (ones)' in Mark iv.15. Comparative adjectives, e.g., *jūhiza* 'younger,' are always weak but are declined in the feminine like *managei*, not like *tuggō*.

OBSTRUENTS, RESONANTS, VOWELS

10.5. In forming stops like [p b t d k g] and affricates like [č ǰ], it will be observed that each requires a complete obstruction of the breath passage. True fricatives, e.g., [f ƀ þ đ s z], require a partial obstruction. Stops, affricates, and fricatives are accordingly classified as **obstruents**; as a rule, they are nonsyllabic. Liquids and nasals, on the other hand, are as a group less obstructed in formation and may alternate between nonsyllabic and syllabic function, e.g., NE [l/l̥] in [bætliŋ] beside [bætl̥] and [n/n̥] in [lajtniŋ] beside [lajtn̥]. Still less obstructed are such semivowel-and-vowel alternants as NE [j/i] in [indjən/indiən] and [w/u] in [bivwæk/bivuæk]. Such alternants, together with liquids and nasals, form a class of **resonants**. Unlike obstruents and resonants, **vowels** are always syllabic and relatively unobstructed in their formation. It must be noted, however, that these distinctions are more relative than absolute. Thus [h], though sometimes genuinely fricative, can be formed with less obstruction than is required for a vowel, and [s š], though not often considered as syllabics, serve in syllabic function in NE [pst] 'listen!' [š] 'be quiet!'

PHONETIC CLASSIFICATION OF VOWELS

10.6. The formation of vowels and their phonetic interrelationships can be described most simply in terms of the positions assumed by the tongue and lips, though in reality the quality of a vowel is determined by the overall contour and condition of the resonating cavity, so that the position assumed by one movable organ may be offset to some extent by compensatory adjustments of other movable organs.

10.7. A vowel is described as **high** (close) or **low** (open), depending upon the height of the tongue in the mouth. In pronouncing [ī ē ę̄ ā], for example, it will be observed that the tongue is close to the palate for [ī] but lowered progressively for [ē ę̄ ā]. A similar lowering can be observed in pronouncing [ū ō ǭ ā]. For [ə] the tongue is approximately midway between high and low:

	FRONT	CENTRAL	BACK
High	ī		ū
High-mid	ē		ō
Mid		ə	
Low-mid	ę̄		ǭ
Low		ā	

The tongue may also be narrowed and raised slightly by tensing it, e.g., for [ī ē ū] as opposed respectively to [i e u].

It will be noticed further that the tongue rises toward the front palate for the **front** (palatal) vowels [ę̄ ē ī], whereas the ascent is toward the back palate for the **back** (velar) vowels [ǭ ō ū]. For the **central** vowels [ā ə] neither the front nor the back of the tongue predominates.

With respect to the shape of the lips, vowels are classified as **lip-rounded** (or simply **rounded**), e.g., [ū u ō ǭ], **unrounded**, e.g., [ī i ē ę̄], or **neutral**, e.g., [ə ā].

For **oral** vowels the velum is raised to meet the back wall of the pharynx, thus preventing the breath from passing through the nasal cavities. For **nasal** vowels, e.g., those of Modern French, the velum is lowered, and the breath flows simultaneously through the mouth and the nasal cavities.

A **diphthong**, in a narrow sense of the term, is a combination of a vowel with a semivowel in the same syllable. If the semivowel glide element occurs first and the vowel element second, e.g., NE [je] in [jes] and [we] in [wet], the combination is called a **rising** (crescendo) diphthong. If the vowel element occurs first, e.g., NE [aj] in [ajl] and [aw] in [krawt], the combination is described as a **falling** (decrescendo) diphthong. In Indo-European phonology the term "diphthong" is often used with a broader meaning, also including falling combinations of vowels with liquids and nasals ([el er em en], etc.) and sometimes the corresponding rising combinations as well ([le re me ne], etc.).

The factors of length, pitch, and stress, though relevant to the description of vowels, have wider applications and will be considered separately (see 11.8; 12.8; 17.7).

11
STRONG FORMS OF ADJECTIVES; PHONOLOGIC AND ANALOGIC CHANGE

The Prodigal Son: Luke xv.11–16

(11) . . . mannē sums áihta twans sununs. (12) jah qaþ sa jūhiza izē du attin: atta, gif mis sei undrinnái mik dáil áiginis. jah disdáilida im swēs sein. (13) jah afar ni managans dagans brāhta samana allata sa jūhiza sunus jah afláiþ in land faírra wisandō. jah jáinar distahida þata swēs seinata libands usstiuriba. (14) biþē þan frawas allamma, warþ hūhrus abrs and gawi jáinata, jah is dugann alaþarba waírþan. (15) jah gaggands gahaftida sik sumamma baúrgjanē jáinis gáujis, jah insandida ina háiþjōs seináizōs haldan sweina. (16) jah gaírnida sad itan haúrnē þōei matidēdun sweina, jah manna imma ni gaf.

(12) *seins** always refers to the subject of its own clause; use of a genitive like *is* in this context is extremely rare.

(15) háiþjōs seináizōs] 'to his field,' a genitive of place.

---

abrs 11.1 great, mighty
afleiþan I go away
áigin n. property
áihta had (3 sg.)
alaþarba 10.4 very poor
alls 11.1 all, every, whole
baúrgja m. citizen
dáils f. share, portion
disdáiljan divide, share
distahjan waste, scatter
duginnan III begin
frawisan V (+D) spend, exhaust
gaggan go
gahaftjan sik join
gaírnjan yearn, long
gif give! (2 sg.)
háiþi f. field, heath
haldan VII tend, hold, feed
haúrn n. husk, horn
hūhrus m. famine, hunger
jáins 11.1 that
jūhiza younger
land n. land
liban live
manags 11.1 many, much, great
matjan eat

mik A, mis D me
sad (= saþ) itan eat one's fill
samana adv. together
sei f. which, who
seins* 11.1 his, his own
sums 11.1 a certain, some
sunus m. son
swein n. swine, pig
swēs sg. 3.1 possessions
twái m., A twans two
þō-ei n. A pl. that, which
undrinnái is coming to
usstiuriba riotously

11.1. When not declined weak (10.4), adjectives and past participles follow the strong declension, e.g., *blinds* 'blind.'

	MASCULINE	NEUTER	FEMININE
sg. N	blinds	blind, blindata	blinda
A	blindana	blind, blindata	blinda
G	blindis	blindis	blindáizōs
D	blindamma	blindamma	blindái
pl. N	blindái	blinda	blindōs
A	blindans	blinda	blindōs
G	blindáizē	blindáizē	blindáizō
D	blindáim	blindáim	blindáim

These endings are partly those of nouns like m. *dags*, n. *waúrd*, f. *giba* and partly those of pronouns:

m. sg.	A	*-ana*	as in	*þana* and *ina*
	D	*-amma*	as in	*þamma* and *imma*
pl.	N	*-ái*	as in	*þái*
	G	*-áizē*	as in	*þizē* and *izē*
n. sg.	N-A	*-ata*	as in	*þata* and *ita*
	D	*-amma*	as in	*þamma* and *imma*
pl.	G	*-áizē*	as in	*þizē* and *izē*
f. sg.	G	*-áizōs*	as in	*þizōs* and *izōs*
pl.	G	*-áizō*	as in	*þizō* and *izō*
m.-n.-f. pl.	D	*-áim*	as in	*þáim* and *im*

A few adjectives (and all possessives) are invariably strong, e.g., *alls* 'all,' *jáins* 'that,' *sums* 'some,' *meins* 'my.'

11.2. The noun endings of a few strong adjectives follow other vowel-declension nouns, e.g., m. *niujis* 'new' like *harjis* (2.3), *wilþeis* 'wild' like *haírdeis* (2.3); n. *waílamēri* 'of good repute' like *kuni* (3.1); f. *wōþi* 'sweet' like *bandi* (6.3). The extant forms of a few other adjectives differ from these only in the nominative singular of all genders and in the neuter accusative and gen-

itive singular: m.-f.˙ *brūks*, n. *brūk* 'useful,' n. G *skeiris* 'clear' (*i*-declension, 9.1); m. *manwus*, n. *manwu* 'ready,' f. *þaúrsus* 'withered' (*u*-declension, 9.3).
11.3. The N sg. *-s* does not occur after *r* preceded by a short vowel or after *s*, e.g., *unsar* 'our,' *láus* 'empty.' Possessives in *-r* and predicate adjectives have no n. N-A *-ata*.
11.4. After vowels or diphthongs, *b d* are replaced respectively by *f þ* when occurring finally or before final *-s*, but *b d* may be leveled in spelling: G *twalibē*, N *twalif* or *-lib* 'twelve'; m. sg. D *gōdamma*, N *gōþs* or *gōds* 'good.'
11.5. Decline like *blinds* (or according to 11.3–4, as indicated): *arms* 'poor,' *diups* 'deep,' *frōþs* (11.4) 'wise,' *izwar* (11.3) 'your,' *baúrans* 'born,' *nasiþs* (11.4) 'saved.'

PHONEMES AND ALLOPHONES

11.6. The **segmental phonemes** of a language or dialect are its contrasting classes of vowel and consonant sounds. NE /i æ/, for example, contrast in *it at*, /l r/ in *led red*. (The diagonals / / indicate that the symbols are phonemic.) Two or more speech sounds that occur as members of the same phoneme constitute its **allophones**. Thus a speaker of English may pronounce *middle* with voiced-postdental-velarized-syllabic [ɫ̥], *mirthless* with partly voiceless-dental-centralized-nonsyllabic [l̪], and *billion* with voiced-postdental-palatalized-nonsyllabic [ʎ]. Neither these nor other types of English *l*-sounds contrast with each other; all are members of a single phoneme.

The phonemic status of speech sounds may vary greatly from language to language or from dialect to dialect. English /l/ and /r/ contrast, for example, but Japanese [l] and [r] do not. Conversely, Welsh contrasts voiced /l/ with voiceless /l̥/, whereas English [l] and [l̥] occur only as **co-allophones**, that is, as allophones of the same phoneme.
11.7. When co-allophones alternate in conformity with their phonetic environment, they are in **complementary distribution (complementation)**. Thus, in its place of articulation, dental [l̪] in *mirthless* conforms with dental /þ/, postdental [ɫ̥] in *middle* with postdental [d]. In its manner of articulation, NE /p/ is exploded and aspirated initially in *pat* [pʰæt] but is exploded without aspiration in *spat* [spæt], in which the exhalation for /s/ lowers the breath pressure. For [p'] in *apt* [æp't], *chapman* [čæp'mən], on the other hand, the breath remains pent up; it is released only in articulating the following stop or nasal. Less commonly, co-allophones may occur in the same phonetic environment; they are then in **free variation**. Thus NE [pʰ p p'] may occur finally, as in *tap*.
11.8. **Prosodic (suprasegmental) phonemes** embrace contrastive features of length (e.g., L *mālus* 'apple tree' vs. *malus* 'bad,' It. *cassa* 'case' vs. *casa* 'house'), stress (NE *ínsult* vs. *insúlt*), pitch (NE yes↗ 'really?' vs. yes↘ 'of course!'), and juncture (NE *night + rate* with open juncture vs. *nitrate* with close juncture).

PHONOLOGIC CHANGE

11.9. Changes in the phonemic status of speech sounds form two major patterns: if some or all allophones of originally separate phonemes coalesce and so no longer contrast with each other, the result is a **merger**; if co-allophones acquire separate phonemic status, the result is a **split**.

The processes involved in phonologic change are of two general types, **conditioned** and **unconditioned**.

(a) Conditioned changes occur only in certain phonetic contexts. Among the varieties of conditioned change, the most common is **assimilation**, through which the articulations of different neighboring sounds are harmonized. In OE *henep* > NE *hemp*, for example, /n/ has become bilabial /m/ by assimilation to bilabial /p/; in OE *ǣmette* > NE *ant*, /m/ has been assimilated to /t/; in IE *jug-tós* > *juk-tós* p.p. 'yoked,' voiced /g/ became voiceless in combination with the following voiceless /t/. In **dissimilation**, on the other hand, like neighboring sounds become less similar in articulation, as in L *marmor* > OFr. *marbre* > NE *marble*. Loss of syllables through dissimilation, as in NE *gently* for **gentle-ly*, is called **haplology**. Other varieties of conditioned change include transposition or **metathesis** (NE *aks* beside *ask*) and addition or **excrescence** (Sp. *e-straic* for English *strike*, NE *ath-a-letic*, ME *soun* > NE *sound*). Conditioned change in juncture, as in NE *moum-pitcher* for *moving picture*, *jeat-chet?* for *did you eat yet?*, *gov'ment* for *government*, is called **sandhi**.

(b) Unconditioned changes are not limited to certain sound combinations. Proto-Italic /x/, for instance, became /h/ in Old Latin and was subsequently lost, and Indo-European /ā ō/ merged in preliterate Germanic, regardless of the phonetic contexts in which these phonemes occurred.

11.10. Though both phonetic and phonemic analyses help to explain how phonologic changes occur, neither explains why. Subconscious mimicry and leveling may spread such innovations from speaker to speaker and from word to word, but only rarely is the source of a change identifiable. The phonemic system of a language may be modified if its speakers absorb a large foreign-speaking substratum whose members pronounce the language with the speech habits and contrasts of their native tongue. Bilingualism in border areas may have a similar effect, eventually modifying the pronunciation of monoglots. It appears likely, too, that the phonemic systems of languages tend to be symmetrical, so that a disruption in one segment of a system may bring about a realignment of other segments. When the speakers of a language become separated into groups, whether through migration or through the presence of topographic or social barriers, dialectal differences often arise. When the contact between two related dialects has been lost, they may become progressively divergent, especially if subject to different local influences. Social ascendancy of individual dialects, linguistic fashions and shibboleths, taboos, class consciousness, and perhaps other influences as well may be contributing factors.

ANALOGIC CHANGE

11.11. Speech is dependent upon a complex of neuromuscular habit patterns. In a narrow sense, **analogic change** is a process by which linguistic usage is altered or created to conform with these patterns. In learning English, for example, a child soon acquires the habit of forming *s*-plurals in such words as *boys.* If he extends this habit to *sheep* and *man*, the analogic plurals *sheeps* and *mans* result. Similarly, "incorrect" weak preterits like *knowed* and *growed* are based on the same habit that produces the "correct" form *sowed*, which is in turn an analogic replacement of a strong preterit (OE *sēow*). Pronunciation, syntax, and meaning as well may be modified by analogy, an analogic replacement often completely superseding the corresponding historic development.

In a broader sense, analogic change includes some inventive processes. Thus **folk etymology (metanalysis)** attempts to make forms more meaningful: *spittin' image* for *spit and image*, Irish English *Mary McDillon* for *Mary Magdalene*. **Contamination** alters one word or phrase through association with another, as in *whirlicane* < *whirlwind* : *hurricane*, *why for* <*why* : *what for*.

12
IMPERATIVE; FIRST PERSON PRONOUN; INDO-EUROPEAN /p t k s/

The Return of the Prodigal: Luke xv.17–24

(17) Qimands þan in sis qaþ: ƕan filu asnjē attins meinis ufarassáu haband hláibē, iþ ik hūhráu fraqistna. (18) usstandands gagga du attin meinamma jah qiþa du imma: atta, frawaúrhta mis in himin jah in andwaírþja þeinamma; (19) ju þanaseiþs ni im waírþs ei háitáidáu sunus þeins; gatawei mik swē áinana asnjē þeináizē. (20) jah usstandands qam at attin seinamma. naúhþanuh þan faírra wisandan gasaƕ ina atta is jah infeinōda jah þragjands dráus ana hals is jah kukida imma. (21) jah qaþ imma sa sunus: atta, frawaúrhta in himin jah in andwaírþja þeinamma; ju þanaseiþs ni im waírþs ei háitáidáu sunus þeins. (22) qaþ þan sa atta du skalkam seináim: spráutō bringiþ wastja þō frumistōn jah gawasjiþ ina jah gibiþ figgragulþ in handu is jah gaskōhi ana fōtuns is; (23) jah bringandans stiur þana alidan ufsneiþiþ, jah matjandans wisam wáila; (24) untē sa sunus meins dáuþs was jah gaqiunōda, jah fralusans was jah bigitans warþ. jah dugunnun wisan.

(17) *qimands þan in sis qaþ*] cf. 12.4 and verses 18, 20, 23.
(18) *in andwaírþja þeinamma*] 'in thy presence' = 'before thee.'
(20) *naúhþanuh . . . wisandan*] see 12.4.
(22), (23) *bringiþ* for *briggiþ*, *bringandans* for *briggandans*. An occasional *n* for [ŋ] is especially characteristic of Luke.

áins one
aljan bring up, fatten
andwaírþi n. presence
asneis m. hireling, servant
bigitan V find
dáuþs dead
driusan II fall
ei that
figgragulþ n. finger ring
fōtus m. foot
fraqistnan perish
frawaúrhta, with mis I have sinned

frumists foremost, best
gaqiunan be made alive
gaskōhi n. pair of sandals
gatawei make! (imper. sg. 2)
gawasjan clothe
háitáidáu I be called
hals m. neck
handus f. hand
ƕan filu how many, how much
im am
infeinan be moved, pity
ju now, already
kukjan (+D) kiss
meins my, mine
naúh-þan-uh yet, still
skalks m. servant
spráutō quickly
stiur m. calf, steer
swē as, like, about
þanaseiþs more, further
þeins thy, thine
þragjan rush, run
ufarassus m. abundance
ufsneiþan I slay
usstandan VI rise up
wáila (?waíla) well
waírþs worthy
wasti f. garment
wisan V feast

12.1. The imperatives of *baíran* 'bear,' *sōkjan* 'seek,' *salbōn* 'anoint,' and *haban* 'have' are the following:

	baíran	sōkjan	salbōn	haban
sg. 2	baír	sōkei	salbō	habái
3	baíradáu	sōkjadáu	[salbōdáu]	[habadáu]
du. 2	baírats	[sōkjats]	[salbōts]	[habáits]
pl. 1	baíram	sōkjam	[salbōm]	[habam]
2	baíriþ	sōkeiþ	salbōþ	habáiþ
3	[baírandáu]	[sōkjandáu]	[salbōndáu]	habandáu

Before a vowel, *áu* is replaced by *aw*: infin. *gatáujan* 'make, do,' imper. sg. 2 *gatawei*.

12.2. Conjugate in the imperative like:

(a) *baíran*: *qiman* 'come,' *niman* 'take,' *haldan* 'hold, tend'
(b) *sōkjan*: *dōmjan* 'judge,' *rōdjan* 'speak,' *wēnjan* 'hope'
(c) *salbōn*: *frijōn* 'love,' *idreigōn* 'repent,' *mitōn* 'consider'
(d) *haban*: *arman* 'pity,' *þahan* 'be silent,' *witan* 'watch'

12.3. The first person pronoun is declined as follows:

	'I'	'we two'	'we'
N	ik	wit	weis
A	mik	ugkis	uns, unsis
G	meina	ugkara*	unsara
D	mis	ugkis	uns, unsis

The nominative is used chiefly for emphasis. The other case forms serve also as reflexive pronouns of the first person.

12.4. A participle modifying the subject or object of a finite verb often replaces a second finite verb: *qimands þan in sis qaþ* 'coming then (=when he came) to himself, he said,' *naúhþanuh þan faíran wisandan* (A) *gasahv ina* (A) *atta is* 'his father saw him being then (=when he was) still far away.'
12.5. A direct object need not be repeated: *þana galáusidēdi . . . gawandidēdi* 'had freed him . . . had converted (him),' *jah bringandans stiur þana alidan ufsneiþiþ* 'and bringing (see 12.4) the fatted calf, slay (it).'

COMPARATIVE AND INTERNAL RECONSTRUCTION

12.6. In **comparative reconstruction**, the essential features of an unrecorded parent language like Indo-European are determined through comparing those of its most archaic known descendants. Thus a comparison of Sk. *ásmi*, Gk. Lesb. *émmi* and Lith. *esmì*, 'am' suggests that they have come from a common parent form, but to reconstruct it we must explain their mutual differences. First, we find /a/ in Sk. *ásmi* beside /e/ in Gk. Lesb. *émmi* and Lith. *esmì*, but comparative evidence shows that /a/ < /e/ is to be expected in Indo-Iranian, as also in Sk. *dáša* = Gk. *déka* 'ten.' Next, /mm/ in Gk. Lesb. *émmi* beside /sm/ in Sk. *ásmi* and Lith. *esmì* shows a Lesbian-Thessalian assimilation, as in Lesb. *ámme* beside Sk. *asmā́n* 'us.' Finally, the accentuation of Lith. *esmì* is an innovation, as also in *esì* = Sk. *ási* 'thou art.' After such archaic forms of 'am' are explained, the parent form is reconstructed as *ésmi*.

Internal reconstruction, on the other hand, is based on analysis of individual languages. Comparative evidence does not explain, for example, the fact that IE *-os-* might produce *-as-* or *-az-* in Gothic medial syllables, as in *hláiwasnōs* 'graves' beside *arhvaznōs* 'arrows.' In this instance Gothic provides the explanation: through dissimilation, *-as-* occurs after a voiced consonant, *-az-* after a voiceless consonant.

INDO-EUROPEAN OBSTRUENTS

12.7. Germanic has distinct reflexes for the following reconstructed Indo-European obstruent phonemes:

	LABIAL	DENTAL	PALATAL OR VELAR	LABIOVELAR
Stops:				
Voiceless	p	t	k	k^w
Voiced	b	d	g	g^w
Voiced aspirated	b^h	d^h	g^h	g^{wh}
Fricative		s		

/s/ represented [z] before voiced obstruents, [s] elsewhere. For practical purposes, /b^h d^h g^h g^{wh}/ are here transcribed respectively as /bh dh gh g^wh/.

ACCENTUATION IN INDO-EUROPEAN AND GERMANIC

12.8. The parent Indo-European accent was characterized principally by tone (pitch) and by movability. The primary accent, a higher tone, fell in some words on the root syllable, in others on a suffix or ending; in still others it alternated from form to form, as in Gk. N *patḗr*, V *páter*, A *patéra*, G *patrós*, D (originally locative) Homeric *patéri*. In the earliest known Germanic, Italic, and Celtic, however, the dominant feature of accent was stress, and primary stress was fixed on initial syllables, as in early OE *fǽder* 'father' (all cases) beside Gk. *patḗr*, *páter*, etc.

VOICELESS REFLEXES OF INDO-EUROPEAN /p t k s/

12.9. IE /p t k s/ produced both voiceless and voiced reflexes in Germanic. Only the voiceless reflexes will be considered in this chapter.

Within the Proto-Germanic period, IE /p t k s/ produced respectively /f þ x s/ under two conditions: (a) when occurring word-initially:

/p/ Gk. Dor. *pṓs*, L *pēs*	/f/ Go. *fōtus* 'foot'
/t/ Gk. Dor. *tū́*, L *tu*	/þ/ Go. *þu* 'thou'
/k/ L *cor*, OIr. *cride*	/x/ Go. *haírtō* 'heart'
/s/ IE m. N *so*, Sk. *sá*	/s/ Go. *sa* 'this, that'

(b) when occurring medially or finally—but only if the nearest preceding Indo-European vowel or other syllabic ([l̥ r̥ m̥ n̥ ŋ̥]) had already borne primary accent:

/p/ IE *klépō*, L *clepō*	/f/ Go. *hlifa* 'I steal'
/t/ IE *wértō*, L *vertō* 'I turn'	/þ/ Go. *waírþa* 'I become'
/k/ Gk. *déka*, L *decem*	/x/ Go. *taíhun* 'ten'
/s/ Sk. *ǰṓṣati* 'partakes, likes'	/s/ Go. *kiusiþ* 'chooses'

12.10. Certain consonant clusters conditioned the shift.

(a) IE /p t k/ remained when directly preceded by /s/:

/sp/ L *spuere*	Go. *speiwan* 'spit, spew'
/st/ Sk. *ásti*, L *est*	Go. *ist* 'is'
/sk/ L *piscis*	Go. *fisks* 'fish'

In some words IE /s/ might or might not occur initially before /p t k/. If this "s movable" remained, /p t k/ did not shift: L *taurus*, NE *steer*. If the /s/ did not remain, /p t k/ shifted: Gk. *stégos* and *tégos*, OE *þæc* 'roof' > NE *thatch*.

(b) /t/ remained in the clusters /pt kt/:

/pt/	Gk. *kléptēs*	/ft/	Go. *hliftus* 'thief'
/kt/	L *octo*	/xt/	Go. *ahtáu* 'eight'

(c) In pre-Germanic times /ts tt/ had already become /ss/ (shortened to /s/ after long vowels, after vowels plus semivowels, and before /r/), and /ttr/ had become /str/:

/ts/	Sk. *vivitsati* 'wishes to see'	/s/	Go. *ga-weisōn* 'visit'
/tt/	Sk. *sattás* 'seated'	/ss/	OI OE OS *sess* 'seat'
/ttr/	IE *pāttro-*	/str/	OI *fōstr* 'fosterage'

EXERCISE

Supply the missing consonants in accordance with 12.9–10: IE *péku*, L *pecu*, Go. ( )*aí*( )*u* 'cattle'; Sk. *spardhā* 'contest,' Go. *s*( )*aúrds* 'racecourse'; Sk. *bhrā́tā*, Go. *brō*( )*ar* 'brother'; Gk. *steíkhō* 'I go,' Go. *s*( )*eiga* 'I ascend'; L *canis*, Go. ( )*unds* 'dog'; OIr. *scāth*, Go. *s*( )*adus* 'shadow'; L *captus* 'seized,' Go. ( )*a*( )*s* 'joined'; L *rēctus*, Go. *raí*( )*s* 'right, straight'; IE *gʷét-*, Go. *qi*( )*an* 'say'; IE *gʷett-*, Go. *ga-qi*( ) 'consent'; IE *wejtto-*, Go. *un-wei*( ) 'unlearned'; IE *mits-*, Go. *mi*( )*ō* 'reciprocally'; L *dént-*, Go. *tun*( )*us* 'tooth'; IE *bhlāttr-*, Go. *-blō*( )*eis* 'worshiper'; Gk. *polú*, Go. ( )*ilu* 'many, much'

CONDITIONED MERGER WITH PRIMARY SPLIT

12.11. The developments noted above in 12.10 are examples of **conditioned merger**. After /s/, IE /p t k/ did not shift but merged respectively with Gc. /p t k/. Similarly, IE /t/ in the clusters /pt kt/ did not become /þ/ but merged with Gc. /t/. IE /ts tt/ merged with pre-Gc. /s(s)/ and IE /ttr/ with pre-Gc. /str/. Moreover, under certain conditions yet to be considered, IE /t s/ merged with /∅/ ("zero"); that is, they were lost: Sk. *bhárēt* but Go. *baírái* 'he may bear,' Gk. Dor. *phéromes* but Go. *baíram* 'we bear.' When an allophone thus breaks away from its former co-allophones and merges with another phoneme or with /∅/, the result is a **primary split**.

13
PRETERIT-STEM OPTATIVE; SECOND PERSON PRONOUN; VERNER'S LAW

The Prodigal's Elder Brother: Luke xv.25–32

(25) Wasuþ-þan sunus is sa alþiza ana akra, jah qimands atiddja nēƕ razn jah gaháusida saggwins jah láikins. (26) jah atháitands sumana magiwē frahuh ƕa wēsi þata. (27) þaruh is qaþ du imma þatei brōþar þeins qam, jah afsnáiþ atta þeins stiur þana alidan untē háilana ina andnam. (28) þanuh mōdags warþ jah ni wilda inn gaggan. iþ atta is usgaggands ūt bad ina. (29) þaruh is andhafjands qaþ du attin: sái swa filu jērē skalkinōda þus, jah ni ƕanhun anabusn þeina ufariddja, jah mis ni áiw atgaft gáitein ei miþ frijōndam meináim biwēsjáu; (30) iþ þan sa sunus þeins, saei frēt þein swēs miþ kalkjōm, qam, ufsnáist imma stiur þana alidan. (31) þaruh qaþ du imma: barnilō, þu sinteinō miþ mis wast jah is, jah all þata mein þein ist; (32) wáila wisan jah faginōn skuld was, untē brōþar þeins dáuþs was jah gaqiunōda, jah fralusans jah bigitans warþ.

(25) *wasuþ-þan* for *was-uh-þan*; see commentary on Mark iv.5, p. 38. Cf. *frah-uh*, *þar-uh*, *þan-uh* in the following verses. *qimands atiddja*] see 12.4.

(27) *þatei* may introduce either direct or indirect quotations.

(28) *bad* for *baþ*; see 4.3a.

---

afsneiþan I kill, cut off
alþiza older, elder
anabusns f. command, commandment
atgaggan, pret. -iddja go, approach
atgiban give, give up
barnilō n. son, small child
biwisan V 13.1 make merry
brōþar m. brother
faginōn rejoice
frijōnds m. friend
gáitein n. kid

háils hale, safe
ƕa n. what
is art
kalkjōm f. D harlots
láiks m. dance, dancing
magus m. boy
mōdags angry
nēƕ near
ni áiw, ni ƕanhun never
razn n. house
sa-ei (he) who
saggws m. song
sinteinō always
skalkinōn serve
skuld wisan be proper
swa so
þan-uh (and) then
þar-uh there(upon)
þu 13.3 thou
ufargaggan, pret. -iddja transgress
usgaggan go forth

13.1. The preterit-stem optative of a strong or weak verb has the same stem as its preterit indicative plural:

	INFINITIVE	PRETERIT INDICATIVE PLURAL	PRETERIT OPTATIVE SINGULAR 1
'be'	wisan	wēs-um	wēs-jáu
'call'	háitan	haíháit-um	haíháit-jáu
'save'	nasjan	nasidēd-um	nasidēd-jáu

All verbs have the same preterit-stem optative endings:

	SINGULAR	DUAL	PLURAL
1	wēsjáu	—	wēseima
2	wēseis	[wēseits]	wēseiþ
3	wēsi		wēseina

The term "optative" is used in Germanic grammar because these forms have developed from Indo-European optatives. There were two such moods in early Indo-European, also in early Greek: the optative and the subjunctive. The subjunctive was lost; its meanings were taken over by the optative. Accordingly later grammars refer to the optative as the subjunctive, and even grammars of Gothic may designate these forms as subjunctive rather than optative.

13.2. The preterit-stem optative is used chiefly (a) to express unreal conditions, present or past:

wáinei þiudanōdēdeiþ 'would that ye reigned!'
wēseis hēr 'if thou hadst been here'

(b) in the past, to express:

exhortation: *anabáuþ im ei mann ni qēþeina* 'he commanded them that they should not tell any man'
uncertainty: *ni kunnandans ƕaþar skuldēdi máiza* 'not knowing which should be greater'
supposition: *hugidēdun þatei is bi slēp qēþi* 'they supposed that he was speaking of sleep'
purpose: *ei afdáuþidēdeina ina* 'that they might put him to death'
possibility: *ƕa wēsi þata* 'what that might be'
indirect discourse: *þadei háusidēdun ei is wēsi* 'where they heard he was'

(c) in the past after *faúrþizei* 'before':

faúrþizei Abraham waúrþi, im ik 'before Abraham was, I am'

13.3. The second person pronoun is declined as follows:

	'thou'	'ye two'	'ye'
N	þu	—	jus
A	þuk	igqis	izwis
G	þeina	igqara	izwara
D	þus	igqis	izwis

The nominative is used chiefly for emphasis. The other cases serve also as reflexive pronouns of the second person.

VERNER'S LAW: VOICED REFLEXES OF INDO-EUROPEAN /p t k s/

13.4. In 12.9 it has been observed that IE /p t k s/ produced respectively /f þ x s/ within the Proto-Germanic period when occurring (a) in word-initial position and (b) medially or finally—but only if the nearest preceding vowel or other syllabic had borne primary accent. Additional examples of this development are included in the exercise below.

13.5. If the nearest preceding Indo-European vowel or other syllabic had not borne primary accent, the Germanic reflexes of medial or final IE /p t k s/ were to be respectively the corresponding voiced fricatives /ƀ ð ǥ z/:

/p/	Sk. *kapā́lam* 'skull'	/ƀ/	Go. *háubiþ* 'head'
/t/	IE *wēntós*, L *ventus*	/ð/	Go. *winds* 'wind'
/k/	IE *pl̥kenós*	/ǥ/	Go. *fulgins* 'hidden'
/s/	Sk. *bhárasē* (medial 2 sg.)	/z/	Go. *baíraza* 'art borne'

Proclitics, that is, originally separate forms that had become phrase-bound, and thus had come to precede the primary accent, were also subject to this development; for example:

/k/ L *com-mū́nis* < *kom-mójnis*	/ǥ/ Go. *ga-máins* 'common'
/s/ Gk. *dus-* 'ill-, mis-'	/z/ Go. *tuz-wḗrjan* 'doubt'

But voiceless clusters remained voiceless; see 12.10.

EXERCISE

Supply the missing consonants in accordance with 12.9–10 or 13.5; the non-Germanic forms indicate the parent accentuation:
Sk. *bhrā́ta*, Go. *brō( )ar* 'brother'; Gk. *patḗr*, Go. ( )*a*( )*ar* 'father'; Gk. *déka*, L *decem*, Go. *taí( )un* 'ten'; Gk. *dekás*, Go. *ti*( )- 'decade'; Sk. *ápara-* 'behind,' Go. *a*( )*ar* 'after'; Sk. *sr̥prás* 'greasy, slippery,' Go. ( )*al*( )*ōn* 'anoint'; IE *juwŋ̥kós*, L *juvencus* 'bullock,' Go. *jug*( )*s* 'young' beside *juwŋ̥́kis-*, Go. *jū*( )*i*( )*a* 'younger'; IE *wértō*, L *vertō* 'I turn,' Go. *waír*( )*a* 'I become' beside *wortéjō* > Go. *fra-war*( )*ja* 'I destroy'; IE *pērsnā́*, L *perna* 'ham, haunch,' Go. ( )*aír*( )*na* 'heel'; IE *dń̥t-* > Go. *tun*( )*us* 'tooth' beside IE *ékwo-* plus *dń̥t-* > Go. *aíƕa-tun*( )*i* 'horsetooth, bramble'; Gk. *oktṓ*, Go. *a*( )*áu* 'eight'; L *con-véntio*, Go. ( )*a-qum*( )*s* 'assembly'; IE *km̥tóm*, Gk. *(he)katón*, Go. ( )*un*( ) 'hundred'

13.6. It is easier to formulate Verner's law than to explain its operation. The following considerations, though leaving many questions unanswered, appear to be relevant:

(a) It is clear that primary accent, whether based chiefly on pitch or chiefly on stress, requires an increased expenditure of effort (fortis articulation), whereas lesser degrees of accent demand reduced effort (lenis articulation).

(b) It is not uncommon for voiceless fricatives like /f þ x s/ to become lenited and then voiced when occurring under a reduced accent. In Middle English, for instance, *of* [of] occurred as both adverb and preposition. It still has voiceless [f] in our stressed adverb *off*, but [f] in our weakly stressed preposition has become voiced: [f] > [v̥] > [v]; by analogy, [v] has been introduced into the stressed forms of the preposition as well. The same voicing appears in ME *þat* [þat] > NE [ðæt] and ME *is* [is] > NE [iz].

(c) The [ƀ ð ǥ] that arose through Verner's law merged respectively with /ƀ ð ǥ/ < IE /bh dh gh/ and so came to contrast with their former coallophones /f þ x/.

SECONDARY SPLIT

13.7. Unlike IE /p t k/, IE /s/ was already fricative ([z] before voiced obstruents, [s] elsewhere), but its development in Proto-Germanic is comparable with theirs, both initially (*sēt-´* > *sēð-* 'seed') and noninitially (*wés-* > *wes-* 'feast, dine' beside *wes-´* > *wez-* 'indulge oneself'). Under the Proto-Germanic initial primary stress, forms like the last two were accented alike: *wés-* 'feast' and *wéz-* 'indulge oneself,' in which *s z* were now independent of their environment and so contrasted. When a factor governing the distribution of coallophones is changed or lost, so that their occurrence is no longer wholly predictable, the result is a **secondary split**.

13.8. Gothic often fails to show the effects of Verner's law, e.g., *ufar* vs. OS *oƀar*, OHG *ubar*, *waúrþan* for Pre-Go. **waúrdun*, *þahan* for Pre-Go. **þagan*, *nasjan* for Pre-Go. **nazjan*. This feature is variously ascribed to the influence of nonnative (captive) speakers, to analogic leveling, or to earlier fixation of primary stress.

14 RELATIVE AND EMPHATIC DEMONSTRATIVE PRONOUNS; PRESENT-STEM ACTIVE OPTATIVE; INDO-EUROPEAN /b d g bh dh gh/

The Old Law and the New: Matt. v.17–20

(17) Ni hugjáiþ ei qēmjáu gataíran witōþ aíþþáu praúfētuns; ni qam gataíran ak usfulljan. (18) amēn áuk qiþa izwis: und þatei usleiþiþ himins jah aírþa, jōta áins aíþþáu áins striks ni usleiþiþ af witōda untē allata waírþiþ. (19) iþ saei nu gataíriþ áina anabusnē þizō minnistōnō jah láisjái swa mans, minnista háitada in þiudangardjái himinē; iþ saei táujiþ jah láisjái swa, sah mikils háitada in þiudangardjái himinē. (20) qiþa áuk izwis þatei nibái managizō waírþiþ izwaráizōs garaíhteins þáu þizē bōkarjē jah Fareisaiē, ni þáu qimiþ in þiudangardjái himinē.

(18) *untē allata waírþiþ*] 'until everything is fulfilled.'
(20) *managizō . . . þáu*] 'more . . . of your justice than (that) . . . .'

---

af (+D) from, of, by
amēn amen
Fareisaiē G of the Pharisees
garaíhtei f. justice
gataíran IV destroy, break
hugjan suppose, think
izwar pl. your, yours
jōta m. iota, jot
láisjan teach
managiza greater, more
mikils great
minnists least, smallest
nibái, niba unless, except
nu now, therefore
sah 14.2 he (emphatic)
striks m. tittle, bit
táujan do, make
þáu than, then, else
usfulljan fulfill
usleiþan I pass, come out

14.1. Relative pronouns are formed by adding *-ei* to the first and second person pronouns (*ikei*, *þuei*, *juzei*, etc.) and to *sa*, *þata*, *sō*. Before *-ei*, weakly stressed *a* is lost, and *z* replaces *s*. *saei*, *þatei*, *sōei* is thus declined:

sg. N	saei (izei)	þatei	sōei (sei)
A	þanei	þatei	þōei
G	þizei	þizei	þizōzei
D	þammei	þammei	þizáiei
pl. N	þáiei (izei)	þōei	þōzei
A	þanzei	þōei	þōzei
G	þizēei	þizēei	þizōei*
D	þáimei	þáimei	þáimei

14.2. The emphatic demonstrative pronoun, which is formed by adding *-uh* to *sa*, *þata*, *sō*, expresses contrast as well as emphasis. Before *-uh*, weakly stressed *a* is lost, and *z* replaces *s*. *-uh* loses its *u* after a stressed vowel:

sg. N	sah	þatuh	sōh
A	þanuh	þatuh	—
G	þizuh	þizuh	—
D	þammuh	þammuh	—
pl. N	þáih	—	—
A	þanzuh	þōh	—
G	—	—	—
D	—	þáimuh	—

14.3. The present-stem active optatives of *baíran* 'bear,' *nasjan* 'save,' and *salbōn* 'anoint' are the following:

sg. 1	baíráu	nasjáu	salbō
2	baíráis	nasjáis	salbōs
3	baírái	nasjái	salbō
du. 1	baíráiwa	[nasjáiwa]	[salbōwa]
2	baíráits	[nasjáits]	[salbōts]
pl. 1	baíráima	nasjáima	salbōma
2	baíráiþ	nasjáiþ	salbōþ
3	baíráina	nasjáina	salbōna

14.4. Conjugate as above the verbs listed in 10.3abe.
14.5. The present-stem optative is used chiefly (a) to express wishes capable of fulfillment:

ei mis gibáis háubiþ Iōhannis '(I desire) that thou give me the head of John' (contrast *wáinei þiudanōdēdeiþ*, 13.2a)

(b) in the present, to express:

exhortation: *gawaúrkjáima hleiþrōs þrins* 'let us make three tents,' *ni filuwaúrdjáiþ* 'do not use many words'
uncertainty: *ƕas þannu sa sijái?* 'who, then, can this be?'
supposition: *jabái ƕas mein waúrd fastái* 'if anyone keep my word,' *táujiþ jah láisjái* 'shall do and (may indeed) teach'
purpose: *ei waíhtái ni fraqistnái* 'that nothing may be lost'
possibility: *faírgunja miþsatjáu* 'I could remove mountains'
indirect discourse: *jus qiþiþ þatei wajamērjáu?* 'do you say that I blaspheme?'

(c) in the present after *faúrþizei* (cf. 13.2c):

faúrþizei jus bidjáiþ ina 'before ye ask him'

SHIFT OF INDO-EUROPEAN /b d g bh dh gh/

14.6. IE /b d g/ became voiceless in Germanic. Compare:

/b/	Lith. *dubùs*	/p/	Go. *diups* 'deep'
/d/	L *edere*	/t/	Go. *itan* 'eat'
/g/	L *ager*, Gk. *agrós*	/k/	Go. *akrs* 'field'

A preceding IE [z] likewise became voiceless:

[zd]	IE *nizdos*, L *nīdus*	/st/	OE OHG *nest* 'nest'
[zg]	Lith. *mezgù* 'I tie in knots'	/sk/	OHG *masca* 'mesh'

IE /dd/ produced the same Germanic reflex as IE [zd]:

/dd/	IE *maddos* > *ma(d)ᶻdos*	/st/	OE *mæst* 'food, mast'

14.7. IE /bh dh gh/ became respectively PGc. /ƀ ð ǥ/:

/bh/	SK. *nábhas* 'cloud'	/ƀ/	OS *neƀal* 'mist'
/dh/	Sk. *rudhirás*	/ð/	Go. D f. *ráudái* 'red'
/gh/	Sk. *stighnōti*	/ǥ/	Go. *steigiþ* 'ascends'

A preceding IE [z] remained voiced; for example:

[z]	IE *mizdh-*, Av. *miždəm*	/z/	Go. *mizdō* 'reward'

These fricatives and those that developed from IE /p t k s/ through the operation of Verner's law (13.5, 13.7) merged respectively as PGc. /ƀ ð ǥ z/.

As reconstructions, IE /bh dh gh/ imply voiced aspirated stops. The phonetic accuracy of these reconstructions has been questioned. The symbols /bh dh gh/ are in standard use, however, and will be retained here.

14.8. Some apparent exceptions to the shifts described above arose from a split that occurred in Indo-European and pre-Germanic times. /b d g/ and /bh dh gh/, when followed by /t/ or /s/, had already become IE /p t k/, hence L *nūb-ere* 'marry' but perfect *nūp-sī* and p.p. *nūp-tus*; Sk. loc. *pad-í* 'on foot' but pl. *pat-sú*; Sk. *yug-ám* 'a yoke' but p.p. *yuk-tá-* 'yoked.' As a result the allophones that merged with IE /p t k/ before /t/ or /s/ later shifted in Proto-Germanic as if they had always been voiceless:

INDO-EUROPEAN AND PRE-GERMANIC							PROTO-GERMANIC
/b-t/	or	/bh-t/	>	/pt/	(12.10b)	>	/ft/
/b-s/	or	/bh-s/	>	/ps/		>	/fs/
/d-t/	or	/dh-t/	>	/tt/	(12.10c)	>	/s(s)/
/d-s/	or	/dh-s/	>	/ts/	(12.10c)	>	/s(s)/
/d-tr/	or	/dh-tr/	>	/ttr/	(12.10c)	>	/str/
/g-t/	or	/gh-t/	>	/kt/	(12.10b)	>	/xt/
/g-s/	or	/gh-s/	>	/ks/		>	/xs/

An analogic /st/ often displaced /ss/ or /s/ arising from this development. Thus IE *-bhowdh-s-* > *-bhowt-s-* did not become Go. **-báus* but *(ana)báust* 'didst command,' *-t* being introduced from other preterit singular second person forms in which it was regular.

14.9. As a result of dissimilations that occurred separately in Indic and Greek at a very early period, the first of two aspirated stops lost its aspiration when these consonants began consecutive syllables or occurred as segments of the same syllable (Grassmann's law): IE *bhendhonom* > Go. *bindan* 'bind' beside Sk. *bándhanam* (*b* < IE /bh/) 'a binding,' IE *ghn̥dh-* > Go. *gund* 'cancer' beside Gk. *kanthúlē* (*k* < *kh* < IE /gh/) 'a swelling.'

It is conventionally assumed that if an Indo-European aspirated stop was followed directly by one or more unaspirated obstruents, the aspiration was transferred from the beginning of the cluster to the end, and the entire cluster became voiced if its first component was voiced (Bartholomae's law): IE *lubh-tós* > *lub-dhós* > Sk. *lub-dhás* 'covetous' beside *lubh-yāmi* 'I yearn.' If this change, which is clearly reflected in Indo-Iranian, took place in Indo-European times, its effects were largely obliterated by analogic leveling in the other descendant language groups. Germanic appears to show no clear instances.

EXERCISE

Supply the missing consonants in accordance with 14.6–8:

Gk. *déka*, Go. ( )*aíhun* 'ten'; IE *ozdos*, Go. *a*( )*s* 'branch'; L *augēre*, Go. *áu*( )*an* 'increase'; IE *wog-s-* > *woks-*, Go. *wa*( )*sjan* 'grow'; L *scabō* 'I scrape,' Go. *ga-ska( )jan* 'create'; IE *skab-tis* > *skaptis*, Go. *ga-ska( )s* 'creation'; IE *magh-tis* > *maktis*, Go. *ma( )s* 'might'; Sk. *vḗda*, Go. *wái( )* 'I know'; IE *wejd-to-* > *wejtto-*, Go. *un-wei( )* 'unlearned'; IE *bhlād-*, Go. ( )*lō( )an* 'worship'; IE *bhlād-tr-* > *bhlāttr-*, Go. -( )*lō( )eis* 'worshiper'; IE *wedh-*, Go. *ga-wi( )an* 'bind'; IE *wedh-to-* > *wetto-*, Go. *us-wi( )* 'unbound, evil'; IE *wr̥g-*, Go. *waúr( )jan* 'work'; IE *wr̥g-t-* > *wr̥kt-*, Go. *waúr( )a* 'I worked'; IE *ghoŋgh-*, Go. ( )*ag( )an* 'go'; IE *ghoŋgh-t-* > *ghoŋkt-*, Go. *fram-( )ā( )s* 'progress'

15
MINOR NOUN DECLENSIONS; INTERROGATIVES; SHIFT OF $/k^w\ g^w\ g^wh/$

Against Enmities: Matt. v.21–22, 43–48

(21) Háusidēduþ þatei qiþan ist þáim áirizam: ni maúrþrjáis; iþ saei maúrþreiþ skula waírþiþ stauái. (22) aþþan ik qiþa izwis þatei ƕazuh mōdags brōþr seinamma swarē skula waírþiþ stauái; iþ saei qiþiþ brōþr seinamma raka skula waírþiþ gaqumþái; aþþan saei qiþiþ dwala skula waírþiþ in gaíaínnan funins. . . . (43) háusidēduþ þatei qiþan ist: frijōs nēƕundjan þeinana jah fiáis fiand þeinana. (44) aþþan ik qiþa izwis: frijōþ fijands izwarans, þiuþjáiþ þans wrikandans izwis, wáila táujáiþ þáim hatjandam izwis, jah bidjáiþ bi þans usþriutandans izwis, (45) ei waírþáiþ sunjus attins izwaris þis in himinam; untē sunnōn seina urranneiþ ana ubilans jah gōdans, jah rigneiþ ana garaíhtans jah ana inwindans. (46) jabái áuk frijōþ þans frijōndans izwis áinans, ƕō mizdōnō habáiþ? niu jah þái þiudō þata samō táujand? (47) jah jabái gōleiþ þans frijōnds izwarans þatáinei, ƕē managizō táujiþ? niu jah mōtarjōs þata samō táujand? (48) sijáiþ nu jus fullatōjái, swaswē atta izwar sa in himinam fullatōjis ist.

(46) *áinans*] 'only' *ƕō mizdōnō . . . þái þiudō*] see 3.4.

áirizans m. pl. ancients
dwala V m. sg. thou fool
fijan, fian hate
fijands, fiands m. 15.1 enemy
fōn n., G funins fire
frijōn love
frijōnds m. 15.1 friend
fullatōjis perfect
gaíaínna m. a Gehenna
gaqumþs assembly
garaíhts just
gōljan greet
gōþs good
hatan, hatjan hate
ƕas, ƕa, ƕō 15.3 who, what
ƕazuh m. each one
ƕē 15.3 how, wherewith
inwinds perverse, unjust

jabái if, although	staua f. judgment
maúrþrjan murder, kill	swarē without cause, in vain
mizdō f. reward	þiuda f. people, nation; pl. Gentiles
nēƕundja m. neighbor	þiuþjan bless
ni-u not?	ubils evil
raka (term of contempt)	urrannjan cause to come forth
rignjan rain	usþriutan abuse, trouble
sama same	wáila táujan do good
sijáiþ be ye! (opt.)	wrikan V persecute
skula waírþan be liable	

15.1. The minor noun declensions are the following:

		r-DECLENSION (MASC. AND FEM.)		ROOT CONSONANT DECLENSION MASC.	FEM.	*nt*-DECLENSION (MASC.)
		'brother' m.		'month'	'city'	'enemy'
sg.	N	brōþar		mēnōþs	baúrgs	fijands
	V-A	brōþar	A	mēnōþ*	baúrg	fijand
	G	brōþrs		?mēnōþs*	baúrgs	fijandis
	D	brōþr		mēnōþ	baúrg	fijand*
pl.	N	brōþrjus		mēnōþs*	baúrgs	fijands
	A	brōþruns		mēnōþs	baúrgs	fijands
	G	brōþrē		mēnōþē*	baúrgē	fijandē
	D	brōþrum		mēnoþum	baúrgim	fijandam

N-A *fōn* n. 'fire' has G *funins*, D *funin*; also see *manna*, 8.3.

15.2. Decline like:

(a) *brōþar*: *daúhtar* f. 'daughter,' *swistar* f. 'sister'

(b) *baúrgs*: *alhs* 'temple,' *brusts* 'breast,' *miluks* 'milk,' *spaúrds* 'racecourse'

(c) *fijands*: *bisitands* 'neighbor,' *dáupjands* 'baptist,' *gibands* 'giver,' *nasjands* 'Savior'

15.3. The interrogative pronoun *ƕas* m., *ƕa* n., *ƕō* f. 'who, what' occurs only in singular forms:

N	ƕas	ƕa	ƕō
A	ƕana	ƕa	ƕō
G	ƕis	ƕis	ƕizōs*
D	ƕamma	ƕamma	ƕizái

ƕē 'with what, wherewith, how' is the instrumental of *ƕa*.

15.4. The interrogative adjectives *ƕileiks* 'what sort,' *ƕēláuþs** (f. *-láuda*) 'how great' and their correlatives *swaleiks* 'such,' *swaláuþs* (f. *-láuda*) 'so great' follow *blinds* (11.1). *ƕaþar* 'which (of two)' occurs only in the masculine and neuter nominative singular. The extant forms of *ƕarjis* 'which (of more than two)' follow *niujis* (11.2). The interrogative enclitic *-u* is added to the first word of its clause, e.g., *niu* 'not?' in Matt. v.46–47, above, *skuldu ist* 'is it lawful?' *abu þus silbin* 'of thyself?'

SHIFT OF /k^w g^w g^wh/

15.5. The Germanic reflexes of /k^w g^w g^wh/ are only roughly comparable with those of IE /k g gh/. The labiovelars were much more subject to conditioned change and often to analogic leveling, which served to obscure their phonologic development. In Germanic the labiovelars appear partly without the labial feature, partly without the velar feature, and partly with both features.

15.6. [^{w}] in /k^w g^w/ was lost in Germanic before IE *u ū* and before a new *u* that developed within the preliterate period:

/k^w/	k^w*u-*	/xØ/ Go. *-hun* (indefinite enclitic)
	beside k^w*ē*	/x^w/ Go. *ƕē* 'wherewith, how'
/g^w/	g^w*m̥-* > Gc. *k(*^{w}*)um-*	/kØ/ OE *cuman*, OHG *koman* 'come'
	beside g^w*em-*	/k^w/ Go. *qiman*, OHG *queman* 'come'

Forms like Go. p.p. *qumans* 'come' are analogical.

15.7. /k^w/—when not subject to Verner's law (15.12)—and /g^w/ similarly lost [^{w}] before consonants:

/k^w/	*sek*^{w}*tís*	/xØ/ OHG *gi-siht* 'sight, vision'
	beside *sék*^{w}*eti*	/x^w/ Go. *saíƕiþ* 'sees'
/g^w/	g^w*rēso-*	/kØ/ OI *krās* 'tidbit, morsel'
	beside g^w*er-*	/k^w/ OHG *querdar* 'bait'

q in Go. *qrammiþa* 'dampness' may represent a scribal substitution for *k*; cf. OI *krammr* 'damp (with snow).'

15.8. The enclitic *-k*^{w}*e* 'and' also lost [^{w}] in Germanic:

/k^w/	*ne-k*^{w}*e*, L *neque*	/xØ/ Go. *nih* 'and not, nor'
	but *sék*^{w}*e*	/x^w/ Go. *saíƕ* 'see thou'

15.9. It is often assumed that [^{w}] in /k^w g^w/ was lost in Germanic when originally followed by *o ō*:

/k^w/	k^w*olsos*	/xØ/ Go. *hals*, OE *heals* 'neck'
/g^w/	A g^w*ōm*	/kØ/ OSw. OS *kō* 'cow'

But in many instances there is no trace of delabialization. Thus k^w*o-* appears in Go. *ƕas*, *ƕadrē*, *ƕan*, *ƕar*, *ƕarjis*, *ƕaþar* (etc.) and k^w*ōd-* in Go. *ƕōta* 'threat.' Although this retention of [^{w}] is often ascribed to analogic leveling, some investigators now believe that IE *o ō*, presumably being less lip-rounded than *u ū*, would be unlikely (or at least less likely) to absorb the labial element.

15.10. IE /k^w/ became Britannic Celtic, Osco-Umbrian, and Classical Greek /p/. In sporadic instances Germanic shows reflexes of a pre-Germanic /p/ in forms that might be expected to reflect IE /k^w/, e.g., /p/ > *f* in OHG *ofan* beside /k^w/ > *h* in Go. *aúhns* 'oven,' /p/ > *f* in OI *ulfr* beside /k^w/ > *g* (by Verner's law) in OI *ylgr* 'she-wolf.' The *p*-forms, which have no satisfactory phonologic explanation, appear to be due partly to pre-Germanic borrowing and partly to contamination.

15.11. Initially, /g^wh/ lost [^{w}] as above in 15.6:

/g^wh/ g^w*hn̥-* > Gc. *ǥ(^{w})un-* /ǥ∅/ OE *gūþ* 'fight, battle'

But the Germanic development of initial /g^wh/ is only sparsely represented and therefore difficult to determine, and the problem is further complicated by mutually contradictory etymologies. Thus the Germanic word for 'warm' (OS OHG *warm*, OE *wearm*, etc.) is variously traced to g^w*hermos*/g^w*hormos* (Gk. *thérmos*, L *formus*) or to *wer-*/*wor-* (Arm. *vaṙim* 'I burn,' Hit. *war-* 'burn,' OCS *variti* 'cook').

15.12. Medially, /k^w/—when subject to the operation of Verner's law—and /g^wh/ merged in Germanic.

(a) After [ŋ], both the labial and velar elements normally survived:

/g^wh/ *seŋ*g^w*heti* [gw] Go. *siggwiþ* 'sings'

But /g^wh/, when becoming voiceless (see 14.8), produced /k^w/, which lost [^{w}] before a consonant, as above in 15.7:

/g^wh/ *leŋ*g^w*h-tos* > *lenk*^{w}*tos* /x∅/ Go. *leihts* 'light'

(b) The labial element was lost as in 15.6, above:

/k^w/ *perk*^{w}*ú-* /ǥ∅/ Go. *faírguni* 'mountain'

(c) Between a vowel and a liquid or nasal, only the labial element survived; in Gothic it appears as *u*:

/k^w/ *sek*^{w}*ní-* > Gc. *se(ǥ)wni-* > *siuns* 'sight, appearance'
/g^wh/ *neg*^{w}*hr-* > Gc. *ne(ǥ)wr-* > **niura* (OHG *nioro* 'kidney')

(d) Before [j] and between vowels, leveling appears to have been active, the result being either /ǥ/ or /w/:

/k^w/ *ə*k^w*jā́* > OE *īeg-* 'river' but MHG *ouwe* 'watery meadow'
/g^wh/ *knejg*^{w}*honom* > Go. *hneiwan* but OE OS OHG *hnīgan* 'bow'

15.13. For reasons already indicated (15.9–11, 15.12d), no phonologic exercise on /k^w g^w g^wh/ is included here.

16
'BE'; PRETERIT-PRESENT VERBS; PROTO-GERMANIC FRICATIVES

The Good Shepherd: John x.11–16

(11) Ik im haírdeis gōds. haírdeis sa gōda sáiwala seina lagjiþ faúr lamba. (12) iþ asneis jah saei nist haírdeis, þizei ni sind lamba swēsa, gasaíƕiþ wulf qimandan jah bileiþiþ þáim lambam jah þliuhiþ, jah sa wulfs frawilwiþ þō jah distahjiþ þō lamba. (13) iþ sa asneis afþliuhiþ untē asneis ist, jah ni karist ina þizē lambē. (14) ik im haírdeis sa gōda; jah kann meina, jah kunnun mik þō meina. (15) swaswē kann mik atta jah ik kann attan, jah sáiwala meina lagja faúr þō lamba. (16) jah anþara lamba áih þōei ni sind þis awistris, jah þō skal briggan, jah stibnōs meináizōs háusjand. jah waírþand áin awēþi, áins haírdeis.

(11) *gōds* for *gōþs*; see 16.3a, below.
(12) *nist*] see 16.1.
(13) *jah ni karist ina þizē lambē*] with *karist* (*kara* plus *ist* 'it concerns') or *kara* alone, the person concerned is expressed by an accusative, the object of the concern by a genitive.
(16) *stibnōs meináizōs háusjand*] objective genitive. The genitive may modify a verb of hearing, asking, desiring, remembering, reminding, calling, helping, sparing, awaiting, expecting, or the like so as to imply its "logical object."

---

afþliuhan II   run away, flee
áih 16.2   (I) have
awēþi n.   flock of sheep
awistr n.   sheepfold
bileiþan I (+D)   leave, forsake
frawilwan III   snatch, catch
kann 16.2   know (1 sg.), knows
kara f.   concern, care
kunnun 16.2   (they) know
lagjan   lay down, lay, set, place
lamb n.   lamb, sheep
sáiwala f.   life, soul, spirit
skal 16.2   (I) must
þliuhan II   flee
wulfs m.   wolf

16.1. The present forms of the verb 'be' are the following:

		INDICATIVE	OPTATIVE
sg.	1	im	sijáu
	2	is	sijáis
	3	ist	sijái
du.	1	siju	sijáiwa
	2	sijuts	sijáits*
pl.	1	sijum	sijáima
	2	sijuþ	sijáiþ
	3	sind	sijáina

j is sometimes omitted: *sium*, *siái*, etc. *nist*, *karist*, *þatist* are respectively contractions of *ni ist*, *kara ist*, *þata ist*. The present-stem optative serves also for an imperative, as in *sijáiþ nu jus fullatōjái* (Matt. v.48, p. 68). The remaining forms of 'be' are expressed by *wisan* V.

16.2. A few verbs, called preterit-presents, have strong past forms that acquired present meanings at a very early period, e.g., IE *wojda* (orig. 'I have seen,' later 'I know') > Sk. *vḗda*, Gk. *oĩda*, Go. *wáit*. This shift in meaning gave rise to the label; in form the present tense is an old preterit, but the meaning is present. Germanic formed new weak preterits and new present verbals for most of these verbs:

ABLAUT CLASS		PRESENT INDICATIVE SINGULAR	PRESENT INDICATIVE PLURAL	PRETERIT INDICATIVE	PAST PARTICIPLE	INFINITIVE OR PRESENT PARTICIPLE
I	'know'	wáit	witum	wissa	—	witan
	'know'	láis	—	—	—	—
II	'profits'	dáug	—	—	—	—
III	'know'	kann	kunnum	kunþa	kunþs	kunnan
	'need'	þarf	þaúrbum	þaúrfta	þaúrfts	þaúrbands
	'dare'	gadars	-daúrsum	-daúrsta	—	-daúrsan
IV	'must, owe'	skal	skulum	skulda	skulds	skulan*
	'think'	man	munum*	munda	munds	munan
	'behoove'	binah	—	—	binaúhts	—
	'suffice'	ganah	—	—	—	—
VI	'have room'	gamōt	—	gamōsta*	—	—
	'fear'	ōg	—	ōhta	—	ōgands
?	'be able'	mag	magum	mahta	mahts	magands
?	'have'	áih	áigum, áihum	áihta	—	áigands, áihands

The past participles *þaúrfts* 'necessary, needy,' *skulds* 'lawful,' *munds* 'thought, supposed,' *binaúhts* 'behooving, proper, lawful,' and *mahts* 'possible' serve as adjectives; *kunþs* serves as both adjective ('known') and noun ('acquaintance').

PROTO-GERMANIC FRICATIVES IN GOTHIC

16.3. The Proto-Germanic fricatives were /ƀ đ z ǥ ǥʷ f þ s x xʷ/.

(a) In Gothic, /ƀ đ/ remained fricative only after a vowel or *ái áu iu*: [ƀ] in *liban* 'live,' *hláibōs* 'loaves,' *háubiþ* 'head,' [đ] in G sg. *gōdis* 'good,' *anabiudan* 'command.' Elsewhere, /ƀ đ/ had already become stops, at first initially and after nasals in Germanic and then in other positions in Pre-Gothic, hence [b] in Go. *baíran* 'bear,' *lamba* 'lambs,' *salbōn* 'anoint,' *arbi* 'inheritance' and [d] in Go. *diups* 'deep,' *land* 'land,' *huzd* 'treasure,' *gards* 'court, dwelling.'

[ƀ đ], when remaining fricative after a vowel or *ái áu iu*, were still further restricted. Finally or before final /s/, they became voiceless and merged respectively with /f þ/; for example:

[ƀ] in pl. *hláibōs* but /f/ in sg. N *hláifs*, A *hláif*
[đ] in G sg. *gōdis* but /þ/ in m. N *gōþs*, n. N-A *gōþ*

In spellings like *hláibs*, *hláib*, *gōds*, *gōd*, *b d* were carried over from those forms in which [ƀ đ] had remained.

(b) In Gothic, /z/ remained medially but merged with /s/ finally, as in G *riqizis* beside N-A *riqis* 'darkness.'

In spellings like *riqiz* for *riqis*, *z* was carried over from those forms in which it had remained in medial position. *us-* > *uz-* by Verner's law (13.5) was assimilated to a following *r*: *ur-reisan* 'arise,' *ur-rists* 'resurrection.'

(c) After [ŋ], /ǥ ǥʷ/ produced respectively Gc. [g gw], e.g., [ŋg] in Go. *laggei* 'length' and [ŋgw] in *siggwiþ* 'sings.' Go. /ǥ/ probably had the allophone [x] both finally and before final /s/ or /t/, as in *dags* 'day,' A *dag*, *magt* 'canst' beside [ǥ] in *dagōs* 'days' and *magum* 'we can.'

(d) Pre-Go. initial *fl-* (labial plus dental) underwent assimilation to *þl-* (dental) in stems ending in /x/ (*þliuh-an* = OS OHG *fliohan* 'flee'), /xs/ (*þlahs-jan* 'terrify'), or /kʷ/ (*þlaq-us* 'soft, tender'). Contrast Go. *flōd-us* = OE OS *flōd* 'flood, stream' D *flaht-ōm* = MGH *flechten* 'braids (of hair).'

(e) /x/ first developed allophonic [h] initially before vowels in Germanic but became /h/ in all positions in historic Gothic. PGc. /xʷ/ appears in Gothic as *ƕ*: PGc. *sexʷanan* > Go. *saíƕan* 'see.'

The spelling of the manuscripts reflects later weakening and loss of /h/. *-h* in *-uh*, *jah*, *nih*, *nuh* is readily assimilated to a following consonant: *wasuþ-þan*, *jad-du*, *niþ-þan*, *nuk-kant*, etc. *h* may be omitted medially before or between consonants (*hiuma* for *hiuhma*, *als* for *alhs*) and finally after originally long vowels bearing weak stress (*ƕarjano* for *ƕarjanoh*). An unetymological *h* may be introduced medially between consonants, e.g., *waurht-* for *waurt-* = OE *wort* 'root.'

16.4. After weakly stressed vowels in Pre-Gothic, medial fricatives were voiceless when the preceding consonants were voiced and, conversely, were voiced when the preceding consonants were voiceless (Thurneysen's law of dissimilation):

/f/ *wald-ufni* 'authority'
/þ/ *mild-iþa* 'mildness'
/s/ D *rim-isa* 'rest'
/x/ D *stáin-ahamma* 'stony'

/ƀ/ *fráist-ubni* 'temptation'
/đ/ *áuþ-ida* 'dryness, desert'
/z/ D *riq-iza* 'darkness'
/ǥ/ D *wulþ-agamma* 'glorious'

This change has no bearing on words plus enclitic *-u* or *-uh*, before which /ƀ đ z/ remained respectively as Go. *b d z*.

j w were voiceless after voiceless consonants: *aúhj-ōdus* 'tumult,' *weit-wōdē* 'of witnesses.' Exceptions to *f/b* and *þ/d* occur, e.g., *sil-ubr* 'silver,' *diup-iþa* 'depth,' *háuh-iþa* 'height.' *h/g* is confined to the suffix *-aha-/-aga-*, in which *h* or *g* may follow a voiced consonant: D *stáin-ahamma*, above, but also *mōd-agamma* 'angry.'

EXERCISE

Supply the missing consonants in accordance with 16.3–4:
PGc. *ǥeƀanan*, Go. *gi*( )*an* 'give'; PGc. *ǥeƀe*, Go. *gi*( ) 'give thou'; IE g^w*e-tete*, PGc. k^w*eþeđe*, Go. *qiþi*( ) 'ye say,' *qiþi*( )*uh* 'and say ye'; PGc. x^w*az*, Go. *ƕa*( ) 'who,' *ƕa*( )*uh* 'each'; IE *-m̥njo-* (suffix), PGc. *-uƀnja-*, Go. *wit-u*( )*ni* 'knowledge,' *wund-u*( )*ni* 'wound, plague'; IE *apó*, PGc. *aƀa*, Go. *a*( ) 'of, from,' *a*( )*u* 'of? from?'; IE *wélīte*, PGc. *wélīđe*, Go. *wilei*( ) 'ye will,' *wilei*( )*u* 'will ye?'; IE sg. N *lewbhos*, PGc. *lewƀaz*, Go. *liu*( )*s*, IE pl. A *lewbhons*, PGc. *lewƀanz*, Go. *liu*( )*ans* 'dear'; pre-Gc. *wélīs* > PGc. *-īz*, Go. *wilei*( ) 'thou wilt,' *wilei*( )*u* 'wilt thou?'; IE *-os-* (suffix), PGc. *-az-*, Go. *hláiwa*( )*nōs* 'graves,' *arƕa*( )*nōs* 'arrows'; IE *lowdh-*, PGc. *lawđ-*, Go. m. *swaláu*( )*s*, f. *swaláu*( )*a* 'so great'

17
WEAK *t*-PRETERITS; *áinshun*; INDO-EUROPEAN /ī ē ā ō ū/

The Ruler's Daughter: Luke viii.41–42, 49–56

(41) Jah sái qam waír þizei namō Iaeirus (sah faúramaþleis swnagōgáis
was), jah driusands faúra fōtum Iēsuis bad ina gaggan in gard seinana;
(42) untē daúhtar áinahō was imma swē wintriwē twalibē, jah sō swalt.
miþþanei þan iddja is, manageins þraíhun ina. . . . (49) naúhþan imma
rōdjandin gaggiþ sums mannē fram þis faúramaþleis swnagōgeis qiþands
du imma þatei gadáuþnōda daúhtar þeina; ni dráibei þana láisari. (50) iþ
is gaháusjands andhōf imma qiþands: ni faúrhtei; þatáinei galáubei, jah
ganasjada. (51) qimands þan in garda, ni fralaílōt áinōhun inn gaggan
alja Paítru jah Iakōbu jah Iōhannēn jah þana attan þizōs máujōs jah áiþein. (52) gaígrōtun þan allái jah faíflōkun þō. þaruh qaþ: ni grētiþ,
untē ni gaswalt ak slēpiþ. (53) jah bihlōhun ina gasaíƕandans þatei gaswalt. (54) þanuh is usdreibands allans ūt jah faírgreipands handu izōs
wōpida qiþands: mawi, urreis! (55) jah gawandida ahman izōs, jah ustōþ
suns. jah anabáud izái giban mat. (56) jah usgeisnōdēdun fadrein izōs.
iþ is faúrbáud im ei mann ni qiþeina þata waúrþanō.

(41) *bad* for *baþ* (16.3a); cf. *-báud* for *-báuþ* in verses 55-56.

(42) *was imma*] 'he had' *áinahō*] *ainoho* MS *sō swalt*] 'she was dying'; her death is reported below in verse 49.

(49) *gaggiþ*] historical present *fram*] 'from (the household)'

(55) *ustōþ* for *usstōþ* *anabáud* for *anabáuþ* *giban*] see 17.4.

(56) *usgeisnōdēdun fadrein* (8.5) *faúrbáud* for *faúrbáuþ* *qiþeina* for *qēþeina* *þata waúrþanō*] 'what had happened.'

áinaha wk. adj. only
áinshun (see 17.3)
áiþei f. mother
alja except
bihlahjan VI laugh at
dráibjan trouble
fadrein n. sg. parents
faírgreipan I take hold of

faúramaþleis m. ruler
faúrbiudan II order, charge
faúrhtjan fear
flōkan* VII bewail
fralētan VII let, allow
gadáuþnan die
gaggan 17.1 go, come, walk
galáubjan believe
ganasjan save
gards m. household, court
gaswiltan III die, be dying
gawandjan bring back, return
grētan VII weep
Iaeirus Jairus
Iakōbu A James
inn adv. in, within
mats m. food
mawi f., G máujōs maiden
naúh-þan yet, still
Paítru A Peter
slēpan VII sleep
swiltan III be dying
swnagōgáis, -eis G of the synagogue
twalibē G twelve
þreihan I crowd, press upon
urreisan I arise
usdreiban I put out, drive out
usgeisnan be amazed
wintrus m. winter, year
wōpjan cry out

17.1. *gaggan* 'go,' originally a strong verb of Class VII, once has the weak preterit *gaggida* and otherwise *iddja*, *iddjēs*, etc., but retains the strong past participle *gaggans*. *káupatjan* 'buffet' has pret. *káupasta* and pp. *káupatiþs**.

17.2. In addition to *káupatjan*, six weak verbs have past forms with *t*-suffixes. Before these suffixes, a *g* or *k* occurring in the present is replaced by *h*:

	INFINITIVE	PRETERIT INDICATIVE	PAST PARTICIPLE
'bring'	briggan	brāhta	brāhts*
'use'	brūkjan	brūhta	brūhts*
'buy'	bugjan	baúhta	-baúhts
'think'	þagkjan	þāhta	-þāhts
'seem'	þugkjan	þūhta	-þūhts
'work, make'	waúrkjan	waúrhta	-waúrhts

This alternation reflects the split described in 14.8. Thus /g/ in IE *wr̥g-* produced /k/ in Go. *waúrkjan*, but IE *wr̥g-t-* > *wr̥kt-* became PGc. *wurxt-* and Go. pret. *waúrht-*.

17.3. In the indefinite negative pronoun *ni áinshun* 'no one, not any, none,' *-hun* is indeclinable. The element *áins-* is declined in part like *blinds* (11.1) but has *-ē-* or *-ō-* where *blinds* has final *-a*:

	MASCULINE	NEUTER	FEMININE
N	áinshun	áinhun	áinōhun
A	áinnōhun, áinōhun	áinhun	áinōhun
G	áinishun	—	—
D	áinummēhun	—	—

Contrast also m. A *áin-(n)ō-hun* with *blind-ana* and m. D *áin-ummē-hun* with *blind-amma*.
17.4. The infinitive of a transitive verb may express the passive: *qēmun mōtarjōs dáupjan* 'publicans came to be baptized,' *anabáud izái giban mat* 'he bade her to be given food.'

INDO-EUROPEAN RESONANTS AND VOWELS

17.5. The parent resonants were /j w l r m n/. With pauses counted as consonants, a single resonant was syllabic between consonants but was nonsyllabic between vowels or between vowel and consonant: *stigh-/stejgh-*, *duk-/dewk-*, *ghl̥t-/ghelt-*, *wr̥t-/wert-*, *dekm̥/dekom*, *dn̥t-/dont-*, *tŋ̥g-/toŋg-*. Between consonant and vowel, a resonant was nonsyllabic after short vowel plus consonant (*sed-jō*) but was syllabic-nonsyllabic after long vowel plus one consonant (*sāg-ijō*) or after short vowel plus more than one consonant (*kerdh-ijos*).
17.6. The Indo-European short vowels (in addition to [i] and [u], above) included /e a o ə/ and probably /ь/. /ə/ ("schwa" or "schwa primum") was a weakly accented central vowel. /ь/ ("schwa secundum"), which may have been a parasitic vowel, was to merge in Germanic with /u/ before a liquid or nasal but with /e/ elsewhere: *tьlonom* > Go. *þulan* 'endure,' *nьmonós* > Go. *numans* 'taken' but *sьdonós* > OE p.p. *seten* 'sat.' The Indo-European long vowels were /ī ē ā ō ū/. Indo-European combinations like /aj ej oj aw ew ow/ or /ja je jo wa we wo/, though conventionally interpreted as diphthongs, can be analyzed more simply as clusters of vowels plus resonants or resonants plus vowels.
17.7. The Proto-Germanic accent was predominantly characterized by stress, with primary stress being fixed on word-initial syllables. Vowels bearing primary or secondary stress underwent little more than changes in quality; of the vowels of weakly stressed syllables, however, some were shortened and some were lost within preliterary times. Unless otherwise indicated, all following references to vowel changes apply only to Germanic syllables bearing primary or secondary stress.

INDO-EUROPEAN /ī ē ā ō ū/

17.8. In pre-Germanic and Proto-Germanic times, Indo-European long vowels were shortened before liquid or nasal plus consonant: IE *pērs-*, Sk. *pārṣ-* but Go. *faírzna* 'heel'; IE *wēntós* but L *ventus*, Go. *winds*, OE OFris. OS *wind* 'wind.' The shortening occurred also before semivowel plus consonant (Sk. *nāus* 'ship' beside OI *naust* 'boat shed'), though in some instances the semivowel was lost (Gk. *kṓmē* beside Go. *háims* 'village').
Otherwise, the long vowels developed as described below.
(a) IE /ā ō/ merged as /ō/ in Germanic:

/ā/ L *frāter* /ō/ Go. *brōþar* 'brother'
/ō/ L *flōs* /ō/ Go. *blōma* 'flower'

Before a vowel, this /ō/ produced Pre-Go. [ǭ] (Go. *au*):

/ā/ IE *sāwel-/sāwol-*, L *sōl* [ǭ] Go. *sauil* 'sun'
/ō/ IE *d(e)rōw-/drū-* [ǭ] Go. *trauan* 'trust'

[w] was lost after /ō/ in Pre-Gothic: *trō(w)an* > *trǭan* > Go. *trauan*. Where IE /ōw ū/ alternated, as in *d(e)rōw-/drū-*, some scholars would trace Go. *au* to the ablaut alternant with /ū/, which appears in OI *trūa*, OS *trūōn*, OHG *trūen* 'trust.'

(b) IE /ē ī ū/ remained in Proto-Germanic, /ī/ being represented by *ei* in Gothic spelling:

/ē/ Gk. *mḗn* 'month' Go. *mēna* 'moon'
/ī/ L *suīnus* 'porcine' OE *swīn*, Go. *sweins* 'pig'
/ū/ L *pūs* 'pus,' Sk. *pūtís* Go. *fūls* 'foul'

Before a vowel, /ē/ produced Pre-Go. [ę̄] (Go. *ai*):

/ē/ OCS *vějati* [ę̄] Go. *waian* 'blow'

Unlike Gothic, most Germanic dialects have separate reflexes for IE /ē/ and for a close /ẹ̄/ of mixed and partly disputed origin, as respectively in OI *dāđ* 'deed'–*hēr* 'here' = WS OE *dǣd–hēr*, OS *dād–hēr hīr*, OHG *tāt–hiar* beside Go. *gadēþs–hēr*.

EXERCISE

Supply the missing Gothic vowels in accordance with 17.8ab:
L f. *quā*, Go. *ƕ(*) 'who'; IE *dhōm-*, Go. *d(*)*m-* 'discernment'; IE *stāwejō*, Go. *st(*)*ja* 'I judge'; IE *stāwā*, Go. f. *st(*)*a* 'judgment'; IE *sē-* plus *-tís*, L *sē-men*, Go. *-s(*)*þs* 'seed'; IE *sējeti*, Go. *s(*)*iþ* 'sows'; Sk. *prītás* 'pleased, content,' Go. *un-fr(*)*deins* 'neglect'; IE *bhrūg-*, L *frūg-* 'edible,' Go. *br(*)*ks* 'useful'; Gk. Dor. f. *hā*, Go. *s(*) 'this, that, the'; Go. G *tōjis*, D *tōja*, N-A *t(*)*i* 'deed'

UNCONDITIONED MERGER

17.9. In **unconditioned merger**, all allophones of separate phonemes coalesce, as in IE /ā ō/ > Gc. /ō/, or an entire phoneme merges with /∅/, as in the Classical Latin loss of /h/.

18
COMPARISON; INDO-EUROPEAN
/a o ə/

God and Mammon: Matt. vi.24–32

(24) Ni manna mag twáim fráujam skalkinōn; untē jabái fijáiþ áinana
jah anþarana frijōþ, aíþþáu áinamma ufháuseiþ iþ anþaramma frakann.
ni maguþ guda skalkinōn jah mammōnin. (25) duþþē qiþa izwis: ni
maúrnáiþ sáiwalái izwarái ƕa matjáiþ jah ƕa drigkáiþ nih leika izwaramma ƕē wasjáiþ; niu sáiwala máis ist fōdeinái jah leik wastjōm? (26) in-
saíƕiþ du fuglam himinis, þei ni saiand nih sneiþand nih lisand in banstins, jah atta izwar sa ufar himinam fōdeiþ ins. niu jus máis wulþrizans
sijuþ þáim? (27) iþ ƕas izwara maúrnands mag anaáukan ana wahstu
seinana aleina áina? (28) jah bi wastjōs ƕa saúrgáiþ? gakunnáiþ blōmans háiþjōs, ƕáiwa wahsjand; nih arbáidjand nih spinnand. (29) qiþuh
þan izwis þatei nih Saúlaúmōn in allamma wulþáu seinamma gawasida
sik swē áins þizē. (30) jah þandē þata hawi háiþjōs himma daga wisandō jah gistradagis in aúhn galagiþ guþ swa wasjiþ, ƕáiwa máis izwis leitil
galáubjandans? (31) ni maúrnáiþ nu qiþandans: ƕa matjam aíþþáu ƕa
drigkam aíþþáu ƕē wasjáima? (32) all áuk þata þiudōs sōkjand; wáituh
þan atta izwar sa ufar himinam þatei þaúrbuþ–

(24) *untē jabái . . . aíþþáu*] 'for either . . . or.'
(25) *fōdeinái . . . wastjōm*] see 18.2 and cf. *þáim* in verse 26.
(29) *qiþuh*] *qiþa* plus *-uh*; cf. *wáituh* in verse 32.
(30) *izwis <wasjiþ>*] zeugma; the verb serves for both clauses.

---

aleina f. ell, cubit
anaáukan VII add, add to
arbáidjan toil, work
aúhns ?m. oven
bansts m. barn
blōma m. flower
drigkan III drink
duþē, duþþē therefore, because
fōdeins f. food
fōdjan feed

frakunnan (+D) 16.2 despise
gakunnan consider, recognize, read
gawasjan sik clothe oneself
gistradagis ?tomorrow (for afardaga?)
hawi n. grass
ƕáiwa how
insaíƕan V look, regard
leitil galáubjandans of little faith
lisan V gather
magan* 16.2 be able
máis more, rather
mammōnin D mammon, wealth
maúrnan be anxious
nih and not, nor, not even
nih . . . nih neither . . . nor
Saúlaúmōn Solomon
saúrgan be concerned
sneiþan I reap, cut
sōkjan seek, argue
spinnan III spin
twáim D two
þandē if, since (also: as long as, when, until)
þaúrban* 16.2 need
þei which
ufar (+ D/A) over, beyond
ufh//áusjan (+D) obey
wahstus m. growth, size
wasjan clothe, dress
witan 16.2 know
wulþrs 18.1 of worth
wulþus m. splendor, glory

18.1. Adjectives are compared by suffixing *-iz-* (or *-ōz-*) in the comparative and *-st-* (or *-ōst-*) in the superlative:

	POSITIVE	COMPARATIVE	SUPERLATIVE
'many, much'	manags	managiza	managists
'wise'	frōþs	frōdōza	—
'poor'	arms	—	armōsts

On the declension of adjectives in the comparative degree see 10.4. Superlative forms are declined strong or weak. When strong, they follow *blinds* (11.1) but do not have the pronominal ending *-ata* in the neuter singular nominative-accusative.

Adjective forms in *-uma* are inflected like comparatives but are intensives that do not imply an actual comparison. These adjectives form the superlative with *-umist-*: *aftuma* 'latter, following,' *aftumists* 'last'; *aúhuma* 'high,' *aúh(u)mists* 'highest'; *fruma* 'former, prior,' *frumists* 'first'; *hleiduma* 'the left'; *iftuma* 'next, following'; *innuma* 'inner'; *hindumists* 'hindmost, uttermost'; *spēdumists* 'last, latest.'

In each of the following adjectives the positive has one root or stem, and the comparative and superlative have another:

'good'	gōþs	batiza	batists
'little'	leitils	minniza	minnists
'great'	mikils	máiza	máists
'old'	sineigs	—	sinista
'evil'	ubils	waírsiza	—

Comparatives of adverbs end in *-is*, *-s*, or *-ōs*, superlatives in *-ist*: *áiris* 'earlier,' *mins* 'less,' *sniumundōs* 'with greater haste,' *máist* 'at most,' *frumist* 'first.'

18.2. After a comparative, the dative occurs in ablative function and implies 'than': *swinþō mis* 'mightier than I.'

INDO-EUROPEAN /a o ə/

18.3 IE /a o ə/ merged as PGc. /a/:

/a/ L *ager*, Gk. *agrós*	/a/ Go. *akrs* 'field'
/o/ L *octō*, Gk. *oktṓ*	/a/ Go. *ahtáu* 'eight'
/ə/ IE *pətḗr*, Sk. *pitā́*	/a/ Go. *fadar* 'father'

IE /ə/ appears as *a* in most Indo-European language groups but as *i* in Indo-Iranian and as *o* (< *a*) in Slavic.

The same merger occurred before or after resonants; for example:

/aj/	IE *kájkos*, L *caecus* 'blind'	/aj/	Go. *háihs* 'one-eyed'
/oj/	Gk. Dor. m. pl. *toí*	/aj/	Go. *þái* 'these, those'
/aw/	L *auris*	/aw/	Go. *áusō* 'ear'
/ow/	IE *rowdh-*	/aw/	Go. f. D *ráudái* 'red'
/wa/	L *vas* 'bail, surety'	/wa/	Go. *wadi* 'pledge'
/wo/	IE *dhwolos*	/wa/	Go. *dwals* 'foolish'

In Gothic stem syllables, PGc. /aj aw/ appear respectively as *aj aw* before vowels but as *ái áu* before consonants or finally.

IE [aŋk] and [oŋk], when not affected by Verner's law, merged as PGc. [aŋx]. In this combination, however, [ŋ] was subsequently lost, and the preceding [a] underwent compensatory lengthening and nasalization to [$\bar{a}^n$] > Pre-Go. *ā*:

INDO-EUROPEAN	GERMANIC	GOTHIC
wáŋk-	waŋx- > $\text{w}\bar{\text{a}}^{\text{n}}\text{k}$-	un-wāhs 'blameless'
tóŋk-	þaŋk- > $\text{þ}\bar{\text{a}}^{\text{n}}\text{x}$-	þāhō 'clay'

Native Pre-Go. [āx] (never [ā] alone) had only this source.

EXERCISE

Supply the missing sounds in accordance with 18.3:
L *alius*, Go. ( )*ljis* 'other'; L *hostis*, Go. *g*( )*sts* 'stranger'; IE *ləd-*, L *lassus* 'tired,' Go. *l*( )*ts* 'lazy'; Lith. Let. *vaĩ*, Go. *w*( ) 'woe,' *w*( )*a-* 'evil'; Gk.

oĩda, Go. *w*( )*t* 'I know'; Gk. *aũ ge* 'another time, again,' Go. ( )*k* 'for' because'; Osc. *loufir* 'wishes,' Go. *us-l*( )*beiþ* 'allows'; OL *tongeō* 'I know,' Go. *þ*( )*gkja* 'I thiṇk'; IE *toŋg-* plus *-t-* > *toŋkt-* (14.8), Go. *þ*( )*hta* 'I thought'; L *ad* 'to,' Go. ( )*t* 'at, by, from'; OL m. A'*oinom* (CL *ūnum*), Go. ( )*nana* 'one'; IE *páŋk-*, Go. *f*( )*han* 'seize'; L *augere*, Go. ( )*kan* 'add, increase'; IE *stət-*, L *status* 'position,' Go. *st*( )*þs* 'place'

EMERGENCE OF PRE-GOTHIC /ę̄/ AND /ǭ/

18.4. It has been observed above that PGc. /aj/ and /aw/ appear respectively in Gothic stem syllables as *aj aw* before vowels but as *ai au* (here marked *ái áu*) when final or before consonants: *waja-* 'evil' but *wái* 'woe,' *tawida* 'he did, made' but infin. *táujan*. These alternations reflect two parallel developments in Pre-Gothic.

(a) When not followed by a vowel in Pre-Gothic, [j] became syllabic, producing [i]: IE *gn̥j-om* > PGc. *kunj-an* > Pre-Go. and Go. *kun-i* 'race, brood.' Finally after a consonant, as in *kun-i*, the [i] merged with Go. /i/.

But if Pre-Go. /a/ preceded, the [i] contracted with it to form an originally long low-mid front vowel, viz., /ę̄/: IE *toj* > PGc. *þaj* > Pre-Go. *þa-i* > *þę̄* m. 'these, those.'

As already noted in 17.8b, [ę̄] also developed in Pre-Gothic as an allophone of /ē/ occurring before a vowel: IE *sējonom*, with loss of [j], > Pre-Go. *sę̄an* 'sow.' This [ę̄] merged with the /ę̄/ that had arisen through contraction, so that both are represented by *ai* in Gothic spelling. In comparative grammar, however, they must be sharply distinguished: *þái* (= Gk. Dor. *toí*) 'these, those' beside *saian* 'sow' (cf. *-sēþs* 'seed'). This merger appears to have played an important role in the development of Pre-Go. /i/ (Chapter 19).

(b) When not followed by a vowel in Pre-Gothic, /aw/ underwent a parallel vocalization and contraction, producing an originally long low-mid back vowel, viz., /ǭ/: IE *awgonom* > PGc. *awkanan* > Pre-Go. *a-ukan* > *ǭkan* 'increase.' As observed in 17.8a, another [ǭ] developed in Pre-Gothic as an allophone of /ō/ before a vowel, as in IE *stāwā* > Pre-Go. *stō(w)a* > *stǭa* f. 'judgment.' Pre-Go. /ǭ/ and [ǭ] merged and are spelled alike with *au* in Gothic, though in comparative grammar they must be carefully distinguished: *áukan* (L *augere*) 'increase' beside *staua* 'judgment' (cf. *stōjan* 'judge'). In turn, this merger appears to have had an important effect on the development of Pre-Go. /u/ (Chapter 20).

19
'WILL'; INDEFINITE *missō*, *ƕas*, *sums*, *mannahun*, *saƕazuh*; INDO-EUROPEAN /e/ AND [i]

On Humility: Mark ix.33–41

(33) Jah qam in Kafarnaum, jah in garda qumans frah ins: ƕa in wiga miþ izwis missō mitōdēduþ? (34) iþ eis slawáidēdun; du sis missō andrunnun ƕarjis máists wēsi. (35) jah sitands atwōpida þans twalif jah qaþ du im: jabái ƕas wili frumists wisan, sijái alláizē aftumists jah alláim andbahts. (36) jah nimands barn gasatida ita in midjáim im, jah ana armins nimands ita qaþ du im: (37) saei áin þizē swaleikáizē barnē andnimiþ ana namin meinamma, mik andnimiþ; jah saƕazuh saei mik andnimiþ, ni mik andnimiþ, ak þana sandjandan mik. (38) andhōf þan imma Iōhannēs qiþands: láisari, sēƕum sumana in þeinamma namin usdreibandan unhulþōns, saei ni láisteiþ uns, jah waridēdum imma untē ni láisteiþ unsis. (39) iþ is qaþ: ni warjiþ imma; ni mannahun áuk ist saei táujiþ maht in namin meinamma jah magi spráutō ubilwaúrdjan mis; (40) untē saei nist wiþra izwis, faúr izwis ist. (41) saei áuk allis gadragkjái izwis stikla watins in namin meinamma untē Xristáus sijuþ, amēn qiþa izwis ei ni fraqisteiþ mizdōn seinái.

(33) *qumans*] see 19.3   *miþ izwis missō*] see 19.2a.
(35) *ƕas*] see 19.2b.
(38) *sumana*] see 19.2c.
(41) *stikla*] instrumental dative   *mizdōn seinái*] see 19.4.

---

aftumists last, aftermost
allis in general, at all, wholly, indeed
andrinnan III dispute, race
arms m. arm
atwōpjan call
fraqistjan spoil, destroy
gadragkjan give to drink
gasatjan set, lay, place, establish
ƕarjis who, which (of more than two)
láistjan follow

mahts f. might, virtue, miracle
máists greatest, chief
midjis adj. middle, midst
missō 19.2a each other, reciprocally
mitōn consider, think
ni mannahun 19.2e no one
saƕazuh saei 19.2d whosoever
sandjan send
sitan V sit
slawan be silent
stikls m. cup
swaleiks such
twalif twelve
ubilwaúrdjan (+D) speak evil of
warjan (+D/A) forbid
watō n. water
wiljan 19.1 will, wish, desire

19.1. The present of the verb 'will' was originally optative ('would'); it retains preterit-stem optative endings:

sg. 1	wiljáu	du. 1	—	pl. 1	wileima
2	wileis	2	wileits	2	wileiþ
3	wili			3	wileina

Modeled after these forms are the new infinitive *wiljan*, the new present participle *wiljands*, and a new weak preterit: sg. 1 indicative *wilda*, optative *wildēdjáu*, etc.

19.2. In the foregoing reading, indefinite pronouns are expressed as follows:

(a) 'each other, one another' by the reciprocal adverb *missō*, which may occur with or without a reflexive

(b) 'anyone' by the masculine interrogative pronoun *ƕas*, to which corresponds the neuter *ƕa* 'anything'

(c) 'a certain one, someone' by the adjective *sums* (11.1), which occurs also in the phrasings *sums . . . sums* 'the one . . . the other' and *sumái* (or *sumáih*) . . . *sumáih* 'some . . . others'

(d) 'whosoever' by m. *saƕazuh saei*, which with the alternants *ƕazuh saei* and *saƕazuh izei* appears only in the singular nominative (other alternants will be noted in the following chapter)

(e) 'no one' by *ni mannahun*, in which *manna* is declined as in 8.3; *-hun* is indeclinable. Cf. *ni áinshun* 'no one,' 17.3. *ni ƕashun* m. 'no one' and *nist saei* 'there is no one who' appear only in the nominative singular.

19.3. The past participle of an intransitive verb expresses a state resulting from a previous occurrence or action, e.g., *ƕa wēsi þata waúrþanō* 'what it might be that had come to pass,' *in garda qumans* 'when he had come into the household.'

19.4. The dative in ablative function, expressing leaving, loss, and the like, often occurs with verbs having the preverb *af-* or *fra-*: *afstandand sumái galáubeinái* 'some will leave the faith,' *fraliusands áinamma þizē* 'losing one of them.'

INDO-EUROPEAN /e/ AND [i]

19.5. IE /e/ was subject to two Proto-Germanic changes.

(a) Before a consonant or finally, IE /ej/ produced [ij] > [ī], which merged with IE = PGc. /ī/ (17.8b):

/ej/ Gk. *steíkhō* 'I go, walk'	/ī/ Go. *steiga* 'I ascend'

The Gothic spelling *ei* was taken from Greek; by the time of Wulfila, Gk. *ei* had come to represent a high front vowel.

(b) /e/ was raised before nasal plus consonant: IE *wēntós* > pre-Gc. *wentós* (17.8) > Go. *winds*, OE OFris. OS *wind* 'wind.'

IE [eŋk], when not affected by Verner's law, thus produced [iŋx] but later lost [ŋ] with compensatory lengthening of [i] to [ī^{n}], which subsequently merged with IE = PGc. /ī/, as above:

INDO-EUROPEAN	GERMANIC	GOTHIC
téŋk-	þiŋx- > þī^{n}x-	þeihan 'thrive'

Germanic umlauts of IE /e/ and [i] are not attested in Gothic.

19.6. In Gothic words that were unaffected by the foregoing changes, IE /e/ and [i] appear partly as *i* and partly as *aí*.

(a) The unconditioned Gothic reflex of IE /e/ and [i] is *i*:

/e/ L *edere*	/i/ *itan* 'eat'
[i] L *vidua* 'alone, widowed'	/i/ *widuwō* 'widow'

(b) Before *h ƕ r*, the Gothic reflex of IE /e/ and [i] is *aí* (though only in syllables bearing primary or secondary stress):

/e/ L *pecu*	/e/ *faíhu* 'cattle, wealth'
/e/ L *sequit-ur* 'follows'	/e/ *saíƕiþ* 'sees'
/e/ L *ferō*, Gk. *phérō*	/e/ *baíra* 'I bear'
[i] IE *migh-st-* > *mikst-* (14.8)	/e/ *maíhstus* 'dung'
[i] L *re-lictus* 'left behind'	/e/ *laíƕans* 'lent' (p.p.)
[i] L *vir*	/e/ *waír* 'man'

(c) IE /e/ also appears as Go. *aí* in a syllable occurring in internal open juncture (11.8) with a following syllable that invariably contains a low or mid vowel:

/e/ IE *e-awge*	/e/ *-aí-áuk* 'he added'

EXERCISE

Supply the missing Gothic vowels in accordance with 19.5–6:
IE *senti*, Osc. Umbr. *sent*, Go. *s*( )*nd* 'they are'; IE *leŋ*^{w}*h-t-* > *leŋk*^{w}*t-* (14.8), Go. *l*( )*hts* (15.7) 'light'; Gk. *deíknūmi* 'I show,' Go. *ga-t*( )*han* 'tell'; L *clepō*, Go. *hl*( )*fa* 'I steal'; L *precor* 'I pray,' Go. *fr*( )*hna* 'I ask, inquire'; L *vertō* 'I turn,' Go. *w*( )*rþa* 'I become'; L *is*, Go. ( )*s* 'he'; L *dictus* 'said' (p.p.), Go. *ga-t*( )*hans* 'told'; IE *bhewdh-*, Go. *anab*( )*dan* 'command'; IE *wéŋkō*, L *vincō* 'I conquer,' Go. *w*( )*ha* 'I fight'; Gk. *ei* 'if,' Go. ( ) 'that'; L *et* 'and, but,' Go. ( )*þ* 'but'; Gc. *eþ* 'but' plus *þaw* 'else, otherwise' > Go. ( )*þþáu* 'or'; L *pellis*, Go. *-f*( )*lls* 'skin'

HISTORIC GOTHIC /e/ AND /i/

19.7. As noted in 18.4a, Pre-Go. /ę̄/ arose from contraction of /aj/ before a consonant or word-end pause (as in *wę̄* 'woe' beside *waja-* 'evil') and from the allophone of /ē/ that occurred before a vowel (as in *sę̄an* 'sow' beside *sēð-* 'seed'). In turn, /ę̄/ probably merged with an allophone of Pre-Go. /i/.

(a) Except in weakly stressed syllables, Pre-Go. /i/ had the allophone [e] before /x x^w r/ (Go. *h ƕ r*) e.g., *fexu* 'cattle, wealth,' *sex*^{w}*ið* 'sees,' *wer* 'man,' also in reduplicating syllables, e.g., *le-lōt* 'permitted,' and in the word for 'or,' viz., *eþþǭ*. In other positions the allophone was [i], as in *nimio* 'takes' < IE *németi*, *ita* 'I eat' < IE *edō*.

In *þar*^{i}*his* 'new' (Matt. ix.16), the first *i*, a scribal addition, bore weak stress. Stressed *i* in sg. *hiri*, du. *hirjats*, pl. *hirjiþ* 'come here!' is probably due to analogy with related forms like *hidrē* 'hither.' *ai* (= *ái* or *aí*?) in *bairts* 'bitter,' *haiþn-* 'heathen,' *jain-* 'that,' *sai* 'lo!' and *waila* 'well' is phonologically regular if it represents *ái*.

(b) It appears likely that by the time of Wulfila Gothic vowels were distinguished solely by quality, not by length. If so, Pre-Go. /ę̄/ and [e] had merged as /e/, spelled *ai*, as in fourth-century Greek: *wai* 'woe,' *saian* 'sow,' *wair* 'man,' *lailaik* 'leaped' (in comparative grammar distinguished respectively as *wái*, *saian*, *waír*, *laíláik*).

20
‘ONE,’ ‘TWO,’ ‘THREE’; ‘EACH’; INDO-EUROPEAN [u l̥ r̥ m̥ n̥ ŋ̥]

Jesus Feeds a Multitude: John vi.5–13, 15

(5) þaruh ushōf áugōna Iēsus jah gáumida þammei manageins filu iddja du imma. qaþuh du Filippáu: ƕaþrō bugjam hláibans, ei matjáina þái? (6) þatuh þan qaþ fráisands ina: iþ silba wissa þatei habáida táujan. (7) andhōf imma Filippus: twáim hundam skattē hláibōs ni ganōhái sind þáim, þei nimái ƕarjizuh leitil. (8) qaþ áins þizē sipōnjē is, Andraias, brōþar Paítráus Seimōnáus: (9) ist magula áins hēr saei habáiþ ·e· hláibans barizeinans jah ·b· fiskans; akei þata ƕa ist du swa managáim? (10) iþ Iēsus qaþ: waúrkeiþ þans mans anakumbjan. wasuh þan hawi manag ana þamma stada. þaruh anakumbidēdun waírōs raþjōn swaswē fimf þūsundjōs. (11) namuh þan þans hláibans Iēsus jah awiliudōnds gadáilida þáim anakumbjandam, samaleikō jah þizē fiskē, swa filu swē wildēdun. (12) þanuh, biþē sadái waúrþun, qaþ du sipōnjam seináim: galisiþ þōs aflifnandeins dráuhsnōs, þei waíhtái ni fraqistnái. (13) þanuh galēsun jah gafullidēdun ·ib· táinjōns gabrukō us fimf hláibam þáim barizeinam þatei aflifnōda þáim matjandam. . . . (15) iþ Iēsus . . . afiddja aftra in faírguni, is áins.

(6) *þatei habáida táujan*] ‘what he was to do.’
(7) *twáim hundam skattē*] ‘for (= costing) two hundred denarii.’
(9) *·e·*] *fimf*   *·b·*] *twans* (20.1) occurs in *Skeireins* VIIa 12.
(12) *dráuhsnōs*] the *h* is probably scribal. *Skeireins* VIId 15 has *dráusnōs* ‘pieces’; cf. *driusan* II ‘fall, drop.’
(13) *·ib·*] *twalif*   *þatei aflifnōda*] collective singular.

---

afgaggan 17.1 depart
aflifnan remain, be left
aftra again, back
akei but, however
anakumbjan recline
Andraias Andrew

awiliudōn   give thanks

barizeins   (made of) barley

bugjan   buy

dráu(h)snōs f.   pieces

faírguni n.   mountain

Filippus, D -áu   Philip

fimf   five

fisks m.   fish

fraqistnan   be lost, perish

gabruka f.   (broken) bit

gadáiljan   divide

gafulljan   fill

galisan V   gather

ganōhs   enough

gasitan V   sit, sit down

gáumjan (+D/A)   observe

hund n.   hundred

ƕarjizuh m.   each, every, every one

ƕaþrō   whence

leitils   little

magula m.   little boy

Paítráus G   Peter

raþjō f.   number, account

saþs   satisfied

Seimōnáus G   Simon

silba   self

skatts m.   coin, denarius

staþs m.   place

swa filu swē   as much as

swaswē   about, just as

táinjō f.   basket

twái 20.1   two

þūsundi f.   thousand

ushafjan VI   lift up

waíhts f.   thing

waíhtái ni   nothing, lit. 'in nothing

20.1. The numeral *áins* 'one,' declined like *blinds* (11.1), also expresses 'a certain one, a certain' (verses 8–9, above), 'alone, only' (verse 15, above; cf. the plural form in Matt. v.46, p. 68), and 'one . . . another' (Mark iv.8, p. 38).

twái 'two' and *þreis** 'three' are thus declined:

	MASCULINE	NEUTER	FEMININE	MASCULINE	NEUTER	FEMININE
N	twái	twa	twōs	—	—	—
A	twans	twa	twōs	þrins	þrija	þrins
G	twaddjē	twaddjē	—	þrijē	—	—
D	twáim	twáim	twáim	þrim	þrim	—

The extant forms of *bái* 'both' are declined like *twái*.

20.2. Indefinite pronouns for 'each' are formed from *ƕas* 'who, anyone' and from *ƕarjis* 'who, which (of more than two)' by adding *-(u)h*, before which *z* occurs in place of *s* (16.3b). *-(u)h* has no *u* after a long vowel or after stressed *a*:

	MASCULINE	NEUTER	FEMININE
sg. N	ƕazuh, ƕarjizuh	-ƕah, ƕarjatōh	ƕōh, —
A	ƕanōh, ƕarjanōh	-ƕa, —	ƕōh, ƕarjō<h>
G	ƕizuh, -ƕarjizuh	—, —	—, —
D	ƕammēh, ƕarjammēh	ƕammēh, ƕarjammēh	—, —

The only recorded plural form is m. A *ƕanzuh*.

ƕazuh and *ƕarjizuh* occur also as the inflected elements of several compounds with uninflected initial *þis-*, *sa-*, *áin-*:

(a) 'whosoever'—m. N *þisƕazuh saei*, A *þisƕanōh saei*, D *þisƕammēh saei*, also N *(sa)ƕazuh saei* (or *izei*)

(b) 'whatsoever'—n. N-A *þisƕah þei* (or *þatei*), G *þisƕizuh þei*, D *þisƕammēh þei*, also A sg. *þataƕah þei*

(c) 'each one'—m. N *áinƕarjizuh* (all masculine singular forms occur), n. N *áinƕarjatōh*, f. A *áinƕarjōh*

INDO-EUROPEAN [u l̥ r̥ m̥ n̥ ŋ̥]

20.3. Gc. /u/ arose through a merger of vowels that came from the syllabic allophones of IE /w l r m n/ (17.5):

[u]	IE *jugom*, L *jugum*	/u/	Go. *juk* 'yoke'
[l̥]	IE *pl̥nós*, Lith. *pìlnas*	/ul/	Go. *fulls* 'full'
[r̥]	IE *(we)wr̥təmé*	/ur/	OHG *wurtum* 'we became'
[m̥]	IE *g*^{w}*ḿ̥tis*, L *con-ventio*	/um/	Go. *ga-qumþs* 'assembly'
[n̥]	IE *mn̥tís*, OL *mentis* 'mind'	/un/	Go. *ga-munds* 'remembrance'
[ŋ̥]	IE *kŋ̥k-´*	[uŋ]	Go. *huggrjan* 'be hungry'

Gothic shows no clear instances of IE [l̥ r̥ m̥ n̥ ŋ̥] producing /lu ru mu nu/ rather than /ul ur um un/, nor does the language reflect a Germanic umlaut of /u/.

20.4. IE [ŋ̥k], when not affected by Verner's law, produced Gc. [uŋx], then lost [ŋ] with compensatory lengthening of [u] to [ū^{n}], which later merged with IE=PGc. /ū/ (17.8b):

INDO-EUROPEAN	GERMANIC	GOTHIC
ŋ̥kt-	uŋxt- > ū^{n}xt-	ūhtwō 'dawn'

20.5. When not lengthened, /u/ produced Go. *aú* or *u*.

(a) Unless weakly stressed, /u/ became *aú* before *h* or *r*:

[u]	pre-Gc. *dhuktēr*, Lith. *duktẽ*	/o/	*daúhtar* 'daughter'
[u]	Gk. *thúra*	/o/	*daúr* 'door'
[r̥]	IE *(we)wr̥təmé*, OHG *wurtum*	/o/	*waúrþum* 'we became'

aúftō 'perhaps' may have *aú* (once spelled *u*) through internal open juncture between *uf-* 'if' (OS *of*) and *-tō*; cf. 19.6c.

(b) In other positions /u/ remained as Go. *u*:

[u]	IE *sunus*, OE *sunu*	/u/	*sunus* 'son'

EXERCISE

Supply the missing Gothic vowels in accordance with 20.3–5:
Gk. *hupér*, Go. (   )*far* 'over'; Cz. *vlk*, Go. *w*(   )*lfs* 'wolf'; IE *km̥tóm*, L *centum*, Go. *h*(   )*nd* 'hundred'; IE *tŋ̥gjonom*, Go. *þ*(   )*gkjan* 'seem'; IE *tŋ̥g-t-* > *tŋ̥kt-* (14.8), Go. *þ*(   )*hta* 'it seemed'; IE *dŋ̥t-*, Go. *t*(   )*nþus* 'tooth'; IE *wr̥gjō*, Go. *w*(   )*rkja* 'I work, make'; Gk. *hupó*, Go. (   )*f* 'under, beneath'; IE *duk-* (cf. L p.p. *ductus*), Go. *t*(   )*hans* 'led'; IE *kŋ̥́k-*, Lith. *kanká* 'suffering,' Go. *h*(   )*hrus* 'famine'; Sk. *mr̥t-* 'death,' Go. *m*(   )*rþr* 'murder'; IE *n̥-*, Go. (   )*n-* 'not'

HISTORIC GOTHIC /o/ AND /u/

20.6. It has been observed (18.4b) that /ǭ/ arose in Pre-Gothic stem syllables through contraction of /aw/ before a consonant or pause, as in Pre-Go. *tǭjan* 'do, make' beside pret. *tawiða*, and from the allophone of /ō/ that occurred before vowels, as in *stǭa* f. 'judgment' beside *stōjan* 'judge.' In turn, this /ǭ/ probably merged with an allophone of Pre-Gothic /u/.

Pre-Go. /u/ possessed the allophones [o] and [u]. [o] occurred (except in weakly stressed syllables) before /x/ (Go. *h*) or /r/, as in *doxtar* 'daughter,' *morþr* 'murder,' and also in the word *oftō* 'perhaps.' In other positions, the allophone was [u]: *ufar* 'over,' *fexu* 'cattle, wealth,' *wiðuwō* 'widow,' weakly stressed *-ux* 'and,' weakly stressed [u] in *fiður-* 'four' (a combining form). Pre-Go. long /ū/, on the other hand, was not lowered before /x/ or /r/: *ūxtwō* > Go. *ūhtwō* 'dawn,' *skūra* > Go. *skūra* 'shower.'

It appears likely that by the time of Wulfila Gothic vowels had come to contrast in quality alone. If so, long /ǭ/ and short [o] merged as /o/, spelled *au*: *taujan* 'do, make,' *staua* f. 'judgment,' *dauhtar* 'daughter,' *maurþr* 'murder,' *aufto* 'perhaps' (in comparative grammar distinguished respectively as *táujan*, *staua*, *daúhtar*, *maúrþr*, *aúftō*). At the same time, *ū u* appear to have merged as /u/, spelled *u*, and *ā a* as /a/, spelled *a*.

For the purposes of comparative grammar, however, etymological distinctions are of prime importance. Thus Go. *ái áu* must be uniformly interpreted as diphthongs, *aí aú a u* as short vowels, and *ai au ā ū* as long vowels, regardless of how these sounds may have been pronounced in the time of Wulfila.

20.7. Historic Go. *iu* may possibly represent /iw/, a vowel, or two successive vowels, as in *ni-u* 'not?' If *iu* represents these vowels, they explain why the masculine *o*-stem noun *stiur* /stí-ur/ 'calf, steer' lacks the nominative singular ending *-s* (2.3). In Gothic, final *-s* was lost after a short vowel plus *r*, and weakly stressed *ur* remained *ur*, as in *fídur-fàlþs* 'fourfold.'

21
PASSIVE OPTATIVE; LONG AND OVERLONG VOWELS IN WEAKLY STRESSED FINAL SYLLABLES

On Almsgiving and Prayer: Matt. vi.1–8

(1) Atsaíƕiþ armaiōn izwara ni táujan in andwaírþja mannē du saíƕan im, aíþþáu láun ni habáiþ fram attin izwaramma þamma in himinam. (2) þan nu táujáis armaiōn, ni haúrnjáis faúra þus, swaswē þái liutans táujand in gaqumþim jah in garunsim ei háuhjáindáu fram mannam; amēn qiþa izwis, andnēmun mizdōn seina. (3) iþ þuk táujandan armaiōn, ni witi hleidumei þeina ƕa táujiþ taíhswō þeina, (4) ei sijái sō armahaírtiþa þeina in fulhsnja, jah atta þeins, saei saíƕiþ in fulhs<n>ja, usgibiþ þus in baírhtein. (5) jah þan bidjáiþ, ni sijáiþ swaswē þái liutans, untē frijōnd in gaqumþim jah waíhstam plapjō standandans bidjan ei gáumjáindáu mannam. amēn qiþa izwis þatei haband mizdōn seina. (6) iþ þu, þan bidjáis, gagg in hēþjōn þeina, jah galūkands haúrdái þeinái bidei du attin þeinamma þamma in fulhsnja, jah atta þeins, saei saíƕiþ in fulh[l]snja, usgibiþ þus in baírhtein. (7) bidjandansuþ-þan ni filuwaúrdjáiþ swaswē þái þiudō; þugkeiþ im áuk ei in filuwaúrdein seinái andháusjáindáu. (8) ni galeikōþ nu þáim; wáit áuk atta izwar þizei jus þaúrbuþ faúrþizei jus bidjáiþ ina.

(1) *in andwaírþja mannē*] 'before men' *du saíƕan*] see 17.4.
(2) *ei háuhjáindáu*] 'that they may be glorified'; see 21.1.
(3) *þuk táujandan* may be governed by *witi* (the Latin versions of MSS Vercellensis and Veronensis have *te facientem*), but it is also possible that this construction may be an accusative absolute. *hleidumei* is the subject of *witi.*
(6) *haúrdái þeinái*] instrumental dative: '(with) thy door.'
(7) *bidjandans-uþ-þan* for *-uh-þan* *þiudō*] see 3.4.

---

andháusjan hear, listen to
armahaírtiþa f. charity, almsgiving, mercy
armaiō f. alms, pity
atsaíƕan V take heed
baírhtei f. brightness

in baírhtein openly
faúrþizei (+opt.) before
filuwaúrdei f. wordiness
filuwaúrdjan use many words
fulhsni n. secret
galeikōn be like
galūkan II shut
gáumjan observe
háuhjan glorify, exalt
haúrds f. door
haúrnjan blow a horn
hēþjō f. room, chamber
hleidumei left (hand)
láun n. reward, wage
liuta m. hypocrite
plapja* f. street, square
taíhswō f. right (hand)
þugkjan seem
usgiban V reward, give out, restore
waíhsta m. corner

21.1. The present-stem passive optatives of *baíran* 'bear,' *sōkjan* 'seek,' *salbōn* 'anoint,' and *haban* 'have' are:

sg.	1	baíráidáu	sōkjáidáu	salbōdáu	habáidáu
	2	baíráizáu	[sōkjáizáu]	[salbōzáu]	habáizáu
	3	baíráidáu	sōkjáidáu	salbōdáu	habáidáu
pl.	1-3	baíráindáu	sōkjáindáu	salbōdáu	habáindáu

21.2. Conjugate in the present-stem passive optative like:
(a) *baíran*: *niman* 'take,' *qiþan* 'say,' *haldan* 'hold, tend'
(b) *sōkjan*: *dōmjan* 'judge, discern,' *wēnjan* 'hope, tend'
(c) *salbōn*: *frijōn* 'love,' *laþōn* 'invite'
(d) *haban*: *áistan* 'revere, regard,' *arman* 'pity'

LONG AND OVERLONG VOWELS IN WEAKLY STRESSED FINAL SYLLABLES

21.3. At an early period, an Indo-European stem vowel contracted with an immediately following vowel. When both vowels were short, their contraction produced a new **long** (bimoric) vowel, which subsequently developed as if it had always been long: *wiro-es* > *wir-ōs*. But if one vowel was long, or if both were, their contraction produced an **overlong** (trimoric) vowel, which is distinguished here by the diacritic ̿: *bhāgā-es* > *bhāg-a̿s*, *bhāgā-ōm* > *bhāg-a̿m* (or *-o̿m*?; the descendant languages that retain this ending do not distinguish the reflexes of *a̿* and *o̿*).

An older opinion assumes that all the contracted vowels, together with others supposed to have undergone compensatory lengthening, were circumflex: *-o-es* > *-õs*, *-āso* > *-ãs*, *-ṓn* > *-õ*, etc.

21.4. In the weakly stressed final syllables of Germanic, **long** vowels remained long only when originally in the following positions:

	PARENT FORM	GOTHIC
(a) In monosyllables	f. A *tām*	*þō* 'this, that'
(b) In medial syllables before consonants	m. A *k*^{w}*omō-k*^{w}*e*	*ƕan-ōh* 'each'
(c) Before final /s/	N pl. *wir-ōs*	*waír-ōs* 'men'
(d) Before final /d/	*k*^{w}*otr-ēd*	*ƕadr-ē* 'whither'

Under otherwise identical conditions, the length of a vowel is greater before voiced obstruents like /z d/ than before voiceless obstruents like /s t/ because the vocal lips continue to vibrate longer; contrast NE *lose* : *loose*, *feed* : *feet*. IE final /s/ became /z/ by Verner's law. IE final /d/ probably survived until late in the Germanic period; its reflex still survives after short vowels in monosyllables.

21.5. With the exceptions above, parent long vowels became short in the weakly stressed final syllables of Germanic, /ā ē ō/ merging with Pre-Go. /a/ and /ī/ with Pre-Go. /i/:

/ā/	Ved. *yugā́*, OL *jugā*	/a/	*juka* 'yokes'
/ē/	IE *tosmē*	/a/	D *þamma* 'this, that'
/ō/	L *ferō*, Gk. *phérō*	/a/	*baíra* 'I bear, carry'
/ī/	IE *tekwī́*	/i/	*þiwi* 'handmaid'

This shortening likewise occurred before resonants; for example:

/āj/	IE loc. *stā́w-āj*	/aj/	D *stau-ái* 'judgment'
/ēw/	IE loc. *sū̆n-ḗw*, Sk. *sūn-ā́u*	/aw/	D *sun-áu* 'son'

By Pre-Gothic times, the **overlong** vowels had become merely long, long /ā/ merging with Germanic and Pre-Gothic /ō/:

	PARENT FORM	GOTHIC
N	*bhāg-ā̄s*	*bōk-ōs* 'letters, writing'
G	*bhāg-ā̄m* (or *-ō̄m*)	*bōk-ō* 'of scriptures'

EXERCISE

Supply the missing Gothic sounds:
Sk. *ádhar-āt* (< *-ōd*) 'from below,' Go. *undar*( ) 'under'; pre-Gc. *welīs*, Go. *wil*( )*s* 'thou wilt,' pre-Gc. sg. 3 *welīt*, Go. *wil*( ); Sk. *vŕ̥̥k-ās* (< *-ōs* < *-o-es*), Go. *wulf*( )*s* 'wolves'; L *edō*, Go. *it*( ) 'I eat'; IE f. *sā*, Sk. *sā́*, Go. *s*( ) 'this, that'; IE I *k*^{w}*osmē*, Go. D *ƕamm*( ) 'whom, what,' *k*^{w}*osmē-k*^{w}*e* > Gc.

D *ƕamm*( )*h* 'each'; Gk. *némō* 'I assign,' Go. *nim*( ) 'I take'; IE n. *ejā*, L *ea*, Go. *ij*( ) 'they'; IE f. *ejās*, Go. *ij*( )*s* 'they'; IE loc. g^{w}*ēnāj*, Go. D *qēn*( ) 'wife, woman'; IE k^{w}*ejlā-ōm* > *-ā̄m* or *-ō̄m*, Go. G *ƕeil*( ) 'of hours'; pre-Gc. pl. I k^{w}*ejlāmis*, Go. D *ƕeil*( )*m* 'hours'; IE *stāwā-es* > *-ā̄s*, Go. f. *stau*( )*s* 'judgments'

22
SHORT VOWELS OF ORIGINALLY MEDIAL AND FINAL SYLLABLES

Christ before Pilate: John xviii.33–40

(33) Galáiþ in praitaúria aftra Peilātus jah wōpida Iēsu qaþuh imma: þu is þiudans Iudaiē? (34) andhōf Iēsus: abu þus silbin þu þata qiþis, þáu anþarái þus qēþun bi mik? (35) andhōf Peilātus: wáitei ik Iudaius im? sō þiuda þeina jah gudjans anafulhun þuk mis. ƕa gatawidēs? (36) andhōf Iēsus: þiudangardi meina nist us þamma faírƕáu; iþ us þamma faírƕáu wēsi meina þiudangardi, aíþþáu andbahtōs meinái usdáudedideina ei ni galēwiþs wēsjáu Iudaium. iþ nu þiudangardi meina nist þaþrō. (37) þaruh qaþ imma Peilātus: an nuh þiudans is þu? andhafjands Iēsus: þu qiþis ei þiudans im ik. ik du þamma gabaúrans im, jah du þamma qam in þamma faírƕáu ei weitwōdjáu sunjái. ƕazuh saei ist sunjōs háuseiþ stibnōs meináizōs. (38) þanuh qaþ imma Peilātus: ƕa ist sō sunja? jah þata qiþands galáiþ ūt du Iudaium jah qaþ im: ik áinōhun faírinō ni bigita in þamma. (39) iþ ist biūhti izwis ei áinana izwis fralētáu in pasxa; wileidu nu ei fralētáu izwis þana þiudan Iudaiē? (40) iþ eis hrōpidēdun aftra allái qiþandans: nē þana, ak Barabban! sah þan was sa Barabba wáidēdja.

(34) *abu*] 'of?' i.e., PGc. *aba* (Go. *af*) with [b] remaining before interrogative *-u*; cf. *wileidu* in verse 39. *þáu*, introducing the second clause, means 'or.'

(36) *aíþþáu*, introducing the clause that states the consequence in a conditional sentence means 'then, in that case.' *usdáudedideina*] MS for *usdáudidēdeina*.

(37) *andhafjands*] 'answered.' Some editors add *qaþ*: 'said in reply.' Compare, however, the present participles on p. 102, verse 24. *stibnōs meináizōs*] see p. 73, commentary on line 16.

(39) *wileidu*] *wileiþ* plus *-u*; cf. *abu* in verse 34.

(40) *nē* is emphatic (< IE *nē*); contrast *ni* (< IE *ne*).

aftra again, a second time
an then?
anafilhan III deliver, commit
Barabba(s), A Barabban Barabbas
bigitan V find, meet
faírƕus m. the world
faírina f. fault, charge
fralētan VII free, let be, let down
galēwjan betray
gudja m. priest
hrōpjan cry out
ƕazuh saei whosoever
Iudaius m. Jew
nē no, nay, not
nuh now? well?
pasxa f. Passover
Peilātus Pilate
praitaúria (ún), praitōria pretorium
silba self
sunja f. truth
þaþrō thence
usdáudjan strive
wáidēdja m. robber, evildoer
wáit-ei perhaps
weitwōdjan testify
wōpjan call

SHORT VOWELS OF ORIGINALLY MEDIAL AND FINAL SYLLABLES

22.1. In the weakly stressed final syllables of Germanic, as already noted, overlong vowels were to become merely long, and long vowels were to become short except in a few phonetic environments (21.4a–d). As a further result of weak stress, in most instances the short vowels of originally final syllables had been lost before the historic period of Gothic:

/a/ Gk. *oĩda*, Sk. *vḗda* /∅/ *wáit* 'I know'
/e/ Gk. *phére* /∅/ *baír* 'bear thou'
[i] L *homini* /∅/ *gumin* 'to a man'
/o/ Gk. *agrós* /∅/ *akrs* 'field'

But the short vowels remained in certain environments.

(a) Short vowels survived in originally monosyllabic forms:

/o/ IE m. *so*, Gk. *ho*, Sk. *sá* /a/ *sa* 'this, that'

(b) A short vowel plus final *-ns* remained in Gothic; for example:

/ons/ Gk. Cret. A *lúkons* /ans/ *wulfans* 'wolves'

(c) So far as Gothic is concerned, Gc. /u/ (< IE [u m̥ n̥], etc.) was regularly lost only when occurring as a vowel in an originally third syllable. Compare the following forms:

[u] IE *péku* /u/ *faíhu* 'cattle, wealth'
[n̥] IE *bhērn̥t* /u/ *bērun* 'they bore'

but:

[m̥] IE A *bhrāterm̥* > Gc. *brōþerun* /Ø/ *brōþar* 'brother'

In weakly stressed final syllables, the Germanic reflexes of IE [u] and [i] tended to survive longer when the preceding syllable was short, as in OE *sun-u* 'son,' OS *sted-i* 'place,' and to be lost earlier when the preceding syllable was long, as in Go. *tagr* = Gk. *dákr-u* 'tear,' Go. *gasts* = L *host-i-s* 'stranger.' In Gothic, however, this phonologic difference was largely obscured by leveling. Regardless of whether the preceding syllable was long or short, the /u/ of *u*-stems was generalized, as in *hand-us* 'hand' as well as in *sun-us* 'son,' whereas the /i/ of masculine singular *i*-stems, which were partly remodeled after *o*-stems, was regularly dropped, as in both *gast-s* 'stranger' and *staþ-s* 'place.'
22.2. IE /oj aj/ merged as PGc. /aj/.

(a) When final, the *j*-element of /aj/ remained in original monosyllables but was lost in forms of more than one syllable:

/oj/ IE *toj*, Gk. Dor. *toí* /aj/ *þái* 'these, those'
/aj/ Gk. medial 3 sg. *phéretai* /aØ/ *baírada* 'is borne'

The parent medial form may have ended in *-toj* rather than *-taj*. Go. *-ái* in the masculine nominative plural of strong adjectives, e.g., *blind-ái*, is due to analogy with *þái*.

(b) When originally followed by a final consonant, the *j*-element of /aj/ remained if the consonant was nonsyllabic:

/oj/ IE *némojt* /aj/ *nimái* 'he may take'

But IE *-ojm̥* became Gc. *-a(j)u(n)*, which lost *-j-* between vowels and *-n* in final position, contracting to Pre-Go. /aw/:

[ojm̥] IE *némojm̥* > Gc. *nema(j)u(n)* /aw/ *nimáu* 'I may take'

Contrast IE [m̥] > Gc. *-un* > -Ø in Go. A *brōþar* in 22.1c.
22.3. /er/, when occurring in an originally medial or final syllable, produced Go. /ar/:

/er/ Sk. *upári* < *uperi*, Gk. *hupér* /ar/ *ufar* 'over'

22.4. Except before [j], /ə/ in an originally medial syllable was lost in pre-Germanic times:

/ə/ IE *dhug(h)ətēr*, Gk. *thugátēr* /∅/ *daúhtar* 'daughter'

/əj/ in originally medial syllables appears to have produced PGc. *-aj-*/*-a-* and will be considered separately.

/ə/ in originally final syllables may have become Gc. /u/:

/ə/ IE *anət-*, L *anas* /u/ OHG *anut* 'duck'

EXERCISE

Supply the missing sounds; omit those that were lost:
Gk. *oīstha*, Go. *wáist*( ) 'knowest'; Gk. *phérete*, Go. *baíriþ*( ) 'ye bear'; L *frātri*, Go. *brōþr*( ) 'to a brother'; Gk. *lúkos*, Go. *wulf*( )*s* 'wolf'; IE m. *dwoj*, Go. *tw*( ) 'two'; Gk. med. 3 pl. *phérontai*, Go. *baírand*( ) 'they are borne'; Gk. *polú*, Go. *fil*( ) 'many'; IE A *kanonm̥*, Gc. *xananun*, Go. *hanan*( ) 'cock'; IE A *agrons*, Go. *akr*( )*ns* 'fields'; IE *kʷosmē* plus *-kʷe*, Go. D *ƕammēh*( ) 'each'; Gk. *póteros*, Go. *ƕaþ*( )*r* 'which (of two)'; L *ne*, Go. *n*( ) 'not'; IE *bhérojm̥*, Go. *baír*( ) 'I may bear'; IE *bhérojs*, Gk. *phérois*, Sk. *bhárēs*, Go. *baír*( )*s* 'thou mayst bear'; IE *kolədos*, Go. *hal*( )*t*( )*s* 'lame'

23
INDO-EUROPEAN FINAL CONSONANTS

The Crucifixion: Mark xv.12–28

(12) Iþ Peilātus aftra andhafjands qaþ du im: ƕa nu wileiþ ei táujáu þammei qiþiþ þiudan Iudaiē? (13) iþ eis aftra hrōpidēdun: ushramei ina! (14) iþ Peilātus qaþ du im: ƕa allis ubilis gatawida? iþ eis máis hrōpidēdun: ushramei ina! (15) iþ Peilātus, wiljands þizái managein fullafahjan, fralaílōt im þana Barabban, iþ Iēsu atgaf usbliggwands ei ushramiþs wēsi. (16) iþ gadraúhteis gataúhun ina innana gardis, þatei ist praitōriaún, jah gahaíháitun alla hansa. (17) jah gawasidēdun ina paúrpurái jah atlagidēdun ana ina þaúrneina wipja uswindandans. (18) jah dugunnun gōljan ina: háils, þiudan Iudaiē! (19) jah slōhun is háubiþ ráusa jah bispiwun ina jah lagjandans kniwa inwitun ina. (20) jah biþē bilaíláikun ina, andwasidēdun ina þizái paúrpurái jah gawasidēdun ina wastjōm swēsáim jah ustaúhun ina ei ushramidēdeina ina. (21) jah undgripun sumana mannē, Seimōna Kwreinaiu, qimandan af akra, attan Alaíksandráus jah Rufáus, ei nēmi galgan is. (22) jah attaúhun ina ana Gaúlgaúþa staþ, þatei ist gaskeiriþ ƕaírneins staþs. (23) jah gēbun imma drigkan wein miþ smwrna, iþ is ni nam. (24) jah ushramjandans ina, disdáiljandans wastjōs is, waírpandans hláuta ana þōs, ƕarjizuh ƕa nēmi. (25) wasuh þan ƕeila þridjō, jah ushramidēdun ina. (26) jah was ufarmēli faírinōs is ufarmēliþ: sa þiudans Iudaiē. (27) jah miþ imma ushramidēdun twans wáidēdjans, áinana af taíhswōn jah áinana af hleidumein is. (28) jah usfullnōda þata gamēlidō þata qiþanō: jah miþ unsibjáim rahniþs was.

(16) *gataúhun ina innana gardis, þatei ist praitōriaún, jah gahaíháitun alla hansa*] The court was that of the pretorial palace, which was guarded by the cohort.

(19) *lagjandans kniwa*] 'laying knees.' i.e., kneeling.

(24) *ushramjandans . . . disdáiljandans . . . waírpandans*] cf. *andhafjands Iēsus* John xviii. 37 and commentary, p. 98.

(28) *þata gamēlidō þata qiþanō*] 'the scripture that said.'

Alaíksandrus, G -áus Alexander
allis at all
andwasjan divest, disrobe
atgiban V give up, deliver
atlagjan lay, put on
attiuhan II draw, bring, take
biláikan VII mock
bispeiwan I spit upon
fullafahjan (+ D/A) satisfy
gadraúhts m. soldier
galga m. cross
gaskeirjan explain, interpret
gatiuhan II lead, bring, take
Gaúlgaúþa Golgotha
gawasjan clothe
háils hail!
hansa f. cohort
hláuts m. lot
ƕaírnei f. skull
ƕarjizuh m. each, each one
ƕeila f. hour, time, season
innana inside (here + G)
inweitan I salute
Kwreinaius m., A -u a Cyrenian
paúrpurái D purple
rahnjan reckon
ráus m. reed
Rufus, G -áus Rufus
slahan VI strike
smwrna D myrrh
staþs m. place
þaúrneins made of thorns
þridja third
ubils evil
ufarmēli n. superscription
ufarmēljan write above
undgreipan I seize
unsibjis wicked
usbliggwan III scourge
usfullnan be fulfilled
ushramjan crucify
uswindan III plait, weave
waírpan III cast
wein n. wine
wipja f. crown

GOTHIC REFLEXES OF INDO-EUROPEAN FINAL CONSONANTS

23.1. As already observed, the Germanic primary stress on word-initial syllables was responsible for both shortenings and losses of vowels in weakened final syllables. Weak articulation likewise caused most Indo-European final consonants to be lost before the historic period of Germanic.

23.2. The only Indo-European final consonants regularly remaining in Gothic were /ns/ and /r/:

/ns/ Gk. Cret. A *lúkons*, Go. *wulfans* 'wolves'
/r/ IE *pətḗr*, Gk. *patḗr*, L *pater*, Go. *fadar* 'father'

23.3. IE final /m/ merged with /n/ in Germanic, as also in Greek and some other descendant language groups. The final /n/ produced by this merger remained only after a short vowel in an original monosyllable or before a particle:

/m/ IE *kʷom*, OL *quom*	/n/ Go. *ƕan* 'when'
/m/ IE m. A *tom* (Gk. *tón*)	/n/ Go. *þan-a* 'this, that'
/n/ IE *en*, OL *en*	/n/ Go. *in* 'in'

Otherwise, PGc. /n/ < IE final /m n/ was lost in Germanic:

/m/ IE A *ghostim*	/∅/ Go. *gast* 'stranger'
/m/ IE f. A *tām*, Sk. *tā́m*	/∅/ Go. *þō* 'this, that'
/n/ IE *kanḗn*, *-ṓn*	/∅/ Go. *hana* 'cock'

23.4. IE final /t d/ were ordinarily lost in Germanic:

/t/ IE *mēnōt*	/∅/ Go. *mēna* 'moon'
/d/ Sk. *ádhar-āt* (< *-ōd*)	/∅/ Go. *undarō* 'under'

But a final dental stop remained (a) before a particle:

/d/ IE *tod*, L *is-tud*	/t/ Go. *þat-a* 'this, that'

(b) in an originally monosyllabic form:

/d/ IE *kʷod*, L *quod*	/t/ OS *hwat*, OE *hwæt* 'what'

If Go. *ƕa* 'what' represents IE *kʷod*, the loss of its final consonant may be due to the use of this form as a weakly accented indefinite pronoun for 'anything.' Another etymology assumes that the parent form was *kʷo*.

23.5. IE final /s/ usually survived in Gothic (cf. Lith. *sūnaũs*, Go. *sunáus* 'of a son') but was lost when, through the loss of a preceding short vowel, it came to stand after:

(a) /m/: IE *némom(e)s*, *-m(o)s* > Go. *nimam* 'we take'
(b) a short vowel plus /r/: IE *wir(o)s* > Go. *waír* 'man'
(c) /s/: IE *dhrus-* plus *-(i)s* > Go. *drus* 'fall'

In this development, final /s/ first became /z/ by Verner's law, then was assimilated to the preceding /m/, /r/, or /s/, and the resulting long consonants were shortened: /mz/ > /mm/ > /m/, /rz/ > /rr/ > /r/, etc. The loss of final /s/ is most noticeable in such forms as *waír* 'man' beside *dags* 'day' (2.3) and *unsar* 'our' beside *meins* 'my' (11.3).

EXERCISE

Supply the missing consonants; omit those that were lost:
IE *jugom*, Sk. *yugám*, L *jugum*, Go. *juk( )* 'yoke'; IE m. A *im*, OL *im*, Go.

i(   )*-a* 'him'; IE f. A *k*^{w}*ām*, Sk. *kā́m*, Go. *ƕō*(   ) 'whom'; IE m. A *k*^{w}*om*, Sk. *kám*, Go. *ƕa*(   )*-a* 'whom'; IE *ad*, L *ad*, Go. *a*(   ) 'from, by, at'; IE *bhrā́ter*, L *frāter*, Go. *brōþa*(   ) 'brother,' IE A pl. *bhrātrn̥s* > Go. *brōþru*(   ), IE A sg. *bhrāterm̥* > Gc. *brōþerun* > Go. *brōþar*(   ); Sk. *bhárēt*, Go. *baírái*(   ) 'he may bear'; IE *ghostis*, L *hostis*, Go. *gast*(   ) 'stranger'; IE *bhéromes,-mos*, Gk. Dor. *phéromes*, L *ferimus*, Go. *baíram*(   ) 'we bear'; IE *k*^{w}*óteros*, Gk. *póteros*, Go. *ƕaþar*(   ) 'which (of two)'; IE *lowsos*, Go. *láus*(   ) 'empty'; IE *agros*, Gk. *agrós*, Go. *akr*(   ) 'field'

24
ADDITIONAL DEVELOPMENTS INVOLVING LIQUIDS AND NASALS

The Death and Burial of Jesus: Mark xv.33–46

(33) Jah biþē warþ ƕeila saíhstō, riqis warþ ana allái aírþái und ƕeila niundōn. (34) jah niundōn ƕeilái wōpida Iēsus stibnái mikilái qiþands: aílōē, aílōē, lima sibakþanei, þatei ist gaskeiriþ: guþ meins, guþ meins, duƕē mis biláist? (35) jah sumái þizē atstandandanē gaháusjandans qēþun: sái Hēlian wōpeiþ. (36) þragjands þan áins jah gafulljands swam akeitis, galagjands ana ráus, dragkida ina qiþands: lēt, ei saíƕam qimáiu Hēlias athafjan ina. (37) iþ Iēsus aftra lētands stibna mikila uzōn. (38) jah faúrahāh als disskritnōda in twa iupaþro und dalaþ. (39) gasaíƕands þan sa hundafaþs sa atstandands in andwaírþja is þatei swa hrōpjands uzōn, qaþ: bi sunjái, sa manna sa sunus was gudis. (40) wēsunuþ-þan qinōns faírraþrō saíƕandeins, in þáimei was Marja sō Magdalēnē jah Marja Iakōbis þis minnizins jah Iōsēzis áiþei jah Salōmē. (41) jah þan was in Galeilaia, jah láistidēdun ina jah andbahtidēdun imma, jah anþarōs managōs þōzei miþiddjēdun imma in Iaírusalēm. (42) jah juþan at andanahtja waúrþanamma, untē was paraskaíwē, saei ist fruma sabbatō, (43) qimands Iōsēf af Areimaþaias, gaguds ragineis, saei was silba beidands þiudangardjōs gudis, ananandjands galáiþ inn du Peilātáu jah baþ þis leikis Iēsuis. (44) iþ Peilātus sildaleikida ei is juþan gaswalt, jah atháitands þan hundafaþ frah ina juþan gadáuþnōdēdi. (45) jah finþands at þamma hundafada, fragaf þata leik Iōsēfa. (46) jah usbugjands lein jah usnimands ita, biwand þamma leina jah galagida ita in hláiwa þatei was gadraban us stáina, jah atwalwida stáin du daúra þis hláiwis.

(36) *swam akeitis*] MS for *swamm akētis* *lēt, ei saíƕam qimái-u Hēlias*] 'wait, so that we see whether Elijah will come.'

(37) *lētands stibna mikila*] 'uttering a great cry.'

(38) *als*] MS for *alhs* (G sg.) *und dalaþ*] 'to the bottom.'

(40) *Marja*] the name of Christ's mother is spelled *Maria.*

(43) *gaguds* for *gaguþs* *þiudangardjōs . . . leikis*] p. 73, commentary on line 16.
(46) *daúra*] 'entrance'; the stone covering its opening served as a door.

áiþei f. mother
akēt ?n. vinegar
alhs f. 15.1 temple
anananþjan dare, be bold
andanahti n. evening
andbahtjan serve, minister
Areimaþaias G of Arimathea
athafjan VI take down
atstandan VI stand near
atwalwjan roll to
beidan I (+G) await
bi sunjái truly
biwindan III wrap, swathe
dalaþ down
disskritnan become torn
dragkjan give to drink
dulƕē why, wherefore
faírraþrō from afar
faúrahāh n. veil, curtain
fragiban V give, grant
fruma sabbatō day before the Sabbath
gadraban VI hew
gafulljan fill
gaguþs godly, pious
Hēlias, A -ian Elijah
hundafaþs centurion
ƕar where
Iakōbis G of James
Iōsēzis G of Joses
iupaþrō from above
juþan already, now
lein n. linen
Magdalēnē Magdalene
minniza less
miþgaggan pret. -iddja accompany
niunda ninth
paraskaíwē Parasceve
Peilātáu D Pilate
qinō f. woman
ragineis m. counselor
riqis n. darkness
saíhsta sixth
Salōmē Salome
sildaleikjan wonder, marvel
swam A sponge
usbugjan buy
uzanan* VI expire

24.1. The time or circumstance of a past occurrence may be expressed by an absolute phrase containing the past participle of *waírþan* in agreement with its accompanying noun, which may be dative, accusative, or (very rarely) nominative:

at andanahtja waúrþanamma	when evening had come
at maúrgin waúrþanana	when morning had come
waúrþans dags gatils	a fitting day having come

ADDITIONAL DEVELOPMENTS INVOLVING LIQUIDS AND NASALS

24.2. Pre-Germanic /str/ arose not only from IE /ttr/ (cf. 12.10c and 14.8) but also from IE initial and medial /sr/:

/sr/ Sk. *srávati* 'flows' /str/ OS OHG *strōm* 'stream'

24.3. In pre-Germanic times a nasal was assimilated to a following stop or fricative: IE *péŋk*^{w}*e* but Gk. *pénte*, OW *pimp* 'five,' and similarly IE *km̥t-* > pre-Gc. *kn̥t-* in 24.4, below.
24.4. In Proto-Germanic the reflex of a parent dental stop was lost between /n/ and [j]: IE *km̥tj-* > pre-Gc. *kn̥tj-* (24.3) > OHG *hunno* 'centurion.' Gc. *-nd-* plus *-j-* as in Go. *sandjan* (rather than **sanjan*) 'send' may come from later word-formation.
24.5. Medial /mn/ apparently underwent dissimilation to /ƀn/ (Go. *bn*, OI OE OFris. *fn*), but numerous exceptions appear, e.g., in OHG *stimna*, OS *stemna*, OE *stemn* beside Go. *stibna*, OE *stefn*, OFris. *stifne* 'voice,' D Go. *namnam* beside OI *nǫfnum* 'names.' The exceptions are generally ascribed to the influence of *m* in the singular forms *namō*, *namins*, *namin*.
24.6. Proto-Germanic developed several long liquids and nasals through assimilation:

/ln/ Let. *vilna*, Lith. *vìlna* /ll/ Go. *wulla* 'wool'
/nw/ IE *minw-*, L *minuō* 'I lessen' /nn/ Go. *minniza* 'less'

In forms bearing reduced syntactic stress, medial /sm/ became /zm/ by Verner's law, then /mm/ by assimilation. When becoming final, /mm/ was shortened to /m/:

/sm/ IE I *k*^{w}*osmē* /mm/ Go. D *ƕamma* 'whom'
/sm/ IE *esmi* /m∅/ Go. *im* 'am'

After a weakly stressed vowel, /nm/ merged with /mm/ and so shared in this development:

/nm/ pre-Gc. *kann̥mis*, Gc. *-ummiz* /m∅/ OE D *hanum* 'cocks'

The Gothic vocabulary inherited from Proto-Germanic shows no instance of a long stop developing from /n/ plus a stop.
24.7. Gothic spelling rarely reflects an excrescent stoppage between PGc. medial /m/ and /r/: *timrjan* or *timbrjan* 'build.'
24.8. PGc. /nn/ was shortened before any consonant but *j*: Go. *kant* 'knowest' beside *kann* 'I know,' *kannjan* 'make known.'
24.9. Gothic lost *h* in the cluster *rhstw*: IE *wr̥kstwom* > Gc. *wurxstwan* > Go. *waúrstw* 'deed, work.'
24.10. /l r m n/ may have become syllabic in Gothic between consonants and finally after a consonant: *akrs* 'field,' A *akr*.

EXERCISE

Supply the missing sounds; omit those that were lost:
IE loc. *swesri*, Go. D *swis*( )*r* 'sister'; IE *km̥tóm*, Lith. *šim̃tas*, Go. *hu*( )*d* 'hundred'; IE *sn̥tjós*, Sk. *satyás*, Go. *sun*( )*jis* 'true'; IE *-m̥njo-* (suffix), Gc. *-uƀnja-*, Go. *witu*( )*ni* (16.4) 'knowledge'; IE *pl̥nós*, Lith. *pìlnas*, Go. *ful*( )*s* 'full'; IE *genw-*, Go. *kin*( )*us* 'cheek'; IE I *tosmē* (cf. Sk. D *tasmai*), Go. D *þa*( )*ma* 'this, that'; PGc. *gumanmiz*, Go. D pl. *guma*( ) 'men'; pre-Gc. I *uksn̥mis*, Go. D *aúhsu*( ) 'oxen'

25
INDO-EUROPEAN [w]
The Resurrection: Mark xvi.1–11

(1) . . . Marja sō Magdalēnē jah Marja sō Iakōbis jah Salōmē usbaúhtēdun arōmata ei atgaggandeins gasalbōdēdeina ina. (2) jah filu áir þis dagis afarsabbatē atidd<j>ēdun du þamma hláiwa at urrinnandin sunnin. (3) jah qēþun du sis missō: ƕas afwalwjái unsis þana stáin af daúrom þis hláiwis? (4) jah insaíƕandeins gáumidēdun þammei afwalwiþs ist sa stáins; was áuk mikils abraba. (5) jah atgaggandeins in þata hláiw gasēƕun juggaláuþ sitandan in taíhswái biwáibidana wastjái ƕeitái; jah usgeisnōdēdun. (6) þaruh qaþ du im: ni faúrhteiþ izwis. Iēsu sōkeiþ Nazōraiu þana ushramidan; nist hēr; urráis. sái þana staþ þarei galagidēdun ina. (7) akei gaggiþ qiþiduh du sipōnjam is jah du Paítráu þatei faúrbigaggiþ izwis in Galeilaian; þaruh ina gasaíƕiþ, swaswē qaþ izwis. (8) jah usgaggandeins af þamma hláiwa gaþlaúhun; diz-uh-þan-sat ijōs reirō jah usfilmei. jah ni qēþun mannhun waíht, ōhtēdun sis áuk. (9) usstandands þan in maúrgin frumin sabbatō, atáugida frumist Marjin þizái Magdalēnē, af þizáiei uswarp sibun unhulþōns. (10) sōh gaggandei gatáih þáim miþ imma wisandam, qáinōndam jah grētandam. (11) jah eis háusjandans þatei libáiþ jah gasaíƕans warþ fram izái, ni galáubidēdun.

(1) *Marja sō Iakōbis*] 'Mary the (mother) of James.'

(2) *þis dagis afarsabbatē*] temporal genitive: 'on the day,' etc.

(4) *þammei*] 'that'; *gáumjan* governs the dative or accusative. *ist*] historical present as also *libáiþ* in verse 11.

(7) *qiþiduh*] *qiþiþ* (imperative) plus *-uh*.

(8) *diz-uh-þan-sat*] the preterit of *dissitan* with interpolated *-uh-þan-* *reirō jah usfilmei*] treated here as a singular.

(9) *frumin sabbatō*] *fruma sabbatō* renders *prosábbaton* 'day before the Sabbath' in Mark xv.42 (p. 106), but here it occurs for *prṓtei sabbátou* 'the first day after the Sabbath.' –The implied subject of *atáugida* s 'he' (Christ); some editors add *sik*: 'showed him-

self.' The following verse, which continued on the recently discovered 188th leaf of the Codex Argenteus, replaces this construction by *atáugiþs warþ*.
(10) *miþ imma wisandam*] 'who had been with him.'

---

abraba exceedingly
afarsabbatē After-Sabbath, Sunday
afwalwjan roll away
áir adv. early
arōmata (Gk.) spices
atáugjan appear, show
biwáibjan clothe, wrap
daúrōm f. D pl. doorposts, doorway
dissitan V seize upon
faúrbigaggan go before
faúrhtjan sis be fearful
frumist adv. first
Galeilaian A Galilee
gasalbōn anoint
gateihan I tell
gaþliuhan II flee
ƕeits white
juggaláuþs m. young man
Nazōraiu A Nazarene
ni waíht f. A nothing
ōgan* sis 16.2 be afraid
Paítráu D Peter
qáinōn lament
reirō f. trembling
sibun seven
taíhswa f. right
usfilmei f. amazement

INDO-EUROPEAN [w]

25.1. Unless otherwise indicated, in this chapter all parent sounds and forms represent Indo-European or pre-Germanic, and all historic sounds and forms represent Gothic. Sounds enclosed within parentheses ( ) were to be lost in preliterate times. For the immediate purpose, Go. *áu iu* will be assumed to retain their earlier Pre-Gothic values, respectively /aw iw/.
25.2. [w] was lost before medial /u/ in Germanic:

[w] *newn̥t-´* > Gc. *ne(w)und-* /Ø/ *niunda* 'ninth'

This loss was often obliterated by analogy; thus Go. *gaswiltan* 'die' has pret. pl. 3 *gaswultun*, not **gasultun*.
25.3. [w] was lost in Pre-Go. /ōwj ōw/:

[w] *stāwéjeti* > Pre-Go. *stō(w)jiþ* /Ø/ *stōjiþ* 'judges'
[w] *stāwā* > Pre-Go. *stō(w)a* /Ø/ *staua* f. 'judgment'

On *au* in *staua* beside *ō* in *stōjiþ* see 17.8a.
25.4. [ew] produced Pre-Go. /iw/. Before consonants in weakly stressed final syllables, the syllabic articulation in /iw/ shifted to the second element, the result being /ju/:

[ew] *sunewes* > Pre-Go. *suniwz* /ju/ *sunjus* 'sons'

Two apparent exceptions occur. *lasiws* 'weak' may reflect the occasional scribal use of *i* for *ei*; *-eiws* would correspond to L *-īvus* as in *captīvus* 'captive.' A *ūhtiug* 'at leisure' is perhaps a scribal error for *ūhteig* 'having time.'

25.5. Pre-Go. /aw iw/ in stem syllables appear respectively in Gothic as *aw iw* before vowels but as *áu iu* in other positions: *tawida* 'he did' but infin. *táujan*, *þiwōs* 'servants' but sg. *þiumagus*, lit. 'servant boy.'

25.6. After a short vowel in some words, IE [w] was lengthened to PGc. [ww], which subsequently produced Go. [ggw] and North Germanic [gg(v)]. The lengthening of [w] is now often ascribed to assimilation of a following /ə/: IE *drewə-* > PGc. *treww-* > OS *triuwi* and OHG *gi-triuwi* beside Go. *triggws*, OI *tryggr* (A *tryggvan*) 'true, faithful.'

25.7. When not subject to the changes noted in 25.2–6, IE [w] produced Pre-Go. and Go. /w/:

(a) Initially: *waír* 'man,' *wlits* 'face,' *wrikan* 'persecute'

(b) Medially before vowels or diphthongs: m. *twái*, f. *twōs*, n. *twa* 'two'

(c) After long vowels (but see 25.3), diphthongs, or consonants, both finally (*lēw* 'occasion,' *fráiw* 'seed,' *waúrstw* 'work') and before *j* (*lēwjan* 'betray,' *hnáiwjan* 'abase,' *ufarskadwjan* 'overshadow') or *s* (*snáiws* 'snow,' *triggws* 'faithful')

In Gothic, PGc. *skaðwaz* 'shadow' transferred from the *o*- to the *u*-declension: N *skadus*, D *-áu*. A suggested explanation assumes that *-w-* in *-aðw-* produced *-u* when becoming final, as in A *skaðw(an)* > Go. *skadu**. But compare *-ad( )* in the last Gothic form in the following exercise.

EXERCISE

Add the missing Gothic sounds; omit those that were lost. Unless otherwise indicated, the parent forms below are Indo-European or pre-Germanic. *juwn̥kós* > *ju( )ggs* 'young,' PGc. *tōwjan* > *t( )i* 'deed,' PGc. pl. N-A *tōwjō* > *t( )ja*; *drewom* > *tr( )** 'tree,' I pl. *drewomis* > D *tr( )am*; *sedh-ewes* > *sid( )s* 'customs'; PGc. *ma(g)wī* > *ma( )i* 'maiden,' G *ma(g)wjōs* > *m( )jōs*; *klojwom* > *hlái( )* 'grave, tomb'; *kwn̥tós* > *h( )unds* 'dog'; N-A *gnewom* > *kn( )** 'knee,' pl. *gnewā* > *kn( )a*; *te(k)wī́* > *þ( )i* 'maidservant,' G *te(k)wjās* > *þ( )jōs*; *sāwelom* > *s( )il* 'sun'; *tr̥n-ewes* > *þaúrn( )s* 'thorns'; *te(k)wo-twom* > *þ( )ad( )* 'servitude'

26
VOCALIZATION AND LENGTHENING OF [j]

On Love: 1 Cor. xiii.1–13

(1) <Jabái razdōm mannē rōdjáu jah aggilē, iþ friaþwa ni habáu, warþ
áiz þuthaúrnjandō> aíþþáu klismō klismjandei. (2) jah jabái habáu praúfētjans jah witjáu alláizē rūnōs jah all kunþi, jah habáu alla galáubein
swaswē faírgunja miþsatjáu, iþ friaþwa ni habáu, ni waíhts im. (3) jah
jabái fraatjáu allōs áihtins meinōs, jah jabái atgibáu leik mein ei gabrannjáidáu, iþ friaþwa <ni> habáu, ni waíht bōtōs mis táujáu. (4) friaþwa
usbeisneiga ist, sēls ist; friaþwa ni aljanōþ; friaþwa ni fláuteiþ, ni ufble-
sada, (5) ni áiwiskōþ, ni sōkeiþ sein áin, ni ingramjada, nih mitōþ ubil,
(6) ni faginōþ inwindiþái, miþfaginōþ sunjái, (7) allata þuláiþ, allata
galáubeiþ, all wēneiþ, all gabeidiþ, (8) friaþwa áiw ni gadriusiþ, iþ jaþþē praúfētja gataíranda, jaþþē razdōs gaƕeiland, jaþþē kunþi gataúrniþ.
(9) suman kunnum jah suman praúfētjam; (10) biþē qimiþ þatei ustaúhan ist, gataúrniþ þatei us dáilái ist. (11) iþ þan was niuklahs, swē
niuklahs rōdida, swē niuklahs frōþ, swē niuklahs mitōda; biþē warþ waír,
barniskeins aflagida. (12) saíƕam nu þaírh skuggwan in frisahtái, iþ þan
andwaírþi wiþra andwaírþi. nu wáit us dáilái; þan ufkunna <swaswē jah
ufkunnada. (13) jah nu bileiband galáubeins, wēns, friaþwa, þōs ·g·, iþ
máista þizō friaþwa.>

(1) *friaþwa* for *frijaþwa*, as below *warþ* 'I have become.'
(3) *ni waíht bōtōs mis táujáu*] lit. 'I do myself nothing of advantage' = 'I gain nothing.'
(5) *ni sōkeiþ sein áin*] 'is not self-seeking.'
(9) *suman*] 'in part'; cf. *us dáilái* below in verse 10.
(10) *ustaúhan*] 'perfect' *us dáilái*] 'in part.'
(11) *was . . . rōdida . . . frōþ . . . mitōda . . . warþ . . . aflagida*] '(I) was . . . (I) spoke . . . (I) understood,' etc. *niuklahs*] 'a child,' lit. 'childish' (Gk. *nḗpios*), an instance of antimeria.
(12) *in frisahtái*] 'in an image' = 'darkly, enigmatically' *andwaírþi wiþra andwaírþi*] 'face to face' *wáit . . . ufkunna . . . ufkunnada*] '(I) know . . . (I) shall know,' etc.

Contrast *witan* 'know' = 'possess knowledge' (verses 2 and 12) with *kunnan* 'know' = 'be acquainted with, be aware of' (verse 9) and *ufkunnan* 'know' = 'recognize' (verse 12).

---

aflagjan put away
áihts f. possession
áiwiskōn act unseemly
áiz n. brass
aljanōn envy
barniskei f. childish thing
bōta f. advantage
fláutjan be pretentious
fraatjan give away as food
fri(j)aþwa f. love, charity
frisahts f. image, example
gabeidan I abide
gabrannjan burn
gadriusan II fall away, fail
gaƕeilan cease
gataúrnan be destroyed
ingramjan provoke
inwindiþa f. iniquity
jaþþē . . . jaþþē whether . . . or, whereas . . . and
klismjan tinkle
klismō f. cymbal
kunnan 16.2 know, be acquainted with
miþfaginōn rejoice with
miþsatjan remove
niuklahs childish (see commentary on verse 11)
praúfet-ja n., -jans m. A prophecies
praúfētjan prophesy
razda f. tongue, language
rūna f. secret, mystery
sēls kind, good
skuggwa m. mirror, glass
þulan endure, bear
þuthaúrnjan sound, trumpet
ufblēsan puff up
ufkunnan know, recognize
usbeisneigs long-suffering
wēnjan hope, expect
wēns f. hope

VOCALIZATION AND LENGTHENING OF [j]

26.1. All parent sounds and forms below are Indo-European or pre-Germanic, and all historic sounds and forms represent Gothic. Parent sounds enclosed within parentheses ( ) were to be lost.

26.2. IE [j] became syllabic in Germanic when a following short vowel was lost in a weakly stressed final syllable.

(a) When coming to stand finally after a consonant, [j] became [i], which merged with Go. /i/:

[j] *gn̥j(om)* /i/ *kuni* 'race, brood'

(b) When coming to stand before final /s/ (< PGc. /z/), both /ej/ and [ij] contracted and merged with /ī/:

/ej/ *ghostej(e)s* /ī/ *gasteis* 'strangers'
[ij] *prij(o)s* /ī/ *freis* 'free'

Compare the development of /īs/ in *welīs* > *wileis* 'thou wilt.'

(c) The same contraction occurred finally, but the resulting /ī/ was shortened, as in *welī(t)* > *wili* 'he will':

[ij] A *kerdhij(om)* /i/ *haírdi* 'herdsman'

sāgi-j(e) > *sōkei* 'seek thou' might appear to contradict this shortening, but here *-ei* is due to analogy with *sōkeis* 'thou seekest.' Other second person singular imperative forms of Class i weak verbs have likewise generalized *-ei*.

26.3. After a short vowel in some forms, IE [j] was lengthened to PGc. *-jj-*, which subsequently produced North Germanic *-gg(v)-* and Go. *-ddj-*. The lengthening is now often ascribed to assimilation of a following /ə/: IE *wojə-* > PGc. *wajj-* > OE *wāg* but OI *veggr*, Go. *-waddjus* 'wall.' Cf. 25.6.

26.4. Otherwise, [j] remained before vowels in Gothic (a) initially, as in *jug(om)* > *juk* 'yoke'; (b) medially after consonants, as in *kapjō* > *hafja* 'I lift'; and (c) between vowels that remained separate vowels, as in n. *trejā* > *þrija* 'three,' except in the parent combination /ēj/ plus a vowel (27.2).

EXERCISE

Supply the missing Gothic sounds:

n. N-A *medhjom* > *mid(* *)*, pl. *medhjā* > *mid(* *)a* 'middle'; N m. *ejes* > (*)s*, n. *ejā* > *i(* *)a*, f. *ejās* > *i(* *)ōs* 'they'; *juwn̥kós* > (*)uggs* 'young'; N *kerdhijos* > *haírd(* *)s* 'herdsman'; pre-Gc. V *lēgije* > *lēk(*) '(thou) physician'

27
STRONG AND WEAK PRESENTS

Skeireins *I.1–31: The Coming of the Redeemer*

' nist saei fraþjai aiþ-
' þau sokjai gþ: al-
' lai uswandidedun:
' samana unbruk-
— jai waurþun:
J ah ju uf dauþaus
atdrusun stauai:
inuh þis qam ga-
mains allaize
nasjands: allai-
ze frawaurhtins
afhrainjan: ni
ibna nih galeiks
unsarai garaih-
tein: ak silba ga-
— raihtei wisands:
E i gasaljands sik
faur uns: ' hunsl
jas-sauþ gþa: þi-
zos manasedais
gawaurhtedi us-
lunein: þata nu
gasaiƕands io-
hannes þo sei us-
tauhana habaida
wairþan fram fin ga-
rehsn miþ sunjai
— qaþ: sai sa ist wiþ-
' rus gþs: saei afni-
' miþ frawaurht þizos manase
'. dais:

(1) *nist saei*] 'there is none who' (Rom. iii.11–12). *nist* is a later insertion. Except for hyphens and for spaces between words, the text is that of the manuscript, Cod. Ambrosianus E.

(6) *dauþaus* modifies *stauai* in line 7.

(13) *ibna... galeiks*] an oblique use of the terms employed in the dispute concerning the relative status of the Father and the Son: Gk. *hísos*, *hómoios*, L *aequalis*, *similis*

(17) *Ei* introduces *þizos manasedais gawaurhtedi uslunein* in lines 19–22: 'that he might accomplish,' etc.

(18) f. *hunsl... gþa*] Eph. v.2.

(19) *jas-sauþ* for *jah sauþ*.

(22) *þata*] 'this, this thing,' i.e., the plan of redemption mentioned in lines 26–27.

(24–27) *þo sei ustauhana habaida wairþan fram fin garehsn*] anastrophe and disjunction. See 28.7a.
(28–31) *sai . . . manasedais*] John i.29.

In the *Skeireins* manuscript, a colon (:) denotes a pause or stop; a raised dot (˙) indicates a shorter pause. A marginal dash (—) draws attention to the colon within the column (the dash in line 1 is a later insertion). The initial letters of the *Skeireins* manuscript, e.g., J in line 6 and E in line 17, serve only to emphasize the colon at the end of the preceding line; when no emphasis is required, as in lines 3 and 7, no initial is used. A quotation dot (') is usually written in the left margin but may also occur within the column, as in line 18.

---

afhráinjan cleanse away
afniman IV take away
atdriusan II fall
dáuþus m. death
fin = fráujin
frawaúrhts f. sin
galeiks like
gamáins common
garēhsns f. plan
gasaljan give, give up
gawaúrkjan accomplish
gþ, gþs, gþa (see 3.1)
hunsl n. offering
ibna equal
inuh þis for this reason
manasēþs f. mankind, world
nasjands m. Savior
sáuþs m. sacrifice
uf (+D/A) under
unbrūks useless
unsar our
usluneins f. redemption
uswandjan go astray
wiþrus m. lamb

STRONG AND WEAK PRESENTS

27.1. The present of Gothic strong verbs reflects a parent **thematic** structure, i.e., one in which a theme vowel, *e/o*, intervened between root and ending, as in the present indicative active of the verb 'bear, carry':

		PARENT FORMS	GOTHIC
sg.	1	bhér-ō	baíra
	2	bhér-e-si	baíris
	3	bhér-e-ti	baíriþ
pl.	1	bhér-o-mes/mos	baíram
	2	bhér-e-te	baíriþ
	3	bhér-o-nti	baírand
du.	1	bhér-ō-wes/wos	baírōs
	2	bhér-o-dus (?)	baírats

Parent thematic verbs had *-o* in the first person singular but no ending. *-ts* in Go. du. 2 *baírats* is difficult to explain, especially if it is believed to occur in place of *-þs*. It has been suggested, however, that the parent ending was *-du-* 'two' plus *-s* from the first person dual and plural, which would produce Go. *-ts*.

Athematic verbs attached endings directly to the root. Although widely attested, their present occurs in Gothic only in the verb 'be': IE *és-mi* > *im*, *és-(s)i* > *is*, *és-ti* > *ist*, etc.

27.2. Weak presents of Class i show one type of development after stems like *nas-* and *stō-* but another type after longer stems in the present indicative active singular and plural:

		SHORT STEM	LONG-OPEN STEM	LONG-CLOSED (OR DISYLLABIC) STEM	
		'save'	'judge'	'seek'	'magnify'
sg.	1	nasja	stōja	sōkja	
	2	nasjis	stōjis	sōkeis	
	3	nasjiþ	stōjiþ	sōkeiþ	(cf. mikileiþ)
pl.	1	nasjam	stōjam	sōkjam	
	2	nasjiþ	stōjiþ	sōkeiþ	
	3	nasjand	stōjand	sōkjand	

Because of their greater stem length, the parent forms for 'seek' and 'magnify' were followed by the syllabic-nonsyllabic allophone of /j/, viz., *-ij-* (17. 5). In turn, *-ij-* contracted before or with the thematic vowels. Before a back theme vowel, *-ij-* contracted to *-j-*: *-ij-ō* > Go. *-ja*, and similarly in the forms *-ij-o-mes* > *-jam*, *-ij-o-nti* > *-jand*. But the contraction with *-e-* produced a long front vowel (/ī/, spelled *ei* in Gothic): *-ij-e-si* > *-eis*, *-ij-e-ti* (and *-te*) > *-eiþ*.

27.3. Gothic weak presents of Class ii reflect a parent stem in *-āje/o-*, in which /ā/ > Gc. /ō/ may well have become overlong by absorbing [j] and the following thematic vowel. Here and below, sounds that were to be lost are enclosed by parentheses ( ): IE *solpā́(jō)* > Go. *salbō* 'I anoint.' A second [j] was likewise absorbed: IE *solpā́(joj)s* > *salbōs* '(thou) mayst anoint.'

27.4. The parent suffix in weak verbs of Class iii appears to have been [əj] rather than its ablaut alternant [ēj].

(a) Thematic /e/ > /i/ contracted with [j] in the suffix, which remained, e.g., *-əj(e)-ti* > *-əj-ti* > Go. *-áiþ* as in *habáiþ* 'has, hath.' Compare the contraction in IE *aj(e)ri* > PGc. *ajri* > Go. *áir* 'early.'

(b) Otherwise, [j] was lost between vowels of noninitial syllables, and /ə/ was lost when coming to stand before a vowel: *-(əj)ō* > Go. *-a* as in *haba* 'I have.' With this loss of schwa compare that in German *hab'ich*. Cf. 22.4.

27.5. It has been shown recently that the present forms of Class iv weak verbs correspond exactly to a Ø-grade stem plus the thematic vowels and endings of strong verbs. Compare the present indicative of the Class iv verb for 'become full'; no dual forms occur:

		PARENT FORMS	GOTHIC
sg.	1	pl̥-n-∅∅- + -ṓ	-fulna
	2	pl̥-n-∅∅- + -é-si	-fulnis
	3	pl̥-n-∅∅- + -é-ti	-fulniþ
pl.	1	pl̥-n-∅∅- + -ó-mes	-fulnam
	2	pl̥-n-∅∅- + -é-te	-fulniþ
	3	pl̥-n-∅∅- + -ó-nti	-fulnand

The second ∅ refers to loss of /ə/ before thematic vowels.

EXERCISE

Add the missing Gothic sounds; omit those that were lost: sg. 1 *sāg-ij-ō* > *sōk*( )*a* 'I seek,' 2 *-ij-e-si* > -( )*s*, 3 *-ij-e-ti* > -( )*þ*, du. 1 *-ij-ō-wes* > ( )*s*, pl. 1 *-ij-o-mes* > -( )*m*, 2 *-ij-e-te* > -( )*þ*, 3 *-ij-o-nti* > -( )*nd*; pl. 3 *solpā́jonti* > *salb*( )*nd* 'they anoint'; sg. 1 *takəjō* > *þah*( ) 'am silent,' pl. 1 *takəjomes* > *þah* ( )*m*, 2 *takəjete* > *þah*( )*þ*, 3 *takəjonti* > *þah*( )*nd*

SPLIT BY ANALOGY

27.6. When allophones are introduced into new phonetic environments through analogic leveling, the result is a **split by analogy**. Thus IE *korjos* would have become Go. **haris* rather than *harjis* 'host' if [j] had not been introduced from other forms of the word. Similarly, regular [ji] in genitive and dative *n*-stem nouns and adjectives (*wiljins*, *midjin*) is carried over to others (*fiskjins*, *wilþjin*) in which *ei* would be expected. Conversely, feminine abstract nouns from Class i weak verbs level *-ei-* for *-ji-*. Thus for **nasjins* 'salvation' (cf. *nasjan* 'save') occurs *naseins*, which is modeled after forms like *láiseins* 'doctrine' (cf. *láisjan* 'teach').

28
HANDWRITING; REVIEW OF PHONOLOGY

Codex Argenteus, fol. 118v: Luke i.6–14

The twenty lines reproduced on the following page are found only in Luke; otherwise, the arches would contain cross-references to other gospels (see 28.5).

Like the Greek alphabet, the Gothic alphabet was used to express both letters and numbers. The values of the Gothic characters are the following:

𐌰	𐌱	𐌲	𐌳	𐌴	𐌵	𐌶	𐌷	𐌸
1	2	3	4	5	6	7	8	9
a	b	g	d	e	q	z	h	þ

𐌹 ï	𐌺	𐌻	𐌼	𐌽	𐌾	𐌿	𐍀	𐍁
10	20	30	40	50	60	70	80	90
i	k	l	m	n	j	u	p	-

𐍂	𐍃	𐍄	𐍅	𐍆	𐍇	𐍈	𐍉	𐍊
100	200	300	400	500	600	700	800	900
r	s	t	w	f	x	ƕ	o	-

In Greek, the characters fitted both letter values and numbers; what remained fixed in Gothic was the number system. The alphabetical order of the characters is shown by their numerical values. If two or three numeral symbols are combined, their values are added, e.g., ·*xib*· (600 + 10 + 2) '612.'

unwaha · jah ni was im barne · unte
was aileisabaiþ stairo · jah ba
framaldra dage seinaize wesun ·
warþ þan miþþanei gudjinoda is
in wikon kunjis seinis in and
wairþja g[u]þs · bi biuhtja gudjinas
saus · hlaut imma urrann du sal
jan · atgaggands in alh fr[auj]ins · jah
manags hiuhma was manageins bei
dandans uta in ƕeilai þymiamins ·
warþ þan imma in siunai aggilus
fr[auj]ins standands af taihswon
hunslastadis þymiamins · jah ga
drobnoda zakarias gasaiƕands ·
jah agis disdraus ina · qaþ þan
du imma sa aggilus · ni ogs þu zaka
ria · unte andhausida ist bida
þeina · jah qens þeina aileisa
baiþ gabairiþ sunu þus · jah hai
tais namo is iohannen · jah wairþiþ

Gothic is written from left to right. Spacing between words is employed only following a raised dot (·) and colon (:) or, rarely, after a quotation dot written within a column.

ï replaces *i* at the beginning of a syllable or word: *ïm*, *fraïtiþ* (= *fra-itiþ*), *usïddja* (= *us-iddja*), *ïohannen*.

(1) *unwaha* ·] · here ends a sentence. *barne*] see 3.4.
(2) The space between *stairo* and *jah* is for ·, which is faded.
(5) *kunjis seinis*] '(for priests) of his lineage,' that of Abia.
(7) *hlauts imma urrann*] 'it became his lot.'
(9) *manageins* is genitive and modifies *hiuhma*.
(11) *warþ . . . in siunai*] 'appeared, came into sight.'
(16) *ogs*] sg. 2 imper. (orig. conjunctive) of *ōgan** 'fear' (16.2).
(19) *gabairid*] *d* for *þ* (16.3a).

Aíleisabaíþ Elizabeth
bida f. prayer
disdriusan II fall upon
fins = fráujins of the Lord
framaldrs very old
gabaíran IV bear
gadrōbnan be troubled
gudjinassus m. priestly office
gudjinōn perform the priestly office
hiuhma m. crowd, throng
hunslastaþs m. altar
saljan make an offering
siuns f. sight
stáirō f. a barren woman
þwmiamins G of incense
unwāhs blameless
ūta adv. outside
wikō f. week
Zakarias, V Zakaria Zachary

GOTHIC HANDWRITING

28.1. The Gothic alphabet is usually divided into two types:

(a) A later type, in Codices Argenteus, Carolinus, Ambrosiani A, C, and E (and originally the Gissensis), is characterized by finished letters, an S-shaped *s*, suspension marks for *m* and *n* (as in Latin), and a closed form of *ƕ* (see the Argenteus, above).

(b) An older type has relatively unfinished letters, a sigma for /s/, a suspension mark for *n* only (as in Greek), and an open *ƕ* (see frontispiece I, line 15, *saƕazuh*). To this type are assigned Codices Ambrosiani B and D, the Naples and Arezzo documents, marginalia on Ambrosiani A and B and Veronensis, and the additions to the Salzburg-Vienna manuscript (though a forthcoming study suggests that the additions show a distinct type of alphabet).

28.2. The foregoing table of Gothic characters contains the later finished letters and suspension marks for *m* and *n*, but with two additions: a sigma of the older script and the symbol for 900, which occurs only in the Salzburg-Vienna manuscript.

28.3. Philostorgius, Sokrates, and Sozomen say that Wulfila "invented" the Gothic alphabet. From this, many scholars have inferred that he selected Greek, Latin, and runic symbols for this purpose. It is now clear, however, that at least some Latin features of the Gothic alphabet are innovations introduced by the Latin-speaking scribes, who followed Wulfila by about two centuries. Moreover, runic influence has been questioned, and its supposed features are explicable in terms of Greek. The symbols for *a b g d e z þ i k l m n u p t w x o* (omega), sigma, 90 (qoppa), and 900 (sampi) are very probably Greek. The symbol for þ (9) has been shown to be a form of theta, and that for *u* a form of omicron. The symbol for *ƕ* (700), a labiovelar fricative, has been analyzed as the labiovelar omicron O plus a mark denoting breath friction. As a careful comparison of the Gothic letters for *e* (5) and *j* (60) will show, the *j*-symbol has only one distinctive feature, namely its descender, to denote the frictionless front glide. Though compared with Latin *G* and Greek xi, Gothic *j* is clearly unlike both. Historic Gothic *i* which was always a vowel or part of a digraph, would not serve for /j/. In their scribal forms, Go. *q h r s* (excluding sigma) and *f* are Latin. The descender that might be expected in *q* (6) regularly occurs in qoppa (90).

28.4. The punctuation of the Codex Argenteus is relatively simple and predictable. To a more limited extent, so is that of Codices B, C, and D. But E (the *Skeireins*), which contains numerous quotations and uses the colon and raised dot for emphasis as well as for pauses, has a more complicated system of punctuation (see p. 119). On the other hand, the Carolinus, the ruined Gissensis, and the first part of Codex A are not punctuated but stichometric; that is, they have been written in sense groups, with certain thought lines beginning at the left margin and others being indented.

28.5. The Argenteus employs the numbered Eusebian sections into which each gospel might be divided so as to facilitate cross-references. Thus the account of Zachary appears in the first section of Luke, numbered "a." If a parallel account existed in another gospel, e.g., John, its section number would appear in Luke under the arch marked $\overline{\textit{ïoh}}$, and the version in Luke would be noted in John by "a" under the arch marked *luk*.

28.6. The Gothic nomina sacra for God, Jesus, Christ, and Lord are contracted respectively as follows (contractions within parentheses occur in the older script):

N	$\overline{\text{gþ}}$	$\overline{\text{ïs}}$ ($\overline{\text{ïus}}$)	$\overline{\text{xs}}$ ($\overline{\text{xus}}$)	$\overline{\text{fa}}$
V	$\overline{\text{gþ}}$	$\overline{\text{ïu}}$	$\overline{\text{xu}}$	$\overline{\text{fa}}$
A	$\overline{\text{gþ}}$	$\overline{\text{ïu}}$	$\overline{\text{xu}}$, $\overline{\text{xau}}$	$\overline{\text{fan}}$, $\overline{\text{fn}}$
G	$\overline{\text{gþs}}$	$\overline{\text{ïuis}}$	$\overline{\text{xaus}}$	$\overline{\text{fins}}$
D	$\overline{\text{gþa}}$	$\overline{\text{ïua}}$, $\overline{\text{ïu}}$	$\overline{\text{xau}}$, $\overline{\text{xu}}$	$\overline{\text{fin}}$

GRECISMS

28.7. Regardless of whether the *Skeireins* originated as a translation from Greek, as a number of scholars believe, its syntax is even more Greek than that of the Gothic Bible. Both documents, in fact, contain so many Greek syntactic features that they are all but useless for the study of Germanic syntax.

The types of Grecisms below require separate attention.

(a) Inverted word order (anastrophe) with separation of nouns from modifiers (disjunction): *þō sei ustaúhana habáida waírþan fram fīn garēhsn* 'the that-fulfilled-was-to-be-by-the-Lord plan' = 'the plan that was to be fulfilled by the Lord'

(b) Loss of syntactic coherence within a sentence (anacoluthon): *waúrd xaus bauái in izwis . . . láisjandans jah talzjandans izwis silbans* 'may the word of Christ dwell within you . . . teaching and admonishing yourselves'

(c) Use of (1) a single finite verb for consecutive clauses or (2) a single participle for consecutive phrases (zeugma): *þandē þata hawi . . . gþ swa wasjiþ, ƕáiwa máis izwis?* 'if God thus clothes the grass . . . how much more (will he clothe) you?' *þana anawaírþan dōm is gasaíƕands jah þatei in galáubeinái þeihan habáida . . .* 'seeing his future discernment and (seeing) that he was to thrive in faith . . . '

(d) Omission of the verb 'be' (schesis onomaton): *áudagái þái hráinjahaírtans* 'blessed (are) the clean of heart'

(e) Use of a participle to indicate the circumstances of an action or state (circumstantial participle), with a participial phrase often assuming the function of a subordinate clause (participial hypotaxis): *in garda qumans frah* . . .'when he had come into the household, he asked . . . ,' *lētands stibna mikila uzōn* 'crying out with a great voice, he expired'

(f) Substitution of an adjective for a noun (antimeria): *niuklahs* 'childish' for 'child' in *þan was niuklahs, swē niuklahs rōdida, swē niuklahs frōþ, swē niuklahs mitōda* 'when I was a child, I spoke as a child, I understood as a child, I thought as a child,' *anþaruþ-þan gadráus ana stáinahamma* 'and then another fell on a stony' (for 'stony place')

(g) Use of the verb 'be' to indicate possession, the owner being expressed by the dative (dative of the possessor): *daúhtar was imma swē wintriwē twalibē* 'a daughter was to him (= he had a daughter) about twelve years old'

(h) Occurrence of a noun in the genitive where an adjective might be expected (a Greek adaptation of the Semitic construct state): *þana faúragaggan inwindiþōs* 'the steward of injustice' = 'the unjust steward'

REVIEW OF PHONOLOGY

28.8. In Indo-European grammar, the term **parent form** may be applied to reconstructions like *pətḗr* 'father,' which represents a word that already existed in Indo-European times. In many instances, however, a parent form represents a later word-formation. Thus Go. *-sēþs*, L *sē-men*, and Lith. *sė-klà* 'seed' share the Indo-European root *sē-* but have three different suffixes. Among the Germanic forms of this 'seed' word, Go. *-sēþs* and OHG *sāt* are feminine and reflect the parent form *sē-tís*, whereas WS OE *sæd*, OFris. *sēd*, OS *sād*, and OI *sāð* (in the sense of 'seed,' not 'chaff') are neuter and derived from *sē-tóm*. Of the parent forms below, some are Indo-European; others represent later word-formations. All their ultimate constituents, however, are attested in at least some Indo-European language groups other than the Germanic.

In each of the following tables supply the missing Gothic consonants or vowels; omit those that were lost.

28.9. Voiceless reflexes of IE /p t k s/ (12.9–10):

péku	( )aí( )u	'cattle, wealth'
speltā́	s( )ilda	'tablet'
ésti	is( )	'is'
klépō	( )li( )a	'I steal'
kleptus	( )li( )us	'thief'
skejris	s( )eirs	'clear'
wértō	waír( )a	'I become'
oktṓw	a( )áu	'eight'
géwseti	kiu( )iþ	'chooses, tests'
tod	( )at-a	'this, that'
mitsōd	mi( )ō	'reciprocally'
n̥-wejttos	unwei( )	'ignorant'
bhlāttrijos	-blō( )eis	'worshiper'

28.10. Verner's law (13.4–5):

úperi	u( )ar	'over, beyond'
solpā́jonom	sal( )ōn	'anoint'
bhrā́tēr, -ōr	brō( )ar	'brother'
pətér	( )a( )ar	'father'
wértō	waír( )a	'I become'
wortéjō	fra-war( )ja	'I destroy'
juwń̥kisēn, -ōn	jū( )i( )a	'younger'
juwn̥kós	jug( )s	'young'
oktṓw	a( )áu	'eight'

pērsnā́ > persnā́	( )aír( )na	'heel'
dń̥tus	tun( )us	'tooth'
ékwo-dn̥tī	aíƕa-tun( )i	'bramble'
dus-́	tu( )-	(proclitic)
kom-́	( )a-	(proclitic)
—́ dek-n̥s	ti( )uns	'decades'
dékm̥	taí( )un	'ten'

Phonologically, final /n/ in this last Gothic form would have been lost. Its occurrence here (as also in *sibun* 'seven' and *niun* 'nine') is due to the influence of the corresponding ordinal numeral, in which /n/ remained in medial position.

28.11. IE /b d g bh dh gh/ (14.6–8):

skabjonom	ga-ska( )jan	'create'
skab-tis > skaptis	ga-ska( )s	'creation'
dwoj	( )wái	'two'
ozdos	a( )s	'branch, twig'
wejd-tos > wejttos	un-wei( )	'ignorant'
awgonom	áu( )an	'increase'
wog-stus > wokstus	wa( )stus	'growth, stature'
bhlā́donti	( )lō( )and	'they worship'
bhlād-trijos > bhlāttrijos	-( )lō( )eis	'worshiper'
ghoŋghonom	( )ag( )an	'go'
ghoŋgh-tis > ghoŋktis	fram-( )ā( )s	'progress'
wedhonom	ga-wi( )an	'bind'
wedh-tos > wettos	us-wi( )	'unbound, evil'
wr̥gjonom	us-waúr( )jan	'work thoroughly'
wr̥g-tos > wr̥ktos	us-waúr( )s	'just, righteous'
kuzdhom	hu( )	'treasure'

28.12. IE /k^w g^w g^wh/ (15.6–12):

sék^we	saí( )	'see thou'
ne-k^we	ni( )	'and not, nor'
g^wēnis	( )ēns	'wife, woman'
seŋg^wheti	sig( )iþ	'sings, chants'
leŋg^wh-tos > leŋk^wtos	lei( )ts	'light, endurable'
perk^wúnjom	faír( )uni	'mountain'
sek^wnís	si( )ns	'appearance'

28.13. Proto-Germanic fricatives in Gothic (16.3–4):

lewbhons	liu( )ans	'dear'
lewbhos	liu( )s	'dear'
wélīte	wilei( )	'ye will'
	wilei( )u	'will ye?'
-ōtú-	gabaúrj-ō( )us	'pleasure'
	mannisk-ō( )us	'humanity'
lowdhā	swa-láu( )a	'so great'
lowdhos	swa-láu( )s	'so great'
g^wétete	qiþi( )	'ye say'
	qiþi( )uh	'and say ye'
-m̥njom	wit-u( )ni	'knowledge'
	wald-u( )ni	'authority'
apó	a( )	'of, from'
	a( )u	'of?, from?'
wélīs	wilei( )	'thou wilt'
	wilei( )u	'wilt thou?'

28.14. IE /ī ē ā ō ū/ (17.8):

bhrā́tēr, -ōr	br( )þar	'brother'
bhlōmonn̥s	bl( )mans	'flowers'
sāwelom	s( )il	'sun'
drōwonom	tr( )an	'trust'
mēnōt	m( )na	'moon'
sḗjeti	s( )iþ	'sows'
sētís	-s( )þs	'seed'
swīnom	sw( )n	'pig, swine'
bhrūgis	br( )ks	'useful'

28.15. IE /a o ə/ (18.3):

ad	( )t	'at, by, from'
stətís	st( )þs	'place'
oktṓw	( )htáu	'eight'
waj	w( )	'woe, alas'
	w( )a-	'evil-'
toj	þ( )	'these, those'
kájkos	h( )hs	'one-eyed'
lowbhéjeti	ga-l( )beiþ	'believes'

toŋgjonom	þ( )gkjan	'think'
toŋg-tós > toŋktós	-þ( )hts	'thought'
pətḗr	f( )dar	'father'
páŋkonom	f( )han	'seize'

28.16. IE /e/ and [i] (19.5–6):

bhéjdhomes, -mos	b( )dam	'we await'
—́ senti	s( )nd	'they are'
wéŋkonom	w( )han	'fight'
édeti	fra-( )tiþ	'devours'
péku	f( )hu	'cattle, wealth'
bhéwdhete	ana-b( )udiþ	'ye command'
migh-stus > mikstus	m( )hstus	'dung'
e+áwge	ana-( )áuk	'he added'
téŋkonom	þ( )han	'thrive'
sék^{w}eti	s( )ƕiþ	'sees'
wiros	w( )r	'man'
klépō	hl( )fa	'I steal'
préknete	fr( )hniþ	'ye ask, inquire'
bhérō	b( )ra	'I bear'

28.17. IE [u l̥ r̥ m̥ n̥ ŋ̊] (20.3–5):

jugom	j( )k	'yoke'
pl̥nós	f( )lls	'full'
g^{w}ḿ̥tis	ga-q( )mþs	'assembly'
mn̥tís	ga-m( )nds	'remembrance'
tŋ̊gjonom	þ( )gkjan	'seem'
tŋ̊g-tós > tŋ̊któs	mikil-þ( )hts	'high-minded'
dhug(h)ətēr > duktēr	d( )htar	'daughter'
sunus	s( )nus	'son'
dhurom	d( )r	'door'
upo	( )f	'under'
mŕ̥trom	m( )rþr	'murder'

28.18. Long and overlong vowels in weakly stressed final syllables (21.3–4):

bhāgā̄s	bōk( )s	'letters'
jugā	juk( )	'yokes'
stāwāj	stau( )	'judgment'

k^{w}omō-k^{w}e	ƕan( )h	'each'
k^{w}ejlā̄m (?-ō̄m)	ƕeil( )	'of hours'
tosmē	þamm( )	'this, that'
sunḗw	sun( )	'to a son'
wirōs	waír( )s	'men'
nemō	nim( )	'I take'
n̥dherōd	undar( )	'under'
g^{w}ēnāj	qēn( )	'to a wife'
sā	s( )	'this, that'
tekwī́	þiw( )	'handmaid'
k^{w}osmē-k^{w}e	ƕamm( )h	'each'
k^{w}osmē	ƕamm( )	'whom, what'
ejā	ij( )	'they'
ejās	ij( )s	'they'
k^{w}otrēd	ƕadr( )	'whither'
k^{w}ejlāmis	ƕeil( )m	'hours'
tām	þ( )	'this, that'

28.19. Short vowels of originally medial and final syllables (22.1–4):

wojda	wáit( )	'I know'
bhére	baír( )	'bear thou'
péku	faíh( )	'cattle, wealth'
bhērn̥t	bēr( )n	'they bore'
bhrāterm̥	brōþar( )	'brother'
bhrātrn̥s	brōþr( )rs	'brothers'
ghostis	gast( )s	'stranger'
kanonm̥	hanan( )	'cock'
ghostins	gast( )ns	'strangers'
bhéreti	baíriþ( )	'bears'
bhérojm̥	baír( )	'I may bear'
bhérojt	baír( )	'he may bear'
bhérontaj (? -toj)	baírand( )	'are borne'
toj	þ( )	'these, those'
agros	akr( )s	'field'
agrons	akr( )ns	'fields'
kolədos	hal( )t( )s	'lame'

28.20. Indo-European final consonants (23.2–5):

k^{w}om	ƕa( )	'when'
k^{w}om	ƕa( )-a	'whom'

jugom	juk( )	‘yoke’
kʷām	ƕō( )	‘whom’
im	i( )-a	‘him’
en	i( )	‘in’
kanḗn, -ṓ	hana( )	‘cock’
bhrā́tēr, -ōr	brōþa( )	‘brother’
bhrātrn̥s	brōþru( )	‘brothers’
mēnōt	mēna( )	‘moon’
n̥dherōd	undarō( )	‘under’
ad	a( )	‘at, by, from’
tod	þa( )-a	‘this, that’
agros	akr( )s	‘field’
bhéromes, -mos	baíram( )	‘we bear’
kʷóteros	ƕaþar( )	‘which (of two)’
lowsos	láus( )	‘empty’

28.21. Additional developments involving liquids and nasals (24.2–10):

swesri	swi( )	‘sister’
km̥tóm	hu( )d	‘hundred’
sn̥tjā́	sun( )ja	‘truth’
-m̥njo- (16.4, 24.5)	fráist-u( )ni	‘temptation’
genwum	kin( )u	‘cheek’
pl̥nos	ful( )s	‘full’
kʷosmē (24.6)	ƕa( )ma	‘whom’
minwisḗn, -ṓ	min( )iza	‘smaller, less’
wr̥g-stwom > wr̥kstwom	waúr( )stw	‘deed, work’

28.22. IE [w] (25.2–7):

juwŋ̥kós	ju( )ggs	‘young’
stāwejeti	stō( )jiþ	‘judges’
stāwā	stau( )a	‘judgment’
sunewes	sun( )s	‘sons’
drewom	-tri( )	‘tree, vine’
drewomis	tri( )am	‘trees’
klojwom	hlái( )	‘grave, tomb’
kwn̥tós	h( )nds	‘dog’
tr̥newes	þaúrn( )s	‘thorns’
wr̥g-stwom > wr̥kstwom	( )aúrst( )	‘deed, work’
sāwelom	s( )il	‘sun’

28.23. Vocalization of [j] (26.2–5):

gn̥jom	kun( )	'race, brood'
gn̥jā	kun( )a	'races, broods'
ejes	( )s	'they'
ejā	i( )a	'they'
ejās	i( )ōs	'they'
prijā	fri( )a	'free'
prijos	fr( )s	'free'
kapjonom	haf( )an	'heave, lift up'
kerdhijos	haírd( )s	'herdsman'
kerdhijom	haírd( )	'herdsman'
trejā	þri( )a	'three'

28.24. Loss of Indo-European intervocalic [j] (27.1–6):

sējeti	s( )iþ	'sows'
sodéjomes, -mos	sat( )am	'we set, place'
bhondhijās	band( )ōs	'bands, bonds'
ájeri	( )r	'early'
gowséjeti	káus( )þ	'chooses, tests'
sodéjeti	sat( )þ	'sets, places'
sāgijeti	sōk( )þ	'seeks'
solpā́jesi	salb( )s	'dost anoint'
solpā́jojs	salb( )s	'mayst anoint'
takəjonom	þah( )an	'be silent'
takəjeti	þah( )þ	'is silent'
takəjnis	þah( )ns	'silence'
sg. 1 sāgijō	sōk( )a	'I seek'
2 sāgijesi	sōk( )s	
du. 1. sāgijōwes, -wos	sōk( )ōs	
pl. 1 sāgijomes, -mos	sōk( )am	
2 sāgijete	sōk( )þ	
3 sāgijonti	sōk( )and	
sg. 1 noséjō	nas( )a	'I save'
2 noséjesi	nas( )s	
pl. 2 noséjete	nas( )þ	
sg. 1 takəjō	þah( )a	'am silent'
2 takəjesi	þah( )s	
pl. 1 takəjomes, -mos	þah( )m	
2 takəjete	þah( )þ	
3 takəjonti	þah( )nd	
kerdhijos (26.2b)	haírd( )s	'herdsman'
kerdhijōs	haírd( )s	'herdsmen'

GLOSSARY

The glossary includes all words of the texts, including proper nouns. References are made to the chapter in which each word occurs, and then to the specific line of the text. Thus "25/4" refers to Chapter 25 of this *Introduction*, verse 4 of Mark xvi, which is the text for that chapter. References to discussions of words within this *Introduction* are by chapter and section, e.g., §8.1 (Chapter 8, section 1).

Following each headword are (1) a listing of occurrences of that form of the word within this text and/or discussions of the word; (2) grammatical information about the word, within brackets; and (3) a gloss or other explanation. All words are listed alphabetically; derived forms are defined and explained under their own entries, with reference to the main entry.

NOUN and ADJECTIVE headwords, including participles, are nominative and singular unless marked otherwise.
VERB headwords are infinitives unless marked otherwise.
Mood is not marked in VERB entries if it is indicative.
Voice is not marked in VERB entries if it is active.
Present participles have ⟨*nt*⟩ as stem class; past participles have ⟨*o*⟩.
Subordinate entries have the same grammatical features as the headword in the set (including the default features described above) unless otherwise indicated.

Uppercase Roman numerals show the class of strong VERBS.
Lowercase Roman numerals show the class of weak VERBS.
"cf." refers the user to a specified section of the book.
"see" and "see also" refer the user to another entry.

[A] = accusative
[adj.] = adjective
[adv.] = adverb
[cj.] = conjunction
[D] = dative
[f.] = feminine
[G] = genitive
[imper.] = imperative
[indef.] = indefinite
[interrog.] = interrogative
[m.] = masculine
[n.] = neuter
[N] = nominative
[num.] = number/numeral
[opt.] = optative
[part.] = participle
[pass.] = passive
[phr.] = phrase
[pl.] = plural
[prep.] = preposition
[pres.] = present
[pret.] = preterit
[pron.] = pronoun
[rel.] = relative
[sg.] = singular
[Voc.] = vocative
[+A], etc. = case government
⟨ ⟩ = stem class
* = unattested form

[1] = 1st person
[2] = 2nd person
[3] = 3rd person

Gk. = Greek
Heb. = Hebrew
Lat. = Latin

aba cf. §8.1 [m.] man, husband

abraba 25/4 [adv.] very, exceedingly

abrs 11/14 [m. ⟨*o*⟩] great, mighty

abu (= *af* + interrog. -*u*) 22/34 [prep., + D] of?

af 1/13, 14/18, 23/21, 23/27, 24/43, 25/3, 25/8, 25/9, 28/12 [prep., + D] from, of, by, on (see also **abu**)

afáikan cf. §6.1 [VIIa] deny
  afaíáik 5/6 [3 sg. pret.]

afar 4/6, 6/11, 8/1, 11/13 [prep., + A] after

afar dagans 2/12 [adv. phr.] after some days

afar-sabbatus [m. ⟨*wa*⟩] After-Sabbath, Sunday
  afarsabbatē 25/2 [G pl.]

afgaggan [VII] go away, depart
  afiddja 20/15; cf. §17.1 [3 sg. pret.]

afhráinjan 27/12 [i] cleanse away

afƕapjan [i] choke
  afƕapidēdun 9/7 [3 pl. pret.]

afƕapjand 10/19 [pres. part., m., of *afƕapjan*] choking

afiddja [3 sg. pret. of *afgaggan* 'go away, depart,' q.v.]

aflagjan [i] put away
  aflagida 26/11 [1 sg. pret.]

aflaílōt [3 sg. pret. of *aflētan* 'leave, let be, forgive,' q.v.]

afleiþan [I] go away
  afláiþ 11/13 [3 sg. pret.]

aflētan [VII] leave, let be, forgive
  aflaílōt 8/10 [3 sg. pret.]
  aflēt 1/12 [2 sg. imper.]
  aflētam 1/12 [1 pl. pres.]

aflifnan [iv] be left, be left over, remain
  aflifnōda 20/13 [3 sg. pret.]

aflifnandeins 20/12 [pres. part., f. A pl. of *aflifnan*] remaining

aflifnōda [3 sg. pret. of *aflifnan* 'remain,' q.v.]

aflinnan [IIIa] depart
  aflunnun 4/3 [3 pl. pret.]

afmáitan [VII] cut off
  afmaímáit 7/12 [3 sg. pret.]

afmarzeins 10/19 [f. ⟨*i*/*ā*⟩] deceitfulness

afniman [IV] take away
  afnimiþ 27/29 [3 sg. pres.]

afsneiþan [I] cut off, kill
  afsnáiþ 13/27 [3 sg. pret.]

aftra 20/15, 22/33, 22/40, 23/12, 23/13, 24/37 [adv.] again, back, a second time

aftumists 19/35 [m. ⟨*o*⟩] last, aftermost

afþliuhan [II] run away, flee
  afþliuhiþ 16/13 [3 sg. pres.]

afwalwiþs 25/4 [past part., m., of *afwalwjan*] rolled away

afwalwjan [i] roll away
  afwalwjái 25/3 [3 sg. pres. opt.]

aggilus 2/4, 2/5, 2/9, 3/7, 28/11, 28/16 [m. ⟨*u*/*i*⟩] angel (from Gk. ἄγγελος)
  aggilē 26/1 [G pl.]

agis 28/15 [n. ⟨*o*⟩] fear
  agisis 3/2 [G sg.]

aglō 10/17 [f. ⟨*n*⟩] anguish, distress
  aglōn 8/6 [A sg.]

ahma [m. ⟨*n*⟩] spirit, the Spirit

ahmam 8/8 [D pl.]
ahman 17/55 [A sg.]
aƕa [f. ⟨*ā*⟩] river, water
aƕái 6/2, 6/4 [D sg.]
áigan* [pret. pres.] have
áih 16/16; cf. §16.2 [1 sg. pres.]
áihta 11/11 [3 sg. pret.]
áigin [n. ⟨*o*⟩] property
áiginis 11/12 [G sg.]
áih [1 sg. pres. of *áigan** 'have,' q.v.]
áihta [3 sg. pret. of *áigan** 'have,' q.v.]
áihts [f. ⟨*i*⟩] possession
áihtins 26/3 [A pl.]
Aíleisabaíþ 28/2, 28/18 Elizabeth
aílōē, aílōē, lima sibakþanei 24/34 (initial Hebrew words of Psalm xxii transliterated into Gothic via Gk.)
áin^{1} 19/37 [n. A sg. of *áins*^{1} 'one']
áin^{2} 16/16 [A sg. of *áins*^{2} 'one, alone, only'] (see also *ni sōkeiþ . . .*)
áin . . . áin . . . áin 9/8, 10/20 [n. ⟨o⟩] one . . . another . . . another
áina^{1} 18/27 [f. A sg. of *áins*^{1} 'one']
áina^{2} 14/19 [f. A sg. of *áins*^{3} 'a certain one']
áinahō 17/42 [f. ⟨*n*⟩ A sg.] only, sole
áinamma [D sg. of *áins*^{3} 'a certain one,' q.v.]
áinana [A sg. of *áins*^{3} 'a certain one,' q.v.]
áinans [A pl. of *áins*^{2} 'one, alone, only,' q.v.]
áinƕarjizuh cf. §20.2c [m.] each one
áinōhun [A sg. of *áinshun* 'one, any,' q.v.]
áins^{1} [num., ⟨*o*⟩] one
áin^{1} 19/37 [n. A sg.]
áina^{1} 18/27 [f. A sg.]
áins^{2} 14/18, 16/16, 20/9, 20/15 [adj., m.] one, alone, only
áin^{2} 16/16 [A sg.] (see also *ni sōkeiþ . . .*)
áinans 15/46 [A pl.]
áins^{3} 18/29, 20/8, 24/36 [indef. pron., m.] one, a certain one
áina^{2} 14/19 [f. A sg.]
áinamma 18/24 [D sg.]
áinana 12/19, 18/24, 22/39, 23/27 [A sg.]
áinshun cf. §17.2 [indef. pron.] one, any
áinōhun^{1} 17/51 [m. A sg.]
áinōhun^{2} 22/38 [f. A sg.]
áir 25/2 [adv.] early
áirizans [m. pl.] the ancients (from *áiris* 'earlier')
áirizam 15/21 [D pl.]
aírþa^{1} 14/18 [f. ⟨*ā*⟩] earth, region
aírþa^{2} 9/5, 9/8 [A sg.]
aírþái 1/10, 6/11, 10/20, 24/33 [D sg.]
aírþōs 9/5 [G sg.]
áiþei 24/40 [f. ⟨*n*⟩] mother
áiþein 17/51 [A sg.]
aíþþáu^{1} 22/36 [cj.] then, in that case
aíþþáu^{2} 10/17, 14/17, 14/18, 18/31, 21/1, 26/1, 27/1 [cj.] or, else (see also *untē jabái . . .*)
áiw [A sg. of *áiws*] (see *ni áiw*)
aíwaggēljō [f. ⟨*n*⟩] gospel (from Gk. *εὐαγγέλιον*)
aíwaggēljōn 8/1 [A sg.]
aíwaggēljōns 8/13 [G sg.]
áiwins [A pl. of *áiws* 'time, age,

eternity,' q.v.]
áiwiskōn [ii] act unseemly
áiwiskōþ 26/5 [3 sg. pres.]
áiws [m. ⟨*wo/i*⟩] time, age, eternity
áiw [A sg.] (see *ni áiw*)
áiwins 1/13 [A pl.]
áiz 26/1 [n. ⟨*o*⟩] brass, metal, coin
ak 1/13, 10/17, 14/17, 17/52, 19/37, 22/40, 27/15 [cj.] but (usually after a negative clause)
akei 20/9, 25/7 [cj.] but, however, still, nonetheless
akēt [?n.] vinegar (from Lat. *acētum*)
akeitis (=*akētis*) 24/36 [G sg.]
akran [n. ⟨*o*⟩] fruit
akran 9/7, 9/8, 10/20 [A sg.]
akranaláus 10/19 [m. ⟨*o*⟩] fruitless
akrs [m. ⟨*o*⟩] field
akra 2/3, 2/5, 13/25, 23/21 [D sg.]
Alaíksandrus [m. ⟨*u*⟩] Alexander
Alaíksandráus 23/21 [G sg.]
alaþarba 11/14 [m. ⟨*n*⟩] very poor
aleina 18/27 [f. ⟨*ā*⟩] ell, cubit
alhs [f. ⟨root noun⟩] temple
alh 28/8 [A sg.]
als (= *alhs*) 24/38 [G sg.]
alidan 12/23, 13/27, 13/30 [past part., m. A sg. of *aljan*] brought up, fattened
alja 17/51 [cj.] except
aljanōn [ii] envy
aljanōþ 26/4 [3 sg. pres.]
all cf. §11.1 [n. ⟨*o*⟩] all the, every, the whole
all 3/5, 5/1, 6/9, 13/31, 18/32, 26/2, 26/7 [n. A sg.]
alla 23/16, 26/2 [f. A sg.]
allái 17/52, 22/40, 24/33, 27/2 [m. N pl.]
alláim 19/35 [D pl.]
alláizē 19/35, 26/2, 27/9, 27/10 [G pl.]
allamma 11/14, 18/29 [D sg.]
allans 17/54 [m. A pl.]
allata 11/13, 26/7 [n. A sg.] (see also *untē allata . . .*)
allōs 26/3 [f. A pl.]
alls 28/9 [m. N sg.]
allaþrō 8/11 [adv.] from all sides
allis 19/41, 23/14 [adv.] at all, wholly, in general, indeed
allōs [f. A pl. of *all* 'every,' q.v.]
alls [m. N sg. of *all* 'every,' q.v.]
alþiza 13/25 [substantive, m. ⟨*jo*⟩] older, elder (from *alþeis* 'old')
amēn 1/13, 14/18, 19/41, 21/2, 21/5 amen, truly (from Heb. *āmēn* via Gk.)
an 22/37 [interrog. particle] then? so?
ana[1] 1/10, 2/3, 2/5, 3/9, 3/10, 9/5, 10/16, 10/20, 13/25, 19/37, 20/10, 24/33 [prep., + D] into, upon, in
ana[2] 12/20, 12/22, 15/45, 18/27, 19/36, 23/17, 23/22, 23/24, 24/36 [prep., + A] into, upon, in
anaáukan 18/27 [VII] add, add to
anabiudan [II: + D of a person, + A of a thing] command, order
anabáuþ (or *-ud*) 7/11, 17/

55 [3 sg. pret.]
anabiudiþ 8/8 [3 sg. pres.]
anabusns [f. ⟨*i*⟩] command, commandment
anabusn 13/29 [A sg.]
anabusnē 14/19 [G pl.]
anafilhan [III] deliver, commit
anafulhun 22/35 [3 pl. pret.]
anakumbjan 20/10 [i] recline (root from Lat. *cumbere*)
anakumbidēdun 20/10 [3 pl. pret.]
anakumbjandam 20/11 [pres. part., D pl., of *anakumbjan*] those who were sitting
anananþjands 24/43 [pres. part., m., of *anananþjan*] being bold
and 5/1, 11/14 [prep., + A] along, among, throughout
andanahti [n. ⟨*jo*⟩] evening
andanahtja 24/42 [D sg.]
andbahtans [A pl. of *andbahts* 'officer, servant,' q.v.]
andbahti [n. ⟨*jo*⟩] service, ministry
andbahtjam 4/10 [D pl.]
andbahtjan [i] serve, minister
andbahtidēdun 24/41 [3 pl. pret.]
andbahts 19/35 [m. ⟨*o*⟩] officer, servant
andbahtans 3/5, 7/1 [A pl.]
andbahtōs 22/36 [N pl.]
andhafjan cf. §5.2 [VI] answer
andhōf 5/6, 17/50, 19/38, 20/7, 22/34, 22/35, 22/36 [3 sg. pret.]
andhafjands 13/29, 22/37, 23/12 [pres. part., m., of *andhafjan*] answering
andháusida 28/17 [past part., f., of *andháusjan*] heard
andháusjan [i] listen to, hear, obey
andháusjáindáu 21/7 [3 pl. pass. pres. opt.] they will be heard
andniman [IVa] receive, take
andnam 5/1, 13/27 [3 sg. pret.]
andnēmun 5/3, 21/2 [3 pl. pret.]
andnimand 10/20 [3 pl. pres.]
andnimiþ 19/37 [3 sg. pres.]
Andraias 20/8 [m.] Andrew
andrinnan [III] dispute, race, contend
andrunnun 19/34 [3 pl. pret.]
andwaírþi [n. ⟨*jo*⟩] presence
andwaírþi [A sg.] (see following phrasal entry)
andwaírþja 12/18, 12/21, 28/5 [D sg.] (see also *in andwaírþja*)
andwaírþi wiþra andwaírþi 26/12 face to face
andwasjan [i] divest, disrobe
andwasidēdun 23/20 [3 pl. pret.]
ansts cf. §9.1 [f. ⟨*i*⟩] grace, favor
anþar 10/19 [n. ⟨*o*⟩] other, second
anþara 16/16 [n. A pl.]
anþarái 22/34 [m. N pl.]
anþaramma 18/24 [m. D sg.]
anþarana 18/24 [m. A sg.]
anþarōs 24/41 [f. N pl.]
anþaruþ-þan (anþar-uh-þan) 9/5 [n.] and another
arbáidjan [i] work, toil

arbáidjand 18/28 [3 pl. pres.]
Areimaþaia Arimathea
Aremaþaias 24/43 [G sg.]
armahaírtiþa 21/4 [f. ⟨*ā*⟩] almsgiving, mercy, charity
armaiōn 21/1, 21/2, 21/3 alms [f. A sg. ⟨n⟩]
armins [A pl. of *arms*[2] 'arm,' q.v.]
arms*[1] cf. §18.1 [m. ⟨*o*⟩] poor
arms[2] [m. ⟨*i*⟩] arm
armins 19/36 [A pl.]
arōmata 25/1 [A pl.] spices (from Gk.)
asneis 16/12, 16/13 [m. ⟨*jo*⟩] hireling, servant
asnjē 12/17, 12/19 [G pl.]
at 9/6, 12/20, 24/42, 24/45, 25/2 [local or temporal prep., + D] at, by, to, from, of, with (introduces absolute phrases in 24/42 and 25/2)
atáugjan [i] show, appear
atáugida 6/9, 25/9 [3 sg. pret.]
atdriusan [II] fall
atdrusan 27/7 [3 pl. pret.]
atgaf [3 sg. pret. of *atgiban* 'give, deliver,' q.v.]
atgaft [2 sg. pret. of *atgiban* 'give, deliver,' q.v.]
atgaggan [VII] come, go, enter, approach
atiddja 13/25 [3 sg. pret.]
atiddjēdun 25/2 [3 pl. pret.]
atgaggands 28/8 [pres. part., m., of *atgaggan*] coming, going, approaching, entering
atgaggandans 10/19 [N pl.]
atgaggandeins 25/1, 25/5 [f. N pl.]
atgiban [V] give, give up, deliver
atgaf 23/15 [3 sg. pret.]
atgaft 13/29 [2 sg. pret.]
atgibáu 26/3 [1 sg. pres. opt.]
athafjan 24/36 [VI] take down
atháitan [VII] summon
athaíháit 7/1 [3 sg. pret.]
atháitands 13/26, 24/44 [pres. part., m., of *atháitan*] summoning
atiddja [3 sg. pret. of *atgaggan* 'come, go, enter, approach,' q.v.]
atiddjēdun [3 pl. pret. of *atgaggan* 'come, go, enter, approach,' q.v.]
atlagjan [i] lay, lay on, put on
atlagidēdun 23/17 [3 pl. pret.]
atsaíƕan [V] observe, give heed to, take heed
atsaíƕiþ 21/1 [2 pl. imper.]
atstandans 24/39 [pres. part., m., of *atstandam*] standing near
atstandandanē 24/35 [G pl.]
atta[1] 12/20, 12/22, 13/27, 13/28, 15/48, 16/15, 18/26, 18/32, 21/4, 21/6, 21/8 [m. ⟨*n*⟩] father, the Father
atta[2] 1/9, 11/12, 12/18, 12/21 [Voc. sg.]
attan 16/15, 17/51, 23/21 [A sg.]
attin 11/12, 12/18, 12/20, 13/29, 21/1, 21/6 [D sg.]
attins 8/12, 12/17, 15/45 [G sg.]
attiuhan [II] draw, bring, take
attaúhun 23/22 [3 pl. pret.]
atwalwjan [i] roll to
atwalwida 24/46 [3 sg. pret.]
atwōpjan [i] call
atwōpida 19/35 [3 sg. pret.]
aþþan 10/15, 15/22, 15/44

[cj.] but, yet, however
aúftō [adv.] perhaps (see *niu aúftō*)
áugō [n. ⟨*n*⟩] eye
  áuganē 8/12 [G pl.]
  áugōna 20/5 [A pl.]
aúhns* [?m.] oven
  aúhn 18/30 [A sg.]
áuk 8/2, 8/12, 14/18, 14/20, 15/46, 18/32, 19/39, 19/41, 21/7, 21/8, 25/4, 25/8 [cj.] for
áukan cf. §6.1 [VIIa] increase
áusō [n. ⟨*n*⟩] ear
  áusōna 8/13 [N pl.]
áuþida [f. ⟨*ā*⟩] desert, wasteland
  áuþida 6/2, 6/5 [A sg.]
  áuþidái 6/1, 6/3, 6/6 [D sg.]
awēþi 16/16 [n. ⟨*jo*⟩] flock of sheep
awiliudōnds 20/11 [pres. part., m., of *awiliudōn*] giving thanks
awistr* [n. ⟨*o*⟩] sheepfold
  awistris 16/16 [G sg.]

·b· (*twái*) 20/9 [num.] two
bad [3 sg. pret. of *bidjan* 'ask, beg, entreat,' q.v.]
bái [num., m.] both
  ba 7/4, 28/2 [n. pl.]
baíran cf. §§5.1, 10.2, 12.1, 14.3, 21.1 [IVb] bear, carry
  baírand 10/20 [3 pl. pres.]
  bar 9/8 [3 sg. pret.]
  bērun 2/13 [3 pl. pret.]
baírhtein [D sg. of *baírhtei* 'brightness'] (see *in baírhtein*)
bandi cf. §6.3 [f. ⟨*ā*⟩] band, bond
bansts [m. ⟨*i*⟩] barn
  banstins 18/26 [A pl.]
bar [3 sg. pret. of *baíran* 'bear, carry,' q.v.]
Barabba 22/40 [m.] Barabbas
  Barabban 22/40, 23/15 [A sg.]
barizeins [m. ⟨*o*⟩] (made of) barley
  barizeinam 20/13 [D pl.]
  barizeinans 20/9 [A pl.]
barn[1] 4/11 [n. ⟨*o*⟩] child
  barn[2] 3/2, 3/4, 4/3, 19/36 [A sg.]
  barna 3/7, 4/7 [D sg.]
  barnē 3/5, 3/9, 3/10, 19/37, 28/1 [G pl.]
barnilō 13/31 [n. ⟨*n*⟩ Voc. sg.] little child, son
barniskei [f. ⟨*n*⟩] childish thing
  barniskeins 26/11 [A pl.]
baþ [3 sg. pret. of *bidjan* 'ask, beg, entreat,' q.v.]
baúrgja [m. ⟨*n*⟩] citizen
  baúrgjanē 11/15 [G pl.]
baúrgs cf. §15.1 city
bēdun [3 pl. pret. of *bidjan* 'ask, pray, entreat,' q.v.]
beidands 24/43 [pres. part., m., of *beidan*, I: +G] awaiting
  beidandans 28/9 [N pl.]
bērun [3 pl. pret. of *baíran* 'bear, carry,' q.v.]
bērusjōs 3/9, 4/3, 4/5 [m. ⟨*jo*⟩ pl.] parents
Bēþlahaím 2/1, 2/6, 3/3 [D sg.] Bethlehem
bi[1] 3/2, 3/3, 8/9, 10/19, 15/44, 18/28, 22/34 [prep., +A] about, regarding
bi[2] 3/5, 4/2, 28/6 [prep., +D] according to, by
bi sunjái 24/39 [adv.] truly, in truth
bida 28/17 [f. ⟨*ā*⟩] prayer,

entreaty
bidjan 21/5; cf. §5.2 [Va: + A or objective G] ask, beg, pray, entreat
bad (or -**þ**) 7/9, 13/28, 17/41, 24/43 [3 sg. pret.]
bēdun 8/9 [3 pl. pret.]
bidei 21/6 [2 sg. imper.]
bidjáis 21/6 [2 sg. pres. opt.]
bidjáiþ[1] 15/44 [2 pl. pres. (hortative) opt.]
bidjáiþ[2] 21/5, 21/8 [2 pl. pres. opt.]
bidjandansuþ-þan (= *bidjandans* + *-uh* + *þan*) 21/7 and when praying
bigitan [V] find, meet, meet with
bigētun 2/11 [3 pl. pret.]
bigita 22/38 [1 sg. pres.]
bigitans 12/24, 13/32 [past part., m., of *bigitan*] found, met, met with
bihlahjan [VI] laugh at, deride
bihlōhun 17/53 [3 pl. pret.]
biláif [3 sg. pret. of *bileiban* 'remain,' q.v.]
biláift [2 sg. pret. of *bileiban* 'remain,' q.v.]
biláikan [VII] mock
biláiláikun 23/20 [3 pl. pret.]
biláist [2 sg. pret. of *bileiþan* 'leave, forsake,' q.v.]
bileiban* [Ia] remain
biláif 4/4 [3 sg. pret.]
biláift 4/7 [2 sg. pret.]
bileiband 26/13 [3 pl. pres.]
bileiþan [I: +D] leave, forsake
biláist 24/34 [2 sg. pret.]
bileiþiþ 16/21 [3 sg. pres.]
binah cf. §16.2 (it) behooves
bindan cf. §4.2 [IIIa] bind
bispeiwan [I] spit upon
bispiwun 23/19 [3 pl. pret.]
biþē 4/1, 4/3, 4/5, 5/9, 7/4, 7/7, 10/17, 11/14, 20/12, 23/20, 24/33, 26/10, 26/11 [cj.] when
biūhti[1] 22/39 [n. ⟨*jo*⟩] practice, custom
biūhti[2] 4/2 [A sg.]
biūhtja 28/6 [D sg.]
biūhtjis 4/3 [G sg.]
biwáibidana 25/5 [past part., m., A sg. of *biwáibjan*, i] clothed, wrapped
biwēsjáu [1 sg. pret. opt. of *biwisan* 'feast, make merry,' q.v.]
biwindan [III] wrap, swathe, wind
biwand 24/46 [3 sg. pret.]
biwisan cf. §13.1 [V] feast, make merry
biwēsjáu 13/29 [1 sg. pret. opt.]
blinda cf. §10.4 [weak adj.] blind
blinds cf. §11.1 [strong adj.]
blōma [m. ⟨*n*⟩] flower
blōmans 18/28 [A pl.]
blōþ 3/10 [n. ⟨*o*⟩] blood
bōkareis [m. ⟨*jo*⟩] scribe
bōkarjē 3/3, 14/20 [G pl.]
bōkarjōs 5/4 [N pl.]
bōtōs [G sg. of *bōta* 'advantage'] (see *ni waíht bōtōs* . . .)
briggan 7/11, 16/16; cf. §17.2 bring
brāhta 7/12, 11/13 [3 sg. pret.]
briggáis 1/13 [2 sg. pres. opt.]
bringiþ 12/22 [2 pl. imper.]
bringandans 12/23 [pres. part., N (for Voc.) pl., of *briggan*] bringing

brinnō 8/10 [f. ⟨*n*⟩] fever

brinnōn 8/9 [D sg.]

brōþar 13/27, 13/32, 20/8; cf. §15.1 [m. ⟨*r*⟩] brother

brōþr 15/22 [D sg.]

brōþrs 7/3, 7/5 [G sg.]

brūkjan cf. §17.2 [i] use

bugjan cf. §17.2 [i] buy

bugjam 20/5 [1 pl. pres.]

dags 4/3; cf. §2.3 [m. ⟨*o*⟩] day

daga 1/11, 2/6, 18/30 [D sg.]

dagam 2/1, 5/1, 6/4 [D pl.]

dagans 4/6, 4/8, 11/13 [A pl.] (see also *afar dagans*)

dagē 6/6, 28/3 [G pl.]

dagis 2/11, 4/3, 25/2 [G sg.]

dáils [f. ⟨*i*⟩] share, portion

dáil 11/12 [A sg.]

dáilái [D sg.] (see *us dáilái*)

dalaþ [adv.] down (see *und dalaþ*)

dáug cf. §16.2 (it) profits

daúhtar 7/7, 17/42, 17/49 [f. ⟨*r*⟩] daughter

daúpiþs 6/4 [past part., m., of *dáupjan*] baptized

dáupidái 5/3, 6/2 [N pl.]

dáupjands 5/1, 6/1 [pres. part., m., of *dáupjan*] baptizing

dáupjandins 7/11 [G sg.] of [St. John] the Baptist

daúr [n. ⟨*o*⟩] entrance

daúra 24/46 [D sg.]

daúram 3/10 [D pl.]

daúrōm 25/3 [f. ⟨*n*⟩ D pl.] doorway

dáuþáus [G sg. of *dáuþus* 'death,' q.v.]

dáuþs 12/24, 13/32 [m. ⟨*o*⟩] dead

dáuþus [m. ⟨*u*⟩] death

dáuþáus 27/6 [G sg.]

diabaúlus 6/7, 6/9 [m. ⟨*u*⟩] devil (from Gk. διάβολος)

disdáiljan [i] divide, share

disdáilida 11/12 [3 sg. pret.]

disdáiljandans 23/24 [pres. part., m., of *disdáiljan*] dividing

disdriusan [II] fall upon

disdráus 28/15 [3 sg. pret.]

dissitan [V] seize upon

diz-uh-þan-sat 25/8 [3 sg. pret.] (*dis-sat* with interpolated *uh-þan*)

disskritnan [iv] become torn

disskritnōda 24/38 [3 sg. pret.]

distahjan [i] waste, scatter

distahida 11/13 [3 pl. pret.]

distahjiþ 16/12 [3 sg. pres.]

diups [f. ⟨*o*⟩] deep

diupáizōs 9/5 [G sg.]

dius* [n. ⟨*o*⟩] wild animal

diuzam 6/6 [D pl.]

diz-uh-þan-sat see *dissitan*

dragkjan [i] give to drink

dragkida 24/36 [3 sg. pret.]

dráibjan [i] trouble

dráibei 17/49 [2 sg. imper.]

dráuhsnōs [A pl. of *dráusna* 'piece,' q.v.]

dráus [3 sg. pret. of *driusan* 'fall,' q.v.]

dráusnōs [f. pl. ⟨*ā*⟩] pieces

dráuhsnōs 20/12 [A pl.]

drigkan 23/23 [III] drink

drigkáiþ 18/25 [2 pl. pres. opt.]

drigkam 18/31 [1 pl. pres.]

driusan [II] fall

dráus 12/20 [3 sg. pret.]

driusands 17/41 [pres. part., m., of *driusan*] falling

du 2/5, 2/10, 3/5, 3/7, 4/7, 5/2, 6/9, 7/1, 7/4, 8/1, 8/6, 8/11, 9/3, 11/12, 12/18, 12/22, 13/27, 13/29, 13/31, 17/49, 18/26,

19/34, 19/35, 19/36, 20/5, 20/9, 20/12, 21/1, 21/6, 22/37, 22/38, 23/12, 23/14, 24/43, 24/46, 25/2, 25/3, 25/6, 25/7, 28/7, 28/16 [prep., + D] to, for, as

duginnan [III] begin
  dugann 11/14 [3 sg. pret.]
  dugunnun 12/24, 23/18 [3 pl. pret.]

dulvē 24/34 [adv.] why, wherefore?

duþē (or *-þþē*) 18/25, 28/17 [adv.] hence, because, moreover, therefore

dwala 15/22 [m. ⟨*n*⟩ Voc. sg.] thou fool!

·e· (*fimf*) 20/9 [num.] five

ei 6/7, 12/19, 12/21, 13/29, 14/17, 15/45, 17/56, 19/41, 20/5, 21/2, 21/4, 21/5, 21/7, 22/36, 22/37, 22/39, 23/12, 23/15, 23/20, 23/21, 24/36, 24/44, 25/1, 26/3, 27/17, 28/17 [cj.] that, so that

-ei [relative particle] (in *saei, sei, sōei, þáiei, þáimei, þammei, þarei, þatei, þei, þizáiei, þizei, þōei*, and *þōzei*, qq. v.)

eis [N pl. of *is* 'he,' q.v.]

fadrein 17/56 [n. ⟨*o*⟩ (uninflected) pl.] parents

faginōn 13/32 [ii] rejoice
  faginōþ 26/6 [3 sg. pres.]

faginōnds 5/9 [pres. part., m., of *faginōn*] rejoicing

fahēþs (or *-ds*) cf. §9.1 [f. ⟨*i*⟩] joy
  fahēdái 10/16 [D sg.]

faíflōkun [3 pl. pret. of *flōkan** 'bewail,' q.v.]

faífráis [3 sg. pret. of *fráisan* 'tempt,' q.v.]

faírgreipands 17/54 [pres. part., m., of *faírgreipan*, I] taking hold of

faírguni [n. ⟨*jo*⟩] mountain
  faírguni 20/15 [A sg.]
  faírgunja 26/2 [A pl.]

faírlvus [m. ⟨*u*⟩] the world
  faírlváu 22/26, 22/37 [D sg.]

faírina [f. ⟨*ā*⟩] fault, accusation
  faírinō 22/38 [G pl.]
  faírinōs 23/26 [G sg.]

faírra[1] 2/9 [prep., + D] far from

faírra[2] 3/8, 11/13, 12/20 [adv.] far, afar

faírraþrō 24/40 [adv.] from afar

faran [VI] go, fare, travel
  fōr 6/5 [3 sg. pret.]

Fareisaius [m. ⟨*u/i*⟩] Pharisee
  Fareisaiē 14/20 [G pl.]
  Fareisaieis 5/4 [N pl.]

faúr 7/10, 8/2, 9/4, 16/11, 16/15, 19/40, 27/18 [prep., + A] for, before, by

faúra 5/7, 17/41, 21/2 [prep., +D] before, for, on account of

faúrahāh 24/38 [n. ⟨*o*⟩] curtain, veil

faúramaþleis[1] 17/41 [m. ⟨*jo*⟩] ruler, chief
  faúramaþleis[2] 17/49 [G sg.]

faúrbáuþ [3 sg. pret. of *faúrbiudan* 'command, forbid,' q.v.]

faúrbigaggan [VII] go before
  faúrbigaggiþ 25/7 [3 sg. pres.]

faúrbiudan [II] command, forbid, order, charge
  faúrbáud (= *-báuþ*) 17/56 [3 sg. pret.]

faúrhtjan [i] fear, be afraid
  faúrhtei 17/50 [2 sg. imper.]

faúrhtjan sis [i] be fearful, be afraid
  faúrhteiþ izwis 25/6 [2 pl. imper.]
faúrþizei 21/8 [cj., + opt.] before
fiáis [2 sg. pres. opt. of *fijan* 'hate,' q.v.]
fiand [A sg. of *fijands* 'enemy,' q.v.]
fidwōr tiguns 6/6 [num., A pl.] forty
figgragulþ [n. ⟨*o*⟩] finger ring
  figgragulþ 12/22 [A sg.]
fijan [iii] hate
  fiáis (= *fijáis*) 15/43 [2 sg. pres. (hortative) opt.]
  fijáiþ 18/24 [3 sg. pres. indic.]
fijands cf. §15.1 [m. ⟨*nt*⟩] enemy
  fiand (= *fijand*) 15/43 [A sg.]
  fijands 15/44 [A pl.]
Filippus 20/7 [m. ⟨*u*⟩] Philip
  Filippáu 20/5 [D sg.]
filu[1] 3/5, 13/29, 20/5 [adj. ⟨*u*⟩] much, many (see also *swa filu swē*)
filu[2] 12/17, 25/2 [adv., + G] very, greatly
filuwaúrdei [f. ⟨*n*⟩] wordiness
  filuwaúrdein 21/7 [D sg.]
filuwaúrdjan [i] use many words, be wordy
  filuwaúrdjáiþ 21/7 [2 pl. pres. (hortative) opt.]
fimf 20/10, 20/13 [num.] five
fin (= *fráujin*) [D sg. of *fráuja* 'lord, Lord,' q.v.]
fins (= *fráujins*) [G sg. of *fráuja* 'lord, Lord,' q.v.]
finþan [IIIa] find out
  funþun 4/5, 4/6 [3 pl. pret.]
finþands 24/45 [pres. part., m., of *finþan*] finding out
fiskans [A pl. of *fisks* 'fish,' q.v.]
fiskē [G pl. of *fisks* 'fish,' q.v.]
fiskja [m. ⟨*n*⟩] fisherman
  fiskjans 8/2 [N pl.]
fisks [m. ⟨*o*⟩] fish
  fiskans 20/9 [A pl.]
  fiskē 20/11 [G pl.]
fláutjan [i] be pretentious
  fláuteiþ 26/4 [3 sg. pres.]
flōkan* [VII] bewail
  faíflōkun 17/52 [3 pl. pret.]
fōdeins [f. ⟨*i*/*ā*⟩] food
  fōdeinái 18/25 [D sg.]
fōdjan [i] feed
  fōdeiþ 18/26 [3 sg. pres.]
fōn [n. ⟨irregular⟩] fire
  funins 15/22 [G sg.]
fōr [3 sg. pret. of *faran* 'go, travel,' q.v.]
fōtus [m. ⟨*u*⟩] foot
  fōtum 17/41 [D pl.]
  fōtuns 12/22 [A pl.]
fraatjan [i] give away as food
  fraatjáu 26/3 [1 sg. pres. opt.]
fragiban [V] give, grant
  fragaf 24/45 [3 sg. pret.]
frahuh (= *frah* + *-uh*) 13/26 and (he) asked
fraíhnan cf. §5.4 [Vb] ask, question
  frah 7/8, 19/33, 24/44 [3 sg. pret.] (see also *frahuh*)
  frēhun 5/5 [3 pl. pret.]
fráisan cf. §6.1 [VIIa] tempt
  faífráis 6/7 [3 sg. pret.]
fráisands 20/6 [pres. part., m., of *fráisan*] tempting
fráistubni [f. ⟨*jā*⟩] temptation
  fráistubnjái 1/13 [D sg.]

fráistubnjōm 6/9 [D pl.]
fraitan cf. §5.1
frēt 13/30 [3 sg. pret.]
frētun 9/4 [3 pl. pret.]
fráiw [n. ⟨*wo*⟩] seed
fráiwa 9/3 [D sg.]
frakunnan [pret. pres., + D] despise
frakann 18/24 [3 sg. pres.]
fralētan [VII] free, let, allow
fralaílōt 17/51, 23/15 [3 sg. pret.]
fralētáu 22/39 [1 sg. pres. opt.]
fralusans 4/5, 12/24, 13/32 [past. part., m., of *fraliusan*, IIa] lost
fram 5/9, 6/4, 6/8, 17/49, 21/1, 21/2, 25/11, 27/26 [prep., + D] from, by, because of
framaldrs [n. ⟨*o*⟩] very old
framaldra 28/3 [N pl.]
fraqistjan [i] destroy
fraqisteiþ 19/41 [3 sg. pres.]
fraqistnan [iv] be destroyed, be lost, perish
fraqistna 12/17 [1 sg. pres.]
fraqistnái 20/12 [3 sg. pres. opt.]
fraþi [n. ⟨*jo*⟩] understanding, knowledge
fraþja 4/11 [D sg.]
fraþjan [VI: + D or + A] understand
fraþjái 27/1 [3 sg. pres. opt.]
frōþ 26/11 [1 sg. pret.]
frōþun 5/5 [3 pl. pret.]
fráuja 8/1, 8/6 [m. ⟨*n*⟩] lord, Lord
fin (= *fráujin*, below)
fins (= *fráujins*, below)
fráujam 18/24 [D pl.]
fráujan 8/9 [A sg.]
fráujin 8/11; (as *fin*) 27/26 [D sg.]
fráujins (as *fins*) 28/8, 28/12 [G sg.]
frawas [3 sg. pret. of *frawisan* 'spend, exhaust,' q.v.]
frawaúrhta 12/21 [1 sg. pret. of *frawaúrkjan*, i] I erred
frawaúrhta mis 12/18 [1 sg. pret. of *frawaúrkjan sis*, i] I sinned
frawaúrhts [f. ⟨*i*⟩] sin
frawaúrhtins 27/11 [A pl.]
frawilwan [III] snatch, catch
frawilwiþ 16/12 [3 sg. pres.]
frawisan [V: + D] spend, exhaust
frawas 11/14 [3 sg. pret.]
frēhun [3 pl. pret. of *fraíhnan* 'ask, question,' q.v.]
frēt [3 sg. pret. of *fraitan* 'devour,' q.v.]
frētun [3 pl. pret. of *fraitan* 'devour,' q.v.]
friaþwa 26/4, 26/8, 26/13 [f. ⟨*wā*⟩] love, charity
friaþwa 26/1, 26/2, 26/3 [A sg.]
frijōn [ii] love
frijōnd 21/5 [3 pl. pres.]
frijōs 15/43 [2 sg. pres. opt.]
frijōþ[1] 15/46 [2 pl. pres.]
frijōþ[2] 18/24 [3 sg. pres.]
frijōþ[3] 15/44 [2 pl. imper.]
frijōndans 15/46 [pres. part., A pl., of *frijōn*] loving
frijōnds cf. §15.1 [m. ⟨*nt*⟩] friend
frijōndam 13/29 [D pl.]
frijōnds 15/47 [A pl.]
frisahtái [D sg. of *frisahts* 'image'] (see *in frisahtái*)
frōdei [f. ⟨*n*⟩] wisdom

frōdein 8/13 [A sg.]
frōþ [1 sg. pret. of *fraþjan* 'understand,' q.v.]
frōþs cf. §18.1 [⟨*o*⟩] wise
frōþun [3 pl. pret. of *fraþjan* 'understand,' q.v.]
fruma 24/42 [m. ⟨*n*⟩] former, prior
fruma sabbatō day before the Sabbath
frumin sabbatō 25/9 [D sg.]
frumist 25/9 [adv.] first
frumists 19/35 [m. ⟨*o*⟩] foremost, best
frumistōn 12/22 [f. A sg.]
fugls [m. ⟨*o*⟩] bird, fowl
fuglam 18/26 [D pl.]
fuglōs 9/4 [N pl.]
fulhsni [n. ⟨*jo*⟩] secret
fulhsnja (or *fulhlsnja*) 21/4, 21/6 [D sg.]
fullafahjan 23/15 [i: + D or + A] satisfy
fullatōjis 15/48 [m. ⟨*jo*⟩] perfect
fullatōjái 15/48 [N pl.]
fullnan cf. §7.1 [iv] become full
fullnōda 3/2, 7/6 [3 sg. pret.]
funins [G sg. of *fōn* 'fire,' q.v.]
funþun [3 pl. pret. of *finþan* 'find out,' q.v.]

·g· (*þreis**) 2/12, 26/13 [num.] three
gabaíran [IV] bring forth
gabaírid 28/19 [3 sg. pres.]
gabar 2/2 [3 sg. pret.]
gabaúrans 2/6, 3/3, 22/37 [past part., m., of *gabaíran*] brought forth
gabei [f. ⟨*n*⟩] riches, wealth
gabeins 10/19 [G sg.]
gabeidan [I] abide
gabeidiþ 26/7 [3 sg. pres.]
gabrannjan [i] burn
gabrannjáidáu 26/3 [3 sg. pass. pres. opt.]
gabruka [f. ⟨*ā*⟩] (broken) bit, fragment
gabrukō 20/13 [G pl.]
gadaban [VI] be fitting
gadōf 5/6 [3 sg. pret.]
gadáiljan [i] divide
gadáilida 20/11 [3 sg. pret.]
gadaúrsan cf. §16.2 dare
gadáuþnan [iv] die
gadáuþnōda 17/49 [3 sg. pret.]
gadáuþnōdēdi 24/44 [3 sg. pret. opt.)
gadōf [3 sg. pret. of *gadaban* 'be fitting,' q.v.]
gadraban 24/46 [past part., n., of *gadraban*, VI] hewn
gadragkjan [i] give to drink
gadragkjái 19/41 [3 sg. pres. opt.]
gadraúhts [m. ⟨*i*⟩] soldier
gadraúhteis 23/16 [N pl.]
gadráus [3 sg. pret. of *gadriusan* 'fall, fail,' q.v.]
gadriusan [II] fall, fall away, fail
gadráus 9/4, 9/5, 9/7, 9/8 [3 sg. pret.]
gadriusiþ 26/8 [3 sg. pres.]
gadrōbnan [iv] be troubled
gadrōbnōda 28/13 [3 sg. pret.]
gaf [3 sg. pret. of *giban* 'give, yield,' q.v.]
gafāhan cf. §6.1 [VIIa] seize
gafulljan [i] fill
gafullidēdun 20/13 [3 pl. pret.]
gafulljands 24/36 [pres. part.,

m., of *gafulljan*] filling
gaggan 13/28, 17/41, 17/51; cf. §17.1 go, come, walk
gagg 21/6 [2 sg. imper.]
gagga 12/18 [1 sg. pres.]
gaggiþ 17/49, 25/7 [3 sg. pres.]
iddja 17/42, 20/5 [3 sg. pret.]
gaggandei 25/10 [pres. part., f., of *gaggan*] going
gaggands 11/15 [pres. part., m., of *gaggan*] going
gaguds (or *-uþs*) 24/43 [adj., m. ⟨*o*⟩] godly, pious
gahaban 7/1 [iii] seize, get, take, have
gahabáidēdun 7/2 [3 pl. pret.]
gahaftjan sik [i] join
gahaftida sik 11/15 [3 sg. pret.]
gahaíháit [3 sg. pret. of *gaháitan* 'promise, call together,' q.v.]
gahaíháitun [3 pl. pret. of *gaháitan* 'promise, call together,' q.v.]
gaháiljan [i] heal
gaháilida 8/12 [3 sg. pret.]
gaháitan [VIIa] promise, call together
gahaíháit 6/9 [3 sg. pret.]
gahaíháitun 23/16 [3 pl. pret.]
gaháusjan [i] hear
gaháusida 13/25 [3 sg. pret.]
gaháusidēdun 8/13 [3 pl. pret.]
gaháusjand 10/15 [3 pl. pres.]
gaháusjands 3/2, 17/50 [pres. part., m., of *gaháusjan*] hearing
gaháusjandans 24/35 [N pl.]
galveilan [iii] cease
galveiland 26/8 [3 pl. pres.]
gaíaínna [m.] a Gehenna (figurative)
gaíaínnan 15/22 [A sg.]
gaígrōtun [3 pl. pret. of *grētan* 'weep,' q.v.]
gaírnjan [i] yearn, desire, long
gaírnida 11/16 [3 sg. pret.]
gáitein* [n. ⟨*o*⟩] kid
gáitein 13/29 [A sg.]
gajukō [f. ⟨*n*⟩] parable
gajukōm 8/1 [D pl.]
gakunnan [iii] consider, recognize, read
gakunnáiþ 18/28 [2 pl. imper.]
galagiþ 18/30 [past part., n., of *galagjan*] lain, put
galagiþs 8/1, 24/47 [past part., m., of *galagjan*] lain, put
galagjan [i] lay, put
galagida 24/46 [3 sg. pret.]
galagidēdun 7/2, 7/13, 25/6 [3 pl. pret.]
galagjands 24/36 [pres. part., m., of *galagjan*] laying, putting
galáiþ [3 sg. pret. of *galeiþan* 'go, travel, come,' q.v.]
galáubei [2 sg. imper. of *galáubjan* 'believe,' q.v.]
galáubeins 26/13 [f. ⟨*i/ā*⟩] faith
galáubein 26/2 [A sg.]
galáubeiþ [3 sg. pres. of *galáubjan* 'believe,' q.v.]
galáubjan [i] believe
galáubei 17/50 [2 sg. imper.]
galáubeiþ 26/7 [3 sg. pres.]
galáubidēdun 25/11 [3 pl. pret.]
galáubjandans [pres. part., m. N pl., of *galáubjan*] believing

(see *leitil galáubjandans*)
galeikan [iii: + D] please
galeikáida 7/7 [3 sg. pret.]
galeikōn [ii] be like
galeikōþ 21/8 [2 pl. imper.]
galeiks 27/13 [adj., m ⟨*o*⟩] like, similar
Galeilaia [f.] Galilee
Galeilaia 24/41 [D sg.]
Galeilaian 8/1, 25/7 [A sg.]
galeiþan [Ia] go, travel, come
galáiþ 4/1, 6/11, 22/33, 22/38, 24/43 [3 sg. pret.]
galiþun 2/9, 4/3, 4/6, 4/11, 7/4 [3 pl. pret.]
galēsun [3 pl. pret. of *galisan* 'gather,' q.v.]
galēwiþs 22/36 [past part., m., of *galēwjan*, i] betrayed
galga [m. ⟨*n*⟩] cross
galgan 23/21 [A sg.]
galisan [V] gather
galēsun 20/13 [3 pl. pret.]
galisiþ 20/12 [2 pl. imper.]
galiþun [3 pl. pret. of *galeiþan* 'go, travel, come,' q.v.]
galiugan [iii] marry
galiugáida 7/3 [3 sg. pret.]
galiugáidēs 7/5 [2 sg. pret.]
galūkan cf. §4.2 [IIa] shut, close
galūkands 21/6 [pres. part., m., of *galūkan*] shutting, closing
gamáins 27/8 [m. ⟨*i*/*jo*⟩] common, unholy
gamarzjan [i] offend
gamarzjanda 10/17 [3 pl. pass. pres.]
gamēlidō 23/28 [past part., n., of *gamēljan*] written, enrolled
gamōt cf. §16.2 (I) have room
ganah cf. §16.2 (it) suffices
ganasjan [i] save, heal
ganasjada 17/50 [3 sg. pres. pass.]
ganisan 5/2 [Va] be saved, be healed
ganiþjis [m. ⟨*jo*⟩] kinsman
ganiþjam 4/3, 4/6 [D pl.]
ganōhs [adj., m. ⟨*o*⟩] enough
ganōhái 20/7 [N pl.]
gaqiunan [iv] be made alive
gaqiunōda 12/24, 13/32 [3 sg. pret.]
gaqumþs [f. ⟨*i*⟩] assembly
gaqumþái 15/22 [D sg.]
gaqumþim 21/2, 21/5 [D pl.]
garaíhtans [A pl. of *garaíhts* 'just,' q.v.]
garaíhtei 27/15 [f. ⟨*n*⟩] justice
garaíhtein 27/14 [D sg.]
garaíhteins 14/20 [G sg.]
garaíhts [adj., m. ⟨*o*⟩] just
garaíhtans 15/45 [A pl.]
gards cf. §9.1 [m. ⟨*i*⟩] household, court
gard 17/41 [A sg.]
garda 17/51, 19/33 [D sg.]
gardis 23/16 [G sg.]
garēhsns [f. ⟨*i*⟩] plan, design
garēhsn 27/26 [A sg.]
garūni [n. ⟨*jo*⟩ N or A sg.] counsel, consultation (see *gatáujands garūni*)
garuns [f. ⟨*i*⟩] street
garunsim 21/2 [D pl.]
gasaíƕan 2/10 [V] see
gasaƕ 8/2, 12/20 [3 sg. pret.]
gasaíƕiþ[1] 25/7 [2 pl. pres.]
gasaíƕiþ[2] 16/12 [3 sg. pres.]
gasēƕun 2/8, 25/5 [3 pl. pret.]
gasaíƕands 8/6, 24/39, 27/23, 28/14 [pres. part., m., of *gasaíƕan*] seeing
gasaíƕandans 17/53 [N pl.]

gasaílvans 25/11 [past part., m., of *gasaíhvan*] seen

gasalbōn [ii] anoint

gasalbōdēdeina 25/1 [3 pl. pret. opt.]

gasaljands 27/17 [pres. part., m., of *gasaljan*, i] giving up, offering

gasatjan [i] set, lay, place, establish

gasatida 19/36 [3 sg. pret.]

gasēlvun [3 pl. pret. of *gasaíhvan* 'see,' q.v.]

gasinþja [m. ⟨*n*⟩] companion

gasinþjam 8/2 [D pl.]

gaskeiriþ 23/22, 24/34 [past part., n., of *gaskeirjan*, i] explained, interpreted

gaskōhi [n. ⟨*jo*⟩] pair of sandals

gaskōhi 12/22 [A sg.]

gastaldan cf. §6.1 [VIIa] possess

gastaístald 6/10 [3 sg. pret.]

gastandan cf. §5.4 [VI] abide, stay, be restored

gastōþun 5/2 [3 pl. pret.]

gaswiltan [III] die, be dying

gaswalt 17/52, 17/53, 24/44 [3 sg. pret.]

gatáih [3 sg. pret. of *gateihan* 'tell,' q.v.]

gataíran 14/17 [IV] destroy, break

gataíranda 26/8 [3 pl. pass. pres.]

gataíriþ 14/19 [3 sg. pres.]

gataúhun [3 pl. pret. of *gatiuhan* 'lead, bring, take,' q.v.]

gatáujan [i] do, make, arrange

gatawei 12/19 [2 sg. imper.]

gatawida 8/3, 23/14 [3 sg. pret.]

gatawidēs 22/35 [2 sg. pret.]

gatáujands garūni 3/2 [participial phr.] consulting

gataúrnan [iv] dissolve, vanish, be torn, be destroyed

gataúrniþ 26/8, 26/10 [3 sg. pres.]

gatawei [2 sg. imper. of *gatáujan* 'do, make, arrange,' q.v.]

gatawida [3 sg. pret. of *gatáujan* 'do, make, arrange,' q.v.]

gatawidēs [2 sg. pret. of *gatáujan* 'do, make, arrange,' q.v.]

gateihan cf. §4.2 [Ib] tell

gatáih 25/10 [3 sg. pret.]

gatiuhan [II] lead, bring, take

gataúhun 23/16 [3 pl. pret.]

gaþaúrsnan [iv] be withered

gaþaúrsnōda 9/6 [3 sg. pret.]

gaþliuhan [II] flee

gaþlaúhun 25/8 [3 pl. pret.]

gáuja [D sg. of *gawi* 'district, area,' q.v.]

gáujē [G pl. of *gawi* 'district, area,' q.v.]

gáujis [G sg. of *gawi* 'district, area,' q.v.]

Gaúlgaúþa Golgotha

Gaúlgaúþa 23/22 [A sg.]

gáumjan [i: + D or + A] observe, perceive

gáumida 20/5 [3 sg. pret.]

gáumidēdun 25/4 [3 pl. pret.]

gáumjáindáu 21/5 [3 pl. pass. pres. opt.]

gawandjan [i] bring back, return

gawandida 17/55 [3 sg. pret.]

gawasida sik [3 sg. pret. of *gawasjan sik* 'clothe oneself,' q.v.]

gawasjan [i] clothe

gawasidēdun 23/17, 23/20 [3 pl. pret.]

gawasjiþ 12/22 [2 pl. imper.]

gawasjan sik clothe oneself
gawasida sik 18/29 [3 sg. pret.]
gawaúrkjan [i] prepare, accomplish
gawaúrhtēdi 27/21 [3 sg. pret. opt.]
gawi 3/5, 11/14; cf. §3.1 [n. ⟨*jo*⟩] district, area
gáuja 3/3, 3/8, 5/8 [D sg.]
gáujē 5/1 [G pl.]
gáujis 11/15 [G sg.]
giban 17/55 [V] give, yield
gaf 9/7, 9/8, 11/16 [3 sg. pret.]
gēbun 2/14, 23/23 [3 pl. pret.]
gibiþ 12/22 [2 pl. imper.]
gif 1/11, 11/12 [2 sg. imper.]
gibu cf. §6.3 [f. ⟨*a*⟩] gift
gistradagis 18/30 [adv.] ?tomorrow (for *afar-daga* 'after a day'?)
gōds (or *-þs*) 16/11 [m. ⟨*o*⟩] good
gōda[1] 9/8 [f. A sg.]
gōda[2] 16/11, 16/14 [m. N sg. (weak)]
gōdans 15/45 [m. A pl.]
gōdōn 10/20 [f. D sg.]
gōljan 23/18 [i] greet
gōleiþ 15/47 [2 pl. pres.]
grēdags 6/6 [m. ⟨*o*⟩] hungry
grētan [VII] weep
gaígrōtun 17/52 [3 pl. pret.]
grētiþ 17/52 [2 pl. imper.]
grētandam 25/10 [pres. part., D pl., of *gretan*] weeping
gþ (= *guþ*) [A sg. of *guþ* 'God,' q.v.]
gþa (= *guda*) [D sg. of *guþ* 'God,' q.v.]
gþs (= *gudis*) [G sg. of *guþ* 'God,' q.v.]

gudja [m. ⟨*n*⟩] priest
gudjans 22/35 [N pl.]
gudjinassus [m. ⟨*u*⟩] priestly function
gudjinassáus 28/6 [G sg.]
gudjinōn [ii] perform a priestly function
gudjinōda 28/4 [3 sg. pret.]
guþ[1] 18/30; cf. §3.1 [m.] God
gþ (= *guþ*[2], below)
gþa (= *guda*, below)
gþs (= *gudis*, below)
guda 18/24; (as *gþa*) 27/19 [D sg.]
gudis 3/7, 4/2, 4/10, 5/1, 5/7, 5/9, 6/3, 24/39, 24/43, 28/6; (as *gþs*) 27/29 [G sg.]
guþ[2] (as *gþ*) 27/2 [A sg.]
guþ[3] 24/34 [Voc. sg.]

-h 10/17 (*þaþrōh*); 18/25 (*nih*); 22/37 (*nuh*) [clitic] and
haban cf. §§7.1, 10.2, 12.1, 21.1 [iii] have, take
habáida (or *habaida*) 9/5, 9/6, 27/25 [3 sg. pret.] (see also *þatei habáida* . . .)
habáidēdun 3/9, 7/13 [3 pl. pret.]
habáiþ[1] 15/46, 21/1 [2 pl. pres.]
habáiþ[2] 20/9 [3 sg. pres.]
haband 10/17, 12/17, 21/5 [3 pl. pres.]
habáu 26/1, 26/2, 26/3 [1 sg. pres. opt.]
habands 3/5, 8/5 [pres. part., m., of *haban*] having
habandō [n. A sg.] (see *jērē habandō*)
hafjan cf. §5.2 [VI] raise
haíháit [3 sg. pret. of *háitan*

'call, order,' q.v.]
háils[1] [adj., m. ⟨*o*⟩] hale, safe
háilana 13/27 [A sg.]
háils[2] 23/18 [interjection] hail!
háims cf. §9.1 [f.] village
haírdeis 16/11, 16/12, 16/14, 16/16; cf. §2.3 [m. ⟨*jo*⟩] herdsman
haírdjam 2/5, 2/9 [D pl.]
haírdjōs 2/3, 2/8 [N pl.]
haírdjōs 2/6 [Voc. pl.]
haírtō cf. §8.1 [n. ⟨*n*⟩] heart
haírtam 10/15 [D pl.]
haírtanē 8/12 [G pl.]
háitan cf. §13.1 [VII] call, order
haíháit 8/3 [3 sg. pret.]
háitada 14/19 [3 sg. pass. pres.]
háitáidáu 12/19, 12/21 [1 sg. pass. pres. opt.]
háitáis 28/29 [2 sg. imper.]
háiþi [f. ⟨*jā*⟩] field, heath
háiþjōs 18/28, 18/30 [G sg.]
háiþjōs seináizōs 11/15 [G of place] to his field
haldan 11/15 [VII] feed
hals [m. ⟨*o*⟩] neck
hals 12/20 [A sg.]
hana cf. §8.1 cock
handus [f. ⟨*u*⟩] hand
handu 12/22, 17/54 [A sg.]
hansa [f. ⟨*ā*⟩] cohort
hansa 23/16 [A sg.]
harjis[1] 2/9; cf. §2.3 [m. ⟨*jo*⟩] host, army
hari 2/8 [A sg.]
harjis[2] 2/8 [G sg.]
hatis cf. §3.1 [n. ⟨*o*⟩] wrath, hatred
hatiza 5/7 [D sg.]
hatizis 3/2, 7/6 [G sg.]
hatjandam 15/44 [pres. part., m. D pl., of *hatjan*, ?i] hating
háubiþ [n. ⟨*o*⟩] head
háubida 3/10 [N pl.]
háubidis 7/9 [G sg.]
háubiþ 7/11, 7/12, 23/19 [A sg.]
háuf [3 sg. pret. of *hiufan* 'mourn,' q.v.]
háuhjan [i] exalt, glorify
háuhjáindáu 21/2 [3 pl. pass. pres. opt.]
haúrds [f. ⟨*i*⟩] door
haúrdái 21/6 [D sg.]
haúrn [n. ⟨*o*⟩] horn, husk
haúrnē 11/16 [G pl.]
haúrnjan [i] blow a horn
haúrnjáis 21/2 [2 sg. pres. opt.]
háusjan [i] hear, listen to, harken
háuseiþ 22/37 [3 sg. pres.]
háusidēdun 2/8, 2/10 [3 pl. pret.]
háusidēduþ 15/21, 15/43 [2 pl. pret.]
háusjand 10/16, 10/20, 16/16 [3 pl. pres.]
háusjandans 10/18, 25/11 [pres. part., m. pl., of *háusjan*] hearing, listening to
hawi[1] 20/10 [n. ⟨*jo*⟩] grass
hawi[2] 18/30 [A sg.]
Hēlias 24/36 Elias
Hēlian 24/35 [A sg.]
hēr 4/7, 20/9, 25/6 [adv.] here
Hērōdēs 3/2, 3/4, 7/1, 7/3, 7/7, 7/10 [m.] Herod
Hērōdis 2/1, 7/3 [G sg.]
Hērōdia 7/3 [f.] Herodia
Hērōdiadins 7/1, 7/9 [G sg.]
hēþjō [f. ⟨*n*⟩] room, chamber
hēþjōn 21/6 [D sg.]
himins 14/18 [m. ⟨*o*⟩] heaven
himin 2/9, 12/18, 12/21 [A sg.]

himina 1/10, 2/4, 3/7 [D sg.]
himinam 1/9, 2/8, 3/2, 15/45, 15/48, 18/26, 18/32, 21/1 [D pl.]
himinē 6/10, 14/19, 14/20 [G pl.]
himinis 2/7, 2/8, 2/14, 18/26 [G sg.]
himma 1/11, 2/6, 18/30 [D sg., (defective) pronominal adj.] this
hiufan [IIa] mourn
háuf 4/5 [3 sg. pret.]
hufum 4/8 [1 pl. pret.]
hufuþ 4/9 [2 pl. pret.]
hiuhma 28/9 [m. ⟨*n*⟩] crowd, throng
hláifs 6/7; cf. §2.3 [m. ⟨*o*⟩] bread, loaf
hláibam 20/13 [D pl.]
hláibans 20/5, 20/9, 20/11 [A pl.]
hláibe 12/17 [G pl.]
hláibōs 20/7 [N pl.]
hláif 1/11 [A sg.]
hláiw [n. ⟨*wo*⟩] grave, tomb
hláiw 25/5 [A sg.]
hláiwa 7/13, 24/46, 25/2, 25/8 [D sg.]
hláiwis 24/46, 25/3 [G sg.]
hláuts [m. ⟨*o*⟩] lot
hláuta 23/24 [D sg.]
hláuts imma urrann 28/7 it became his lot
hleidumei 21/3 [f. ⟨*n*⟩] left (hand), left (side)
hleidumein 23/27 [D sg.]
hrōpjan [i] cry out, call
hrōpidēdun 22/40, 23/13, 23/14 [3 pl. pret.]
hrōpjands 24/39 [pres. part., m., of *hrōpjan*] crying out
hufum [1 pl. pret. of *hiufan* 'mourn,' q.v.]
hufuþ [2 pl. pret. of *hiufan* 'mourn,' q.v.]
hugjan [i] think, suppose
hugidēdun 4/3 [3 pl. pret.]
hugjáiþ 14/17 [2 pl. pres. opt.]
hūhrus 11/14 [m. ⟨*u*⟩] famine, hunger
hūhráu 12/17 [D sg.]
hund [n. ⟨*o*⟩] hundred
hundam 20/7 [D pl.]
hundafaþs (or *-ads*) 24/39 [m. ⟨*i*⟩] centurion
hundafada 24/45 [D sg.]
hundafaþ 24/44 [A sg.]
hundam [D pl. of *hund* 'hundred,' q.v.]
hunsl 27/18 [n. ⟨*o*⟩] offering
hunslastaþs (or *-ads*) [m. ⟨*i*⟩] altar
hunslastadis 28/12 [G sg.]

ƕa[1] 4/7, 13/26, 20/9, 22/38; cf. §15.3 [interrog. pron., n.] what? (why?)
ƕa[2] 18/25, 18/28, 18/31, 19/33, 21/3, 22/35, 23/12, 23/14, 23/24 [A]
ƕa þatei 4/9, 18/28, 19/33 [adv. phr.] why?
ƕaírnei [f. ⟨*n*⟩] skull
ƕaírneins 23/22 [G sg.]
ƕáiwa 18/28, 18/30 [adv.] how?
ƕan 12/17 [adv.] how (before adj. or adv.)
ƕanhun [adv.] ever (but used only in *ni ƕanhun*, q.v.)
ƕar 24/47 [adv.] where?
ƕarjis 19/34; cf. §15.4 [interrog. pron., m.] who? which? (of more than two)
ƕarjizuh (*ƕarjis* + *-uh*) 20/7, 23/24; cf. §20.2 [indef. pron.,

m.] each, each one, every, every one

ƕas[1] 5/5, 18/27, 25/3; cf. §15.3 [interrog. pron., m.] who? what?

ƕis [n. G sg.] (see *ƕis wildēdi*)

ƕas[2] 19/35 [indef. pron., m.] anyone

ƕaþrō 20/5 [adv.] whence?

ƕazuh (*ƕas*[1] + *-uh*) 15/22; cf. §20.2 [indef. pron., m.] each one

ƕazuh saei 22/37 [indef. pron., m.] whosoever (see also *salvazuh saei*)

ƕē 15/47, 18/25, 18/31; cf. §15.3 [adv.] how? wherewith? with what?

ƕeila[1] 23/25, 24/33 [f. ⟨*ā*⟩] hour, time, season

ƕeila[2] 24/33 [A sg.]

ƕeilái 24/34, 28/10 [D sg.]

ƕeilaƕaírbs [m. ⟨*o*⟩] inconstant

ƕeilƕaírbái 10/17 [N pl.]

ƕeits [f. ⟨*o*⟩] white

ƕeitái 25/5 [D sg.]

ƕēláuþs cf. §15.4 how great?

ƕileiks cf. §15.4 what sort?

ƕis wildēdi 7/8 what she wanted

ƕō cf. §15.3 [interrog. pron., f.] who? what?

ƕō 15/46 [A]

Iaeirus 17/41 [m.] Jairus

Iaírusalēm 4/1, 4/4, 4/6, 24/41 [indeclinable] Jerusalem

Iakōbus [m.] James

Iakōbis 24/40, 25/1 [G sg.]

Iakōbu 17/51 [A sg.]

Iaúrdanus* the Jordan

Iaúrdanáus 5/1 [G sg.]

Iaúrdanē 6/2 [D sg.]

·ib· (*twalif*) 20/13 [num.] twelve

ibna 27/13 [adj., n. ⟨*a*⟩ (inflected only in weak declension)] equal

iddja [3 sg. pret. of *gaggan* 'go, come, walk,' q.v.]

idreiga [f. ⟨*ā*⟩] repentance

idreiga 6/1 [A sg.]

idreigōn sik [ii] repent

idreigōdēdun sik 7/4 [3 pl. pret.]

Iēsus 3/1, 4/1, 5/8, 6/4, 6/5, 20/5, 20/10, 20/11, 20/15, 22/34/, 22/36, 22/37, 24/34, 24/37 [m.] Jesus

Iēsu 2/2, 2/11, 3/6, 4/3, 6/7, 22/33, 23/15, 25/6 [A sg.] (see also *ni kara*...)

Iēsua 2/14, 6/8, 6/9 [D sg.]

Iēsuis 17/41, 24/43 [G sg.]

ija[1] 7/3, 7/8 [A sg. of *si* 'she,' q.v.]

ija[2] 7/4 [N pl. of *ita* 'it,' q.v.]

ijōs [A pl. of *si* 'she,' q.v.]

ik 12/17, 15/22, 15/44, 16/11, 16/14, 16/15, 22/35, 22/37, 22/38; cf. §12.3 [personal pron.] I

mik 11/12, 12/19, 16/14, 16/15, 19/37, 22/34 [A sg.]

mis 11/12, 13/29, 13/31, 19/39, 22/35, 24/34 [D sg.] (see also *frawaúrhta mis* and *ni waíht bōtōs*...)

uns[1] (or *unsis*[1]) 1/11, 1/12, 25/3 [D pl.]

uns[2] (or *unsis*[2]) 1/13, 19/38, 27/18 [A pl.]

weis 1/12 [N pl.]

im[1] [1 sg. pres. of *wisan*[1] 'be,' q.v.]

im[2] [D pl. of is[1] 'he,' q.v.]

imma [D sg. of *is* 'he,' q.v.]

in[1] 7/1, 7/9, 7/11, 10/17 [prep., +G] because of (see also *in þizei* and *inuh þis*)

in[2] 1/13, 2/1, 2/8, 2/9, 3/5, 4/1, 4/6, 4/11, 6/2, 6/5, 6/11, 8/1, 9/7, 9/8, 10/18, 11/13, 12/18, 12/21, 12/22, 15/22, 17/41, 18/26, 18/30, 20/15, 21/6, 22/33, 24/38, 24/41, 25/5, 25/7, 25/9, 28/8 [prep., + A] in, into, toward (see also *in baírtein*)

in[3] 1/9, 1/10, 1/13, 2/1, 2/6, 2/10, 2/11, 3/2, 3/3, 3/10, 4/3, 4/4, 4/6, 4/10, 5/1, 5/8, 6/1, 6/2, 6/3, 6/4, 6/6, 7/2, 7/13, 8/1, 8/2, 8/4, 8/9, 8/12, 10/15, 10/17, 12/17, 12/18, 12/21, 14/19, 14/20, 15/45, 15/48, 17/51, 18/29, 19/33, 19/36, 19/38, 19/39, 19/41, 21/2, 21/4, 21/5, 21/6, 21/7, 22/37, 22/38, 22/39, 24/40, 24/41, 24/46, 25/5, 28/5 [prep., + D] in, into, among (see also *in andwaírþja, in frisahtái, warþ . . . in siunai*)

in andwaírþja 21/1, 24/39 [adv. phr.] before

in baírhtein 21/4, 21/6 [adv. phr.] openly

in frisahtái 26/12 [adv. phr.] in an image (i.e., darkly, enigmatically)

in þizei 9/5 [adv. phr.] because

ina [A sg. of *is* 'he,' q.v.]

infeinan [iv] be moved, pity

  infeinōda 12/20 [3 sg. pret.]

ingramjan [i] provoke

  ingramjada 26/5 [3 sg. pass. pres.]

inn 10/19, 13/28, 17/51, 24/43 [adv.] in, within

innana 23/16 [adv., + G] within, inside

ins [A pl. of *is* 'he,' q.v.]

insaian cf. §10.4 [VII] sow in

insaianō 10/15 [past part., n. A sg., of *insaian*] sown in

insaíhvan [V] look, regard, behold

  insaíhviþ 18/26 [2 pl. imper.]

insaíhvandeins 25/4 [pres. part., f. pl., of *insaíhvan*] looking, regarding

insandjan [i] send, send forth

  insandida 3/5, 7/1, 7/11, 11/15 [3 sg. pret.]

inu 4/3 [prep., + A] without, excepting

inuh þis 27/8 [adv. phr.] for this reason

inweitan [I] salute

  inwitun 23/19 [3 sg. pret.]

inwindiþa [f. ⟨*ā*⟩] injustice, inequity

  inwindiþái 26/6 [D sg.]

inwinds [m.⟨*o*⟩] unjust, perverse

  inwindans 15/45 [A pl.]

inwitun [3 sg. pret. of *inweitan* 'salute,' q.v.]

Iōhannēs 5/1, 5/5, 5/7, 6/1, 7/4, 8/1, 19/38, 27/23 [m.] John

  Iōhannē 6/4 [D sg.]

  Iōhannēn[1] 5/9, 17/51 [D sg.]

  Iōhannēn[2] 7/1, 7/6, 28/20 [A sg.]

  Iōhannis 7/9, 7/11, 7/13 [G sg.]

Iōsēf[1] 2/1, 4/5, 24/43 [m.] Joseph

  Iōsēf[2] 2/11 [A sg.]

  Iōsēfa 3/1, 3/7, 4/1, 24/45 [D sg.]

Iōsēzis 24/40, 24/47 [G sg.] of Joses

is[1] 7/12, 11/14, 13/27, 13/29, 17/42, 17/50, 17/54, 17/56,

19/39, 20/15, 23/23, 24/44; cf. §7.3 [personal pron., m.] he
eis 7/2, 19/34, 22/40, 23/13, 23/14, 25/11 [N pl.]
im 7/11, 11/12, 17/56, 19/35, 19/36, 21/1, 21/7, 22/38, 23/12, 23/14, 23/15, 25/6, 28/1 [D pl.]
imma 7/4, 7/7, 7/11, 7/12, 11/16, 12/18, 12/20, 12/21, 13/27, 13/30, 13/31, 17/49, 17/50, 19/38, 19/39, 20/5, 20/7, 22/33, 22/37, 22/38, 23/23, 23/27, 24/41, 28/11, 28/16 [D sg.] (see also *was imma, miþ imma . . . , hláuts imma . . .*)
ina 7/2, 11/15, 12/20, 12/22, 13/27, 13/28, 17/41, 17/42, 17/53, 20/6, 21/8, 23/13, 23/14, 23/16, 23/17, 23/18, 23/19, 23/20, 23/22, 23/24, 23/25, 24/36, 24/41, 24/44, 25/1, 25/6, 25/7, 28/15 [A sg.] (see also *ni karist ina . . .*)
ins 7/1, 8/3, 18/26, 19/33 [A pl.]
is[2] 7/13, 12/20, 12/22, 13/25, 13/28, 20/8, 23/19, 23/21, 23/24, 23/26, 23/27, 24/39, 25/7, 28/4, 28/20 [G sg.]
izē 7/6, 10/15, 11/12 [G pl.]

is[2] [G sg. of *is*[1] 'he,' q.v.]

is[3] 13/31, 22/33, 22/37 [2 sg. pres. of *wisan* 'be,' q.v.]

ist [3 sg. pres. of *wisan* 'be,' q.v.]

ita [personal pron., n.] it
ija[2] 7/4 [N pl.]
ita 10/16, 19/36, 24/46 [A sg.]

itan [V] eat (see *sad itan*)

iþ 2/10, 3/2, 3/7, 3/9, 4/4, 4/9, 5/5, 5/6, 5/9, 6/8, 6/10, 7/6, 7/9, 8/3, 8/6, 8/10, 12/17, 13/28, 13/30, 14/19, 15/21, 15/22, 16/12, 16/13, 17/50, 17/56, 18/24, 18/27, 19/34, 19/39, 20/6, 20/10, 20/15, 21/3, 21/6, 22/36, 22/39, 22/40, 23/12, 23/13, 23/14, 23/15, 23/16, 23/23, 24/37, 24/44, 24/47, 26/1, 26/2, 26/3, 26/8, 26/11, 26/12, 26/13 [cj.] and, but (as in "but to continue the story")

Iudaius 22/35 [m. ⟨*u*/*i*⟩] Jew
Iudaias 3/3 [G sg.]
Iudaiē 3/3, 22/33, 22/39, 23/12, 23/18, 23/26 [G pl.]
Iudaium 22/36, 22/38 [D pl.]

iupaþrō 24/38 [adv.] from above, from on high

izái [D sg. of *si* 'she,' q.v.]

izē [G pl. of *is* 'he,' q.v.]

izō [G pl. of *si* 'she,' q.v.]

izōs [G sg. of *si* 'she,' q.v.]

izwar 15/48, 18/26, 18/32, 21/8 [pronominal adj., 2 pl., m.] your, yours
izwarái 18/25 [f. D sg.]
izwaráizōs 14/20 [f. G sg.]
izwaramma[1] 18/25 [n. D sg.]
izwaramma[2] 21/1 [m. D sg.]
izwarans 15/44, 15/47 [m. A pl.]
izwaris 15/45 [m. G sg.]

izwara [G pl. of *þu* 'thou,' q.v.]

izwis[1] 14/18, 14/20, 15/22, 18/25, 18/29, 19/33, 19/41, 21/2, 21/5, 22/39, 25/7 [D pl. of *þu* 'thou,' q.v.]

izwis[2] 15/44, 15/46, 18/30, 19/40 [A pl. of *þu* 'thou,' q.v.]

·j· (*saíhs tiguns*) 9/8, 10/20

[num., A pl.] sixty

jabái 15/46, 15/47, 19/35, 26/1, 26/2, 26/3 [cj.] if, even if, although (see also *untē jabái*...)

jah 1/10, 1/12, 1/13, 2/1, 2/2, 2/3, 2/4, 2/5, 2/7, 2/8, 2/9, 2/11, 2/12, 2/13, 2/14, 3/1, 3/2, 3/4, 3/5, 3/7, 3/8, 3/9, 3/10, 4/1, 4/2, 4/3, 4/5, 4/6, 4/7, 4/8, 4/9, 4/11, 5/1, 5/2, 5/3, 5/4, 5/5, 5/6, 5/7, 5/9, 6/1, 6/2, 6/3, 6/4, 6/5, 6/6, 6/7, 6/8, 6/9, 6/11, 7/1, 7/2, 7/3, 7/6, 7/7, 7/8, 7/10, 7/11, 7/12, 7/13, 8/1, 8/2, 8/3, 8/4, 8/5, 8/7, 8/8, 8/9, 8/10, 8/11, 8/12, 8/13, 9/4, 9/5, 9/6, 9/7, 9/8, 10/15, 10/16, 10/17, 10/18, 10/19, 10/20, 11/12, 11/13, 11/14, 11/15, 11/16, 12/18, 12/20, 12/21, 12/22, 12/23, 12/24, 13/25, 13/26, 13/27, 13/28, 13/29, 13/31, 13/32, 14/18, 14/19, 14/20, 15/43, 15/44, 15/45, 15/46, 15/47, 16/12, 16/13, 16/14, 16/15, 16/16, 17/41, 17/42, 17/50, 17/51, 17/52, 17/53, 17/54, 17/55, 17/56, 18/24, 18/25, 18/26, 18/28, 18/30, 19/33, 19/35, 19/36, 19/37, 19/38, 19/39, 20/5, 20/9, 20/11, 20/13, 21/2, 21/4, 21/5, 21/6, 22/33, 22/35, 22/37, 22/38, 23/16, 23/17, 23/18, 23/19, 23/20, 23/21, 23/22, 23/23, 23/24, 23/25, 23/26, 23/27, 23/28, 24/33, 24/34, 24/35, 24/36, 24/38, 24/40, 24/41, 24/42, 24/43, 24/44, 24/45, 24/47, 25/1, 25/2, 25/3, 25/4, 25/5, 25/7, 25/8, 25/10, 25/11, 26/1, 26/2, 26/3, 26/9, 26/12, 26/13, 27/6, 28/1, 28/2, 28/8, 28/13, 28/15, 28/18, 28/19, 28/20 [cj.] and, also (see also *jas-sáuþ*)

jáináim [D pl. of *jáins* 'that, yon,' q.v.]

jáinar 2/2, 2/3, 2/8, 3/9, 4/2, 5/2, 8/5, 11/13 [adv.] yonder, there

jáind 5/4 [adv.] thither

jáindrē 5/9 [adv.] thither

jáins cf. §11.1 [demonstrative pron.] that, yon

  jáináim 5/1, 6/4 [m. D pl.]

  jáinata 11/14 [n. A sg.]

  jáinis 11/15 [n. G sg.]

jas-sáuþ (= *jah* + *sáuþ*) 27/19 [m. A sg.] and sacrifice

jaþþē . . . jaþþē 26/8 [cj.] either . . . or

jēr [n. ⟨*o*⟩] year

  jērē 13/29 [G pl.]

jērē habandō 3/5; cf. §3.4 years old

jōta 14/18 [m. ⟨*n*⟩] jot, iota (from Gk. *ἰῶτα*)

ju 12/19, 12/21, 27/6 [adv.] now, already

juggaláuþs [m. ⟨*i*⟩] young man

  juggaláuþ 25/5 [A sg.]

jūhiza 11/12, 11/13 [adj., m., comparative of *juggs*] younger

jus [N pl. of *þu* 'thou,' q.v.]

juþan 24/42, 24/44 [adv.] already, now

Kafarnaum 8/4, 19/33 [indeclinable] Capharnaum (Capernaum)

kalkjō* (?*kalki**) [f.] harlot

  kalkjōm 13/30 [D pl.]

kann [1 sg. pres. or 3 sg. pres. of *kunnan*, 'know, be acquainted with,' q.v.]

kara [f. ⟨*a*⟩] care, anxiety, concern (see *ni kara* ..., *ni karist* ...)

karist (= *kara* + *ist*) it concerns

(see *ni karist* . . .)

karkara [f. ⟨*a*⟩] prison (from Lat. *carcer*)

karkarái 7/2, 8/1 [D sg.]

káupatjan cf. §17.1 buffet

kiusan cf. §4.2–3 [IIa] choose

klismjandei 26/1 [pres. part., f., of *klismjan*, i] tinkling

klismō 26/1 [f. ⟨*n*⟩] cymbal

kniu* cf. §3.3 [m. ⟨*wo*⟩] knee

kniwa [A pl.] (see *lagjandans kniwa*)

kniwam 3/9 [D pl.]

kukjan [i: + D] kiss

kukida 12/20 [3 sg. pret.]

kuni cf. §3.1 [n. ⟨*jo*⟩] race, generation, lineage

kuni 5/7 [Voc. sg.]

kunjis seinis 28/5 [noun phr.] (for priests) of his lineage

kunnan [pret. pres.] know, be acquainted with

kann 16/14, 16/15 [1 sg. pres.]

kann 16/15 [3 sg. pres.]

kunnum 26/9 [1 pl. pres.]

kunnun 16/14 [3 pl. pres.]

kunþi[1] 26/8 [n.⟨*jo*⟩] knowledge

kunþi[2] 26/2 [A sg.]

kunþja 4/11 [D sg.]

Kwreinaius [m.] a Cyrenian

Kwreinaiu 23/21 [A sg.]

·l· (*þrins tiguns*) 9/8, 10/20 [num., A pl.] thirty

lag [3 sg. pret. of *ligan* 'lie, recline,' q.v.]

lagjan [i] lay, lay down, set, place

lagja 16/15 [1 sg. pres.]

lagjiþ 16/11 [3 sg. pres.]

lagjandans kniwa 23/19 [participial phr.] laying knees (i.e., kneeling)

láiks [m. ⟨*i*⟩] dance, dancing

láikins 13/25 [A pl.]

láis cf. §16.2 (I) know

láisareis [m. ⟨*jo*⟩] teacher, master

láisari[1] 17/49 [A sg.]

láisari[2] 19/38 [Voc. sg.]

láisarjam 4/4, 4/6 [D pl.]

láiseins cf. §9.1 [f.] doctrine

láisjan [i] teach

láisjái 14/19 [3 sg. pres. opt.]

láistjan [i] follow

láisteiþ 19/38 [3 sg. pres.]

láistidēdun 24/41 [3 pl. pret.]

lamb [n. ⟨*o*⟩] lamb, sheep

lamba[1] 16/12 [N pl.]

lamba[2] 16/11, 16/12, 16/15, 16/16 [A pl.]

lambam 16/12 [D pl.]

lambē [G pl.] (see *ni karist* . . .)

land [n. ⟨*o*⟩] land, country

land 11/13 [A sg.]

láun [n. ⟨*o*⟩] reward, wage

láun 21/1 [A sg.]

láusjan [i] free, deliver

láusei 1/13 [2 sg. imper.]

leik[1] 18/25 [n. ⟨*o*⟩] body, flesh

leik[2] 7/13, 24/45, 26/3 [A sg.]

leika[1] 3/10 [N pl.]

leika[2] 18/25 [D sg.]

leikis 24/43 [G sg.]

lein [n. ⟨*o*⟩] linen

lein 24/46 [A sg.]

leina 24/46 [D sg.]

leitil galáubjandans 18/30 [participial phr.] of little faith

leitils cf. §18.1 [⟨*o*⟩] little

leitil 20/7 [A sg.] (see also *leitil galáubjandans*)

lētan cf. §6.1 [VIIb] let, let

out, leave, suffer, let be
  laílōt 6/8 [3 sg. pret.]
  lēt 24/36 [2 sg. imper.]
lētands stibna mikila 24/37 [participial phr.] uttering a great cry
libáins [f. ⟨*i*⟩] life
  libáináis 10/19 [G sg.]
liban [iii] live
  libáiþ 25/11 [3 sg. pres.]
libands 11/13 [pres. part., m., of *liban*] living
ligan [V] lie, recline
  lag 8/9 [3 sg. pret.]
lima (see *aílōē* . . .)
lisan [V] gather
  lisand 18/26 [3 sg. pres.]
liubōstōn p. xvii [f. D sg. of superlative of *liubs*] dearest
liuhaþ [n. ⟨*o*⟩] light
  liuhaþ 3/2 [A sg.]
liuta [m. ⟨*n*⟩] hypocrite
  liutans 21/2, 21/5 [N pl.]
liuþareis [m. ⟨*jo*⟩] singer
  liuþarjans 2/8 [A pl.]
lustus [m. ⟨*u*⟩] desire, lust
  lustjus 10/19 [N pl.]

magan* cf. §16.2 [pret. pres.] be able
  mag 18/24, 18/27 [3 sg. pres.]
  magi 19/39 [3 sg. pres. opt.]
  maguþ 18/24 [2 pl. pres.]
Magdalēnē[1] 24/40, 24/47, 25/1 [f.] Magdalene
  Magdalēnē[2] 25/9 [D sg.]
magula 20/9 [m.⟨*n*⟩] little boy
magus [m. ⟨*u*⟩] boy
  magiwē 13/26 [G pl.]
mahts 1/13 [f. ⟨*i*⟩] power, virtue, miracle
  maht 19/39 [A sg.]

máis 18/25, 18/26, 18/30, 23/14 [adv.] more, rather
máists 19/34 [adj., m. ⟨*o*/*n*⟩ (strong)] greatest, chief
  máista 26/13 [m. N sg. (weak)]
máiþms [m. ⟨*o*⟩] gift
  máiþmans 2/13, 2/14 [A pl.]
mammōna [⟨*n*⟩] mammon, wealth (from Aramaic *māmōnā* via Gk.)
  mammōnin 18/24 [D sg.]
manag 20/10; cf. §18.1 [n.⟨*o*⟩] much, many, great
  managa 9/5 [f. A sg.]
  managáim 20/9 [m. D pl.]
  managans 11/13 [m. A pl.]
  managōs 24/41 [f. N pl.]
managei 8/8; cf. §8.1 [f. ⟨*n*⟩] multitude
  manageim 8/1 [D pl.]
  managein 23/15 [D sg.]
  manageins[1] 8/11, 17/42 [N pl.]
  manageins[2] 20/5, 28/9 [G sg.]
managizō[1] 14/20 [n., comparative of *manag*] greater, more
  managizō[2] 15/47 [A sg.]
managōs [f. N pl. of *manag* 'much, many, great,' q.v.]
manasēds (or -*þs*) [f. ⟨*i*⟩] mankind, the world ("man-seed")
  manasēdáis 27/20, 27/30 [G sg.]
manna 8/5, 11/16, 18/24; cf. §8.3 [m. ⟨*n*⟩] man
  mann 8/7, 17/56 [D sg.]
  mannam 21/2, 21/5 [D pl.]
  mannē 8/3, 8/13, 11/11, 17/49, 21/1, 23/21, 26/1 [G pl.]
  mans[1] 8/3, 14/19, 20/10 [A pl.]
  mans[2] 8/6 [G sg.]

mannahun (or *mannhun*) 25/8 [indef. pron., m.] someone (see also *ni mannahun*)
marei [f. ⟨*n*⟩] sea, lake
  marein 8/2 [D sg.]
Maria 2/1. 2/2, 4/5, 4/7 [f.] Mary (mother of Jesus; see also *Marja*)
  Marian 2/11 [A sg.]
  Mariin 3/1, 3/7, 4/1 [D sg.]
Marja 24/40, 24/47, 25/1 [f.] Mary (except the mother of Jesus; see also *Maria*)
  Marjin 25/9 [D sg.]
mat [A sg. of *mats* 'food,' q.v.]
matjan [i] eat
  matidēdun 11/16 [3 pl. pret.]
  matjáina 20/5 [3 pl. pres. opt.]
  matjáiþ 18/25 [2 pl. pres. opt.]
  matjam 18/31 [1 pl. pres.]
matjandans 12/23 [pres. part., m., of *matjan*] eating
  matjandam 20/13 [N pl.]
mats [m. ⟨*i*⟩] food
  mat 17/55 [A sg.]
máujōs [G sg. of *mawi* 'maiden,' q.v.]
maúrgins [m. ⟨*o*⟩] morning
  maúrgin 2/11, 25/9 [D sg.]
maúrnan [iii] be anxious
  maúrnáiþ 18/25, 18/31 [2 pl. imper.]
maúrnands 18/27 [pres. part., m., of *maúrnan*] being anxious
maúrþr [n. ⟨*o*⟩] murder
  maúrþris 3/6 [G sg.]
maúrþrjan [i] murder, kill
  maúrþreiþ 15/21 [3 sg. pres.]

  maúrþrjáis pres.] 15/21 [2 sg.

mawi cf. §6.3 [f. ⟨*ja*⟩] maiden
  máujōs 17/51 [G sg.]
  mawi 17/54 [Voc. sg.]
mein[1] 13/31 [possessive, n.] my, mine
  mein[2] 26/3 [n. A sg.]
  meina[1] 16/14 [n. N pl.]
  meina[2] 16/14 [n. A pl.]
  meina[3] 16/15 [f. A sg.]
  meina[4] 22/36 [f. N sg.]
  meinái[1] 22/36 [m. N pl.]
  meinái[2] p. xvii [f. D sg.]
  meináim 13/29 [m. D pl.]
  meináizōs 16/16, 22/37 [f. G sg.]
  meinamma[1] 12/18 [m. D sg.]
  meinamma[2] 19/37, 19/39, 19/41 [n. D sg.]
  meinis 12/17 [m. G sg.]
  meinōs 26/3 [f. A pl.]
  meins 12/24, 24/34 [m. N sg.]
mēnōþs cf. §15.1 month
mērjands 5/1, 6/1, 8/1 [pres. part., m., of *mērjan*, i] preaching
midjis* [adj., m. ⟨*jo*⟩] middle
  midjáim 19/36 [D pl.]
mik [A sg. of *ik* 'I,' q.v.]
mikils 14/19, 25/4; cf. §18.1 [m. ⟨*o*⟩] great
  mikila [f. A sg.] (see *lē-tands stibna* . . .)
  mikilái 24/34 [f. D sg.]
minnists [adj., m. ⟨*o*/*n*⟩ (strong)] least, smallest
  minnista 14/19 [m. N sg. (weak)]
  minnistōnō 14/19 [f. G pl.]
minniza [⟨*n*⟩] less, smaller
  minnizins 24/40 [m. G sg.]
mis [D sg. of *ik* 'I,' q.v.]
missō 19/33, 19/34, 25/3; cf. §19.2a [adv.] each other, one

another, reciprocally
mitōn [ii] think, ponder, consider
mitōda 26/11 [1 sg. pret.]
mitōdēduþ 19/33 [2 pl. pret.]
mitōþ 26/5 [3 sg. pres.]
miþ 3/1, 3/2, 3/7, 4/1, 4/6, 6/6, 8/2, 8/8, 10/16, 13/29, 13/30, 13/31, 19/33, 23/23, 23/27, 23/28, 27/27, 27/30 [prep., + D] with, among
miþ imma wisandam 25/10 [participial phr.] who had been with him
miþfaginōn [ii] rejoice with
miþfaginōþ 26/6 [3 sg. pres.]
miþgaggan [VII] accompany
miþiddjēdun 24/41 [3 pl. pret.]
miþsatjan [i] remove
miþsatjáu 26/2 [1 sg. pres. opt.]
miþþanei 9/4, 17/42, 28/4 [cj.] while, when
mizdō [f. ⟨*n*⟩] reward
mizdōn[1] 19/41 [D sg.]
mizdōn[2] 21/2, 21/5 [A sg.]
mizdōnō 15/46 [G pl.]
mōdags 13/28, 15/22 [⟨*o*⟩] angry
mōtareis [m. ⟨*jo*⟩] publican
mōtarjōs 5/4, 15/47 [N pl.]
munan cf. §16.2 think
mundōn sis [ii] note, mark
mundōda sis 7/6 [3 sg. pret.]

nadrs* [?m. ?⟨*o*⟩] viper, adder
nadrē 5/7 [G pl.]
nahtamats [m. ⟨*i*⟩] supper
nahtamat 7/7 [A sg.]
nam [3 sg. pret. of *niman* 'take, accept, receive,' q.v.]
namō[1] 1/9, 17/41; cf. §8.1 [n. ⟨*n*⟩] name
namin 8/12, 19/37, 19/38, 19/39, 19/41 [D sg.]
namō[2] 28/20 [A sg.]
namuh (= *nam* + *uh*) 20/11 and (he) took
nasjan cf. §§7.1, 10.2, 13.1, 14.3 [i] save
nasjands 27/10 [pres. part., m., of *nasjan*] savior
naúh [adv.] yet, still
naúh ni 5/8 [adv.] not yet
naúhþan (= *naúh* + *þan*) 17/49 [adv.] (then) yet, still
naúhþanuh (= *naúh* + *þan* + *uh*) 12/20 [adv.] yet, and (then) yet, still, and still
náus cf. §9.1 corpse
Nazaraíþ [indeclinable] Nazareth
Nazaraíþ 4/11, 6/4, 6/11 [D sg.]
Nazaraius [m. ⟨*u*⟩] Nazarene
Nazōraiu 25/6 [A sg.]
nē 22/40 [adv.] not, no, nay
nēƕ 13/25 [adv.] near
nēƕundja [m. ⟨*n*⟩] neighbor
nēƕundjan 15/43 [A sg.]
nēmi [3 sg. pret. opt. of *niman* 'take, accept, receive,' q.v.]
ni 1/13, 3/9, 5/5, 6/8, 7/4, 7/5, 7/10, 9/5, 9/6, 9/7, 10/17, 11/13, 11/16, 13/28, 14/17, 14/18, 14/20, 15/21, 16/12, 16/16, 17/49, 17/50, 17/51, 17/52, 17/56, 18/24, 18/25, 18/26, 18/31, 19/37, 19/38, 19/39, 19/41, 20/7, 20/12, 21/1, 21/2, 21/3, 21/5, 21/7, 21/8, 22/36, 22/38, 23/23, 25/6, 25/8, 25/11, 26/1, 26/2, 26/3, 26/4, 26/5, 26/6, 27/12,

28/1, 28/16 [adv.] not (see also *nih*, *nist*, *nist saei*, *niu*, *þanaseiþs ni*)
ni áiw (or *áiw ni*) 13/29, 26/8 [adv. phr.] never
ni ƕanhun 13/29 [adv. phr.] never
ni kara was Iēsu 6/10 [+G] Jesus had no concern for
ni karist ina þizē lambē 16/13 he has no care for the sheep
ni mannahun 19/39; cf. §19.2e no one
ni sōkeiþ sein áin 26/5 [verb phr.] is not self-seeking
ni waíht bōtōs mis táujáu 26/3 I do myself nothing of advantage (i.e., I gain nothing)
nibái 14/20 [cj.] unless, except
nih[1] (= *ni* + *-h*) 18/25, 18/29, 26/5, 27/13 [cj.] and not, nor, not even
nih[2] . . . **nih** 18/26, 18/28 [cj.] neither . . . nor
niman cf. §8.4 [IV] take, accept, receive
  nam 23/23 [3 sg. pret.] (see also *namuh*)
  nēmi 23/21, 23/24 [3 sg. pret. opt.]
  nimái 20/7 [3 sg. pres. opt.]
  nimand 10/16 [3 pl. pres.]
nimands 19/36 [pres. part., m., of *niman*] taking, accepting, receiving
nist (= *ni* + *ist*) 16/12, 19/40, 22/36, 25/6 is not
nist saei 27/1 there is none who
niu (= *ni* + *-u*) 15/46, 15/47, 18/25, 18/26 [interrog. adv.] not? (presupposes positive answer)
niu aúftō 5/5 [cj.] whether
niuklahs 26/11; cf. §26.1g [m. ⟨*o*⟩] childish
niunda [num., ⟨*n*⟩] ninth
  niundōn[1] 24/33 [f. A sg.]
  niundōn[2] 24/34 [f. D sg.]
nu 14/19, 15/48, 18/31, 21/2, 21/8, 22/36, 22/39, 23/12, 26/12, 26/13, 27/22 [adv.] now, so, therefore
nuh (= *nu* + *-h*) 22/22 [interrog. adv.] now? so? well?
nuta [m. ⟨*n*⟩] catcher
  nutans 8/3 [N pl.]

ōgan* [pret. pres.] be afraid
  ōgs 28/16 [2 sg. imper.]
  ōhtēdun 25/8 [3 pl. pret.]

Paítrus [m.] Peter
  Paítráu 25/7 [D sg.]
  Paítráus 20/8 [G sg.]
  Paítru 17/51 [A sg.]
paraskaíwē 24/42 Parasceve, day before the Sabbath (= preparation day)
pasxa [f.] Passover, Pasch (from Heb. via Gk.)
  pasxa 22/39 [D sg.]
paúrpurái 23/17, 23/20 [D sg.] purple (from Gk. πορφύρα)
Peilātus 22/33, 22/35, 22/37, 22/38, 23/12, 23/14, 23/15, 24/44 [m. ⟨*a*⟩] Pilate
  Peilātáu 24/43 [D sg.]
plapja* [f.] street, square
  plapjō 21/5 [G pl.]
plinsjan [i] dance
  plinsida 7/7 [3 sg. pret.]
praitōriaún 23/16 [m.] pretorium (from Lat. via Gk.)
  praitaúria 22/33 [D sg.]
praúfētja 26/8 [n. N pl.] prophecy (from Gk. προφητεία)
  praúfētjans 26/2 [m. A pl.]
praúfētjan [i] prophesy (from

Gk.)
praúfētjam 26/9 [1 pl. pres.]
praúfētus 5/6, 5/9 [m. ⟨*u*/*i*⟩] prophet (from Gk.)
praúfētuns 14/17 [A pl.]

qáinōndam 25/10 [pres. part., m. D pl., of *qáinōn*, ii] lamenting
qam [3 sg. pret. of *qiman* 'come, arrive,' q.v.]
qaþ [3 sg. pret. of *qiþan* 'say,' q.v.]
qaþuh (= *qaþ* + *uh*) 20/5, 22/33 and (he) said
qēmjáu [1 sg. pret. opt. of *qiman* 'come, arrive,' q.v.]
qēns 7/3, 28/18 [f. ⟨*i*⟩] wife, woman
qēn 7/5 [A sg.]
qēnai p. xvii [D sg.]
qēþun [3 pl. pret. of *qiþan* 'say,' q.v.]
qimáiu (= *qimái* + *u*) 24/36 whether (he) will come
qiman cf. §5.1 [IVa] come, arrive
qam[1] 14/17, 22/37 [1 sg. pret.]
qam[2] 2/4, 3/7, 5/9, 6/4, 6/11, 8/1, 12/20, 13/27, 13/30, 17/41, 19/33, 27/8 [3 sg. pret.]
qēmjáu 14/17 [1 sg. pret. opt.]
qēmun 2/1, 2/10, 2/12, 5/2, 6/2, 8/11, 9/4 [3 pl. pret.]
qimái 1/10 [3 sg. pres. opt.] (see also *qimáiu*)
qimiþ 10/15, 10/17, 14/20, 26/10 [3 sg. pres.]
qimands 8/10, 12/17, 13/25, 17/51, 24/43 [pres. part., m., of *qiman*] coming, arriving
qimandan 16/12, 23/21 [A sg.]
qinō [f. ⟨*n*⟩] woman
qinōns 24/40 [N pl.]
qiþan[1] cf. §5.1 [Va] say, speak, name, tell, call
qaþ 2/5, 3/7, 4/7, 4/9, 5/7, 5/9, 6/3, 6/7, 7/4, 8/6, 11/12, 12/17, 12/21, 12/22, 13/27, 13/29, 13/31, 17/52, 19/35, 19/36, 19/39, 20/6, 20/8, 20/10, 20/12, 22/37 22/38, 23/12, 23/14, 24/39 25/6, 25/7, 27/28, 28/15 [3 sg. pret.] (see also *qaþuh*)
qēþun 8/8, 22/34, 24/35, 25/3, 25/8 [3 pl. pret.]
qiþ 6/7 [2 sg. imper.]
qiþa 12/18, 14/18, 14/20, 15/22, 15/44, 18/25, 19/41, 21/2, 21/5 [1 sg. pres.] (see also *qiþuh*)
qiþeina (= *qēþeina*) 17/56 [3 pl. pret. opt.]
qiþis 22/34, 22/37 [2 sg. pres.]
qiþiþ[1] 15/22, 23/12 [3 sg. pres.]
qiþiþ[2] [2 pl. imper.] (see *qiþiduh*)
qiþan[2] 15/21, 15/43 [past part., n., of *qiþan*[1]] said
qiþanō 23/28 [A sg.]
qiþands 17/49, 17/50, 17/54, 19/38, 22/38, 24/34, 24/36 [pres. part., m., of *qiþan*[1]] saying
qiþandans 18/31, 22/40 [N pl.]
qiþiduh (= *qiþiþ*[2] + *uh*) 25/7 and tell
qiþuh (= *qiþa* + *uh*) 18/29 and I say
qumans 19/33 [past part., m., of *qiman*] come, arrived

·r· (*taíhuntēhund*) 9/8, 10/20 [num., A pl.] a hundred
ragineis 24/43 [m. ⟨*jo*⟩] counselor
rahniþs 23/28 [past part., m., of *rahnjan*, i] counted, reckoned
raíhtis 9/4 [adv.] indeed
raíhtōs waúrkeiþ 6/3 [verb phr.] make straight!
raka 15/22 (abusive epithet, 'fool,' from Aramaic via Gk.)
raþjō [f. ⟨*n*⟩] number, account
  raþjōn 20/10 [D sg.]
ráus [n. ⟨*o*⟩] reed
  ráus 24/36 [A sg.]
  ráusa 23/19 [D sg.]
razda [f. ⟨*ā*⟩] tongue, language
  razdōm 26/1 [D pl.]
  razdōs 26/8 [N pl.]
razn [n. ⟨*o*⟩] house
  razn 13/25 [A sg.]
reirō 25/8 [f. ⟨*n*⟩] trembling
rignjan [i] rain
  rigneiþ 15/45 [3 sg. pres.]
riqis 24/33 [n. ⟨*o*⟩] darkness
rōdjan cf. §8.4 [i] speak
  rōdida 26/11 [1 sg. pret.]
  rōdjáu 26/1 [1 sg. pres. opt.]
rōdjands 8/1 [pres. part., m., of *rōdjan*] speaking
  rōdjandin 17/49 [D sg.]
Rufus [⟨*u*⟩] Rufus
  Rufáus 23/21 [G sg.]
rūna [f. ⟨*ā*⟩] mystery, secret, counsel
  rūnōs 26/2 [A pl.]

sa[1] 2/5, 2/9, 5/5, 5/9, 6/9, 7/8, 9/3, 10/14, 11/12, 11/13, 12/21, 12/22, 12/24, 13/25, 13/30, 16/11, 16/12, 16/13, 16/14, 22/40, 23/26, 24/39, 25/4, 28/16; cf. §2.2–3 [definite article, m.] the
  þái[1] 2/8, 2/10, 2/14, 4/3, 4/5, 9/7, 15/46, 21/2, 21/5, 21/7 [N pl.]
  þáim[1] 2/5, 2/9, 3/2, 4/6, 8/8, 15/21, 15/44, 20/11, 20/13, 25/10 [D pl.]
  þamma[1] 2/5, 6/7, 8/7, 20/10, 22/36, 24/45 [D sg.]
  þana 1/11, 2/10, 12/23, 13/27, 13/30, 17/49, 17/51, 19/37, 22/39, 22/40, 23/15, 25/3, 25/6 [A sg.]
  þans 2/14, 8/3, 15/44, 15/46, 15/47, 19/35, 20/10, 20/11 [A pl.]
sa[2] 2/7, 2/14, 5/9, 6/3, 15/48, 18/26, 18/32, 27/28; cf. §2.2–3 [demonstrative (or personal) pron., m.] this, that, he (she, it) (see also *sah*, *saƕazuh saei*)
  þái[2] 10/15, 10/16, 10/18, 10/19, 10/20, 20/5 [N pl.]
  þáim[2] 1/12, 5/7, 18/26, 20/7, 21/8 [D pl.]
  þamma[2] 8/6, 21/1, 21/6, 22/37, 22/38 [D sg.]
  þis[2] 15/45, 27/8 [G sg.]
  þizē[1] 2/13, 14/20, 18/29, 20/8, 20/11, 24/35 [G pl.]
  þizei[1] 2/10, 16/12, 17/41 [G sg.]
sabbatō 24/42, 25/9 [m., indeclinable] Sabbath (see also *fruma sabbatō*)
sad itan 11/16 [verb phr.] eat one's fill
Saddukaieis 5/4 [m. pl.] Sadducees
sads* (or *-þs**) [adj., m. ⟨*o*⟩] satisfied
  sadái 20/12 [m. N pl.]
saei (= *sa*² + *-ei*) 13/30, 14/19, 15/21, 15/22, 16/12, 19/37,

19/38, 19/39, 19/40, 19/41, 20/9, 21/4, 21/6, 22/37, 24/42, 24/43, 27/29; cf. §14.1 [relative pron., m.] (he) who, which, that (corresponding [f.] is *sōei*, [n.] is *þatei*. See also *þisƕazuh saei*, *nist saei*, *saƕazuh saei*)

þáiei 10/16, 10/20 [N pl.]

saggws [m. ⟨*i*⟩] song, music

saggwins 13/25 [A pl.]

sah (= *sa*² + *-h*) 14/19, 17/41, 22/40; cf. §14.2 [emphatic demonstrative pron., m.] he (she, it) especially

saƕazuh saei (= *sa*² + *ƕazuh saei*) 19/37; cf. §19.2d [indef. pron., m.] whosoever

sái (?*saí*) 2/4, 2/6, 2/7, 4/8, 5/9, 6/5, 8/7, 8/8, 9/3, 13/29, 17/41, 24/35, 25/6, 27/28 [interjection] lo!

saian (or *saijan*) cf. §6.1 [VIIb] sow

saiada 10/15 [3 sg. pass. pres.]

saiand 18/26 [3 pl. pres.]

saijiþ 10/14 [3 sg. pres.]

saísō 9/4 [3 sg. pret.]

saianans 10/16, 10/18, 10/20 [past part., m. N pl., of *saian*] sown

saiands (or *saijands*) 9/3, 10/14 [pres. part., m., of *saian*] sower

saíhstō 24/33 [num., f.] sixth

saíƕan 21/1; cf. §5.1 [Vb] see

saíƕam 24/36, 26/12 [1 pl. pres.]

saíƕiþ 21/4, 21/6 [3 sg. pres.]

sēƕum 19/38 [1 pl. pret.]

sēƕun 24/47 [3 pl. pret.]

saíƕans 5/9 [past. part., m., of *saíƕan*] seen

saíƕandeins 24/40 [f. N pl.]

saijand (see *saian*)

saijands (see *saiands*)

saijiþ [3 sg. pres. of *saian* 'sow,' q.v.]

sáir 3/9 [n. ⟨*o*⟩] sorrow

sáiwala¹ 18/25 [f. ⟨*ā*⟩] soul, life, spirit

sáiwala² 16/11, 16/15 [A sg.]

sáiwalái 18/25 [D sg.]

sakan cf. §5.1 [VI: + D] rebuke

sōk 5/7 [3 sg. pret.]

sakans 6/8 [past part., m., of *sakan*] rebuked

salbōn cf. §§7.1, 10.2, 12.1, 14.3, 21.1 [ii] anoint

saljan 28/7 [i] make an offering

Salōme 24/40, 25/1 [f.] Salome

sama [adj., n. ⟨*n*⟩] same

samō 15/46, 15/47 [A sg.]

samaleikō 10/16, 20/11 [adv.] in like manner, likewise

samana 11/13, 27/4 [adv.] together

samō [A sg. of *sama* 'same,' q.v.]

sandjandan 19/37 [pres. part., m. A sg., of *sandjan*, i] sending

Satanas 10/15 Satan

Saúlaúmōn 18/29 Solomon

saúrga [f. ⟨*ā*⟩] sorrow, care

saúrgōs 10/19 [N pl.]

saúrgan [iii] be concerned, be anxious

saúrgáiþ 18/28 [2 pl. pres.]

sáuþs* [m. ⟨*i*⟩] sacrifice

sáuþ [A sg.] (see *jas-sáuþ*)

sēƕum [1 pl. pret. of *sáiƕan* 'see,' q.v.]

sēƕun [3 pl. pret. of *saíƕan* 'see,' q.v.]

sei (shortened form of *sōei*)

11/12, 27/24 [relative pron., f.] (she) who, which
Seimōn [m.] Simon
Seimōna 23/21 [A sg.]
Seimōnis (or *-náus*) 8/9, 20/8 [G sg.]
Seimōnu 8/2 [A sg.]
sein [possessive, n. (referring to the subject of its own clause)] its, its own
sein (or *seinata*) 11/12, 11/13 [A sg.] (see also *ni sōkeiþ . . .*)
seina[1] 15/45 [possessive, f. (referring to the subject of its own clause)] her, her own
seina[2] 16/11, 21/5 [A sg.]
seinái 19/41, 21/7 [D sg.]
seináizōs [G sg.] (see *háiþjōs seináizōs*)
seins* [possessive, m. (referring to the subject of its own clause)] his, his own
seináim 12/22, 20/12 [D pl.]
seináizē 28/3 [G pl.]
seina 21/2 [N pl.]
seinamma 9/3, 12/20, 15/22, 18/29 [D sg.]
seinana 17/41, 18/27 [A sg.]
seinis [G sg.] (see *kunjis seinis*)
sēls 26/4 [m. ⟨*i/jo*⟩] kind, good
si 7/6, 7/9; cf. §7.3 [personal pron., f.] she
ija[1] 7/3, 7/8 [A sg.]
ijōs 7/10, 25/8 [A pl.]
izái 7/10, 7/12, 17/55, 25/11 [D sg.]
izō 7/11 [G pl.]
izōs 7/7, 17/54, 17/55, 17/56 [G sg.]

sibakþanei (see *aílōē . . .*)
sibun 25/9 [num.] seven
sijái [3 sg. pres. opt. of *wisan* 'be,' q.v.]
sijáima [1 pl. pres. opt. of *wisan* 'be,' q.v.]
sijáiþ [2 pl. pres. opt. of *wisan* 'be,' q.v.]
sijuþ [2 pl. pres. of *wisan* 'be,' q.v.]
sik 27/17; cf. §7.3 [general reflexive pron., A] (see also *gahaftjan sik*, *gawasjan sik*, *idreigōn sik*, *skaman sik*)
sis 10/17, 12/17, 19/34, 25/3, 25/8 [D] (see also *mundōn sis*)
silba 20/6, 24/43, 27/15 [m.] himself
silbin 22/34 [D sg.]
sildaleikjan [i] wonder, marvel
sildaleikida 24/44 [3 sg. pres.]
sind [3 pl. pres. of *wisan* 'be,' q.v.]
sineigs cf. §18.1 old
sinista cf. §18.1 [superlative of *sineigs*, q.v.]
sinteinō 13/31 [adv.] always
sinteins [adj., m. ⟨*o*⟩] daily
sinteinan 1/11 [A sg.]
sipōneis [m. ⟨*jo*⟩] disciple
sipōnjam 20/12, 25/7 [D pl.]
sipōnjē 20/8 [G pl.]
sipōnjōs 5/2, 6/2, 7/13 [N pl.]
sis [D of *sik*, general reflexive pron., q.v.]
sitands 19/35 [pres. part., m., of *sitan*, V] sitting
sitandan 25/5 [A sg.]
siukei [f. ⟨*n*⟩] sickness
siukeins 8/12 [A pl.]
siuns [f. ⟨*i*⟩] sight, appearance

siunái [D sg.] (see *warþ... in siunai*)
skáidan cf. §6.1 [VIIa] sever
skal [1 sg. pres. of *skulan* 'owe, must,' q.v.]
skalkinōn 18/24 [ii] serve
  skalkinōda 13/29 [1 sg. pres.]
skalks [m. ⟨*o*⟩] servant
  skalkam 12/22 [D pl.]
skaman sik [iii] be ashamed
  skamáida sik 7/10 [3 sg. pret.]
skatts [m. ⟨*o*⟩] a coin, denarius
  skattē 20/7 [G pl.]
skip [n. ⟨*o*⟩] ship, boat
  skipam 8/2 [D pl.]
skuggwā [m. ⟨*n*⟩] mirror, glass
  skuggwan 26/12 [A sg.]
skula [m. ⟨*n*⟩] debtor (see *skula waírþiþ*)
  skulam 1/12 [D pl.]
skula waírþiþ 15/21, 15/22 is liable
skulan* cf. §16.2 [pret. pres.] owe, must
  skal 16/16 [1 sg. pres.]
  skulda 4/10 [1 sg. pret.]
skulans 1/12 [pres. part., m., of *skulan**] owing
skuld wisan 7/5, 13/32 [verb phr.] be proper or lawful (impersonal)
skulda [1 sg. pret. of *skulan** 'owe, must,' q.v.]
slahan [VI] strike
  slōhun 23/19 [3 pl. pret.]
slawan [iii] be silent
  slawáidēdun 19/34 [3 pl. pret.]
slēpan cf. §6.1 [VIIa] sleep
  slēpiþ 17/52 [3 sg. pres.]
slōhun [3 pl. pret. of *slahan* 'strike,' q.v.]
smwrna 23/33 [D sg.] myrrh (from Gk. σμύρνα, of Semitic origin)
sneiþan [I] cut, reap
  sneiþand 17/26 [3 pl. pres.]
sniwan cf. §5.3 [Va] hasten
  snáu 5/1 [3 sg. pret.]
  snēwun 5/4 [3 pl. pret.]
sō[1] 6/3, 7/3, 7/7, 8/8, 8/10, 21/4, 22/35, 22/38, 24/40, 24/47, 25/1; cf. §6.3 [definite article, f.] the
  þizái[1] 6/4, 6/6, 6/11, 8/6, 23/15, 23/20, 25/9 [D sg.]
  þizō[1] 6/10, 14/19 [G pl.]
  þizōs[1] 17/51, 27/19, 27/30 [G sg.]
  þō[1] 6/2, 6/10, 8/9, 8/10, 12/22, 27/24 [A sg.]
  þōs[1] 6/9, 21/12 [A pl.]
  þōs[2] 26/13 [N pl.]
sō[2] 17/42 [demonstrative (or personal) pron., f.] this, that, she (he, it) (see also *sōh*)
  þizái[2] p. xvii, 10/20 [D sg.]
  þizō[2] 26/13 [G pl.]
  þizōs[2] 10/19 [G sg.]
  þō[2] 17/52 [A sg.]
  þōs[3] 23/34 [A pl.]
sōei (= *sō* + *-ei*, spelling varies with *sei*, q.v.) [relative pron., f.] (she) who, which, that
  þáimei 24/40 [D pl.]
  þizáiei 25/9 [G pl.]
  þōzei 24/41 [N pl.]
sōh (= *sō* + *-uh*) 25/10; cf. §14.2 [emphatic demonstrative pron., f.] she (he, it) especially
sōk [3 sg. pret. of *sakan* 'rebuke,' q.v.]
sōkjan cf. §§10.2, 12.1, 21.1 [i] seek, argue
  sōkeiþ[1] [3 sg. pres.] (see *ni sōkeiþ . . .*)

sōkeiþ[2] 25/6 [2 pl. pres.]
sōkjái 27/2 [3 sg. pres. opt.]
sōkjand 18/32 [3 pl. pret.]
spaíkulatur [m.] executioner
spaíkulatur 7/11 [A sg.]
spinnan [III] spin
spinnand 18/28 [3 pl. pres.]
spráutō 12/22, 19/39 [adv.] quickly
stáiga [f. ⟨*ā*⟩] path
stáigōs 6/3 [A pl.]
stáinahs cf. §28.7f [adj., ⟨*o*⟩] stony, stony (spot)
stáinahamma 9/5, 10/16 [D sg.]
stáins 25/4 [m. ⟨*o*⟩] stone
stáin 24/46, 25/3 [A sg.]
stáina 6/7, 24/46 [D sg.]
stáirō 28/2 [f. ⟨*n*⟩] barren woman
standands 28/12 [pres. part., m., of *standan*, VI] standing
standandans 21/5 [N pl.]
staþs (or *-ds*) 23/22, 25/6; cf. §9.1 [m. ⟨*i*⟩] place
stada 20/10 [D sg.]
staþ 23/22, 25/6 [A sg.]
staua [f. ⟨*wā*⟩] judgment, sentence
stauái 15/21, 15/22, 27/7 [D sg.]
steigan cf. §4.2 [Ia] ascend
stibna[1] 6/3 [f. ⟨*ā*⟩] voice
stibna[2] [A sg.] (see *lētands stibna . . .*)
stibnái 24/34 [D sg.]
stibnōs 16/16, 22/37 [G sg.]
stikls [m. ⟨*o*⟩] cup
stikla 19/41 [D sg.]
stiur 12/23, 13/27, 13/30 [m. ⟨*o*⟩] calf, steer
stōjan cf. §7.1 judge
striks 14/18 [m.] tittle, bit
sum 9/4, 9/7, 9/8 [indef. pron., n. ⟨*o*⟩] some, one
sumái 24/35 [N pl.]
sumamma 11/15 [D sg.]
sumana 13/26, 19/38, 23/21 [A sg.]
suman 26/9 [adv.] in part (from A sg. of *sum*)
sums 11/11, 17/49; cf. §11.1 [indef. pron., m. ⟨*o*⟩] a certain one, some, someone
sunja 22/38 [f. ⟨*ā*⟩] truth
sunjái 22/37, 26/6, 27/27 [D sg.] (see also *bi sunjái*)
sunjōs 22/37 [G sg.]
sunnō [f./n. ⟨*n*⟩] sun
sunnin 9/6, 25/2 [f. D sg.]
sunnōn 15/45 [n. A sg.]
suns 8/7, 9/5, 10/15, 10/16, 10/17, 17/55 [adv.] at once, soon
sunus 11/13, 12/19, 12/21, 12/24, 13/25, 13/30, 24/39; cf. §9.3 [m. ⟨*u*⟩] son
sunjus 15/45 [N pl.]
sunu 28/19 [A sg.]
sununs 11/11 [A pl.]
swa 13/29, 14/19, 18/30, 20/9, 24/39 [adv.] so, thus
swa filu swē 20/11 as much as
swaíhrō 8/9 [f. ⟨*n*⟩] mother-in-law
swaláuþs cf. §15.4 so great
swaleiks cf. §15.4 [adj., n. ⟨*o*⟩] such
swaleikáizē 19/37 [G pl.]
swalt [3 sg. pret. of *swiltan* 'be dying,' q.v.]
swamm* [m.] sponge
swam 24/36 [A sg.]
swarē 15/22 [adv.] without cause, in vain
swaswē (= *swa* + *swē*) 1/12, 5/6,

15/48, 16/15, 20/10, 21/2, 21/5, 21/7, 25/7, 26/2, 26/12 [adv.] as, even as, about, just as

swē[1] 12/19, 17/42, 18/29, 26/11 [adv.] like, as, approximately

swē[2] 1/10 [cj.] as (see also *swa filu swē*)

swein [n. ⟨*o*⟩] swine, pig

sweina[1] 11/16 [N pl.]

sweina[2] 11/15 [A pl.]

swēs [n. ⟨*o*⟩] possessions, property, one's own

swēs[1] 11/12, 11/13, 13/30 [A sg.]

swēs[2] [adj., ⟨*o*⟩] own

swēsa 16/12 [n. N pl.]

swēsáim 23/20 [f. D pl.]

swiltan [III] be dying

swalt 17/42 [3 sg. pret.]

swnagōgē* [f.] synagogue (from Gk. *συναγωγή*)

swnagōgáis 17/41 [G sg.]

swnagōgeis 17/49 [D sg.]

tagr [n. ⟨*o*⟩] tear

tagra 3/9 [N pl.]

taíhswa [adj., f. ⟨*o*⟩] right

taíhswái 26/5 [D sg.]

taíhswō 21/3 [f. ⟨*n*⟩] right (hand), right (side)

taíhswōn 23/27, 28/12 [D sg.]

táinjō [f. ⟨*n*⟩] basket

táinjōns 20/13 [A pl.]

taui cf. §3.3 [n. ⟨*jo*⟩] deed, work

tōja 3/6 [A pl.]

táujan 21/1; cf. §17.1 [i] do, make (see also *þatei habáida . . .*)

táujáis 21/2 [2 sg. pres. opt.]

táujáiþ [2 pl. pres. opt.] (see *wáila táujáiþ*)

táujand 15/46, 15/47, 21/2 [3 pl. pres.]

táujáu 23/12 [1 sg. pres. opt.] (see also *ni waíht...*)

táujiþ 14/19, 15/47, 19/39, 21/3 [3 sg. pres.]

táujandan 21/3 [pres. part., m. D sg., of *táujan*] doing, making

tigus* [num.] decade, ten

tiguns [A pl.] (see *fidwōr. . .)*

tiuhan cf. §4.2 [IIb] lead

tōja [A pl. of *taui* 'deed,' q.v.]

tuggō cf. §8.1 [f. ⟨*n*⟩] tongue

tuggōnō 8/12 [G pl.]

twa cf. §20.1 [num., n. pl.] two

twa 3/5, 24/38 [n. A pl.]

twáim 18/24 [m. D pl.]

twans 11/11, 23/27 [m. A pl.]

twáim hundam skattē [adj. phr.] for (= costing) two hundred denarii

twalibē [G pl. of *twalif* 'twelve,' q.v.]

twalibwintrus 4/1 [compound adj., m. ⟨*u*⟩] twelve years old

twalif (or *-ib*) 19/35 [num.] twelve

twalibē 17/42 [G pl.]

twans [m. A pl. of *twa* 'two,' q.v.]

þagkjan cf. §17.2 think

þái[1] 2/8, 2/10, 2/14, 4/3, 4/5, 9/7, 15/46, 21/2, 21/5, 21/7 [m. N pl. of *sa*[1] 'the,' q.v.]

þái[2] 10/15, 10/16, 10/18, 10/19, 10/20, 20/5 [m. N pl. of *sa*[2] 'this, that, he,' q.v.]

þáiei [m. N pl. of *saei* '(he) who,' q.v.]

þáih [3 sg. pret. of *þeihan* 'thrive,' q.v.]

þáim[1] 2/5, 2/9, 3/2, 4/6, 8/8, 15/21, 15/44, 20/11, 20/13, 25/10 [D pl. of *sa*[1] 'the,' q.v.]

þáim[2] 1/12, 5/7, 18/26, 20/7, 21/8 [D pl. of *sa*[2] 'this, that, he,' q.v.]

þáim[3] 16/12 [D pl. of *þata*[1] 'the,' q.v.]

þáimei [f. D pl. of *sōei* '(she) who,' q.v.]

þaírh 3/6, 26/12 [prep., + A] through

þamma[1] 2/5, 6/7, 8/7, 20/10, 22/36, 24/45 [D sg. of *sa*[1] 'the,' q.v.]

þamma[2] 8/6, 21/1, 21/6, 22/37, 22/38 [D sg. of *sa*[2] 'this, that, he,' q.v.]

þamma[3] 1/13, 3/7, 3/8, 4/7, 5/5, 5/8, 24/46, 25/2, 25/8 [D sg. of *þata*[1] 'the,' q.v.]

þammei[1] (= *þamma*[2] + *-ei*) 23/12 [D sg. of *saei*[2] '(he) who,' q.v.]

þammei[2] (= *þamma*[2] + *-ei*) 20/5, 25/4 [relative pron. functioning as cj.] that

þan 2/9, 6/9, 7/1, 9/6, 10/15, 10/16, 11/14, 12/17, 12/20, 12/22, 13/30, 17/42, 17/51, 17/52, 18/29, 19/38, 20/6, 20/10, 20/11, 21/2, 21/5, 21/6, 22/40, 23/25, 24/36, 24/39, 24/41, 24/44, 25/9, 26/11, 26/12, 28/4, 28/11, 28/15 [adv./cj.] then, when (see also *þanuh*, *wasuþ-þan*, *wēsun-uþþan*, *bidjandsuþþan*, *diz-uh-þan-sat*, *anþaruþ-þan*)

þana [A sg. of *sa*[1] 'the,' q.v.]

þanaseiþs ni 12/19, 12/21 [adv.] no longer

þandē 18/30 [cj.] if

þans [A pl. of *sa*[1] 'the,' q.v.]

þanuh (= *þan* + *-uh*) 13/28, 17/54, 20/12, 20/13, 22/38 [adv./cj.] (and) then

þar [adv.] there

þarei (= *þar* + *-ei*) 9/5, 10/15, 25/6 [adv.] where

þaruh (= *þar* + *-uh*) 13/27, 13/29, 13/31, 17/52, 20/5, 20/10, 22/37, 25/6, 25/7 [adv.] (and) there, thereupon, therefore

þata[1] 4/11, 10/15, 13/31; cf. §3.1 [definite article, n.] the

- **þáim**[3] 16/12 [D pl.]
- **þamma**[3] 1/13, 3/7, 3/8, 4/7, 5/5, 5/8, 24/46, 25/2, 25/8 [D sg.]
- **þata**[2] 3/2, 3/4, 3/5, 4/3, 5/3, 7/12, 10/16, 10/19, 10/20, 11/13, 15/46, 15/47, 17/56, 18/30, 23/28, 24/45, 25/5 [A sg.]
- **þō**[3] 3/6, 7/6, 16/12, 16/15 [A pl.]

þata[3] 7/5, 13/26, 20/9 [demonstrative pron., n.] this, that, it (he, she)

- **þata**[4] 6/11, 9/4, 9/7, 18/32, 22/34, 22/38, 27/22 [A sg.] (see also *þatuh*)
- **þis**[3] 10/17, 16/16, 24/43, 24/46, 25/3 [G sg.] (see also *inuh þis*)
- **þizē**[2] 3/10, 19/37 [G pl.] (see also *ni karist*...)
- **þizei**[2] 21/8 [G sg.] (see also *in þizei*)
- **þō**[4] 16/14 [N pl.]
- **þō**[5] 16/12, 16/16 [A pl.]

þatáinei (= *þata*[1] + *áin* + *-ei*) 5/6, 15/47, 17/50 [adv.] only

þatei (= *þata*[3] + *-ei*) 1/12, 4/5, 4/6, 4/7, 8/1, 13/27, 14/18, 14/20, 15/21, 15/22, 15/43,

17/49, 17/53, 18/29, 18/32, 20/13, 21/5, 23/16, 23/22, 24/34, 24/39, 24/46, 25/7, 25/11, 26/10; cf. §14.1 [cj. or relative pron., n.] that, who, which (see also *þei*, *hva þatei*)

þōei[1] 16/16 [N pl.]

þōei[2] 11/16 [A pl.]

þatei habáida táujan 20/6 what he was to do

þatuh (= *þata*[4] + *uh*) 20/6; cf. §14.2 [emphatic demonstrative pron., A sg.] it especially

þaþrō 22/36 [adv.] from there, thence, from then on

þaþrōh (= *þaþrō* + *-h*) 10/17 [adv.] afterward

þáu[1] 14/20 [adv.] than

þáu[2] 22/34 [cj.] or

þaúrban* cf. §16.2 [pret. pres.] need, be in want

þaúrbuþ 18/32, 21/8 [2 pl. pres.]

þaúrneins [f. ⟨*o*⟩] made of thorns

þaúrneina 23/17 [A sg.]

þaúrnus [m. ⟨*u*⟩] thorn

þaúrnjus 9/7 [N pl.]

þaúrnuns 9/7, 10/18 [A pl.]

þei[1] (shortened form of *þatei*] 18/26 [relative pron., n.] who

þei[2] (shortened form of *þatei*) 20/7, 20/12 [cj.] so that

þeihan [Ib] thrive

þáih 4/11 [3 sg. pret.]

þein[1] 1/9, 13/31 [possessive, n.] thy, thine

þein[2] 13/30 [n. A sg.]

þeina[1] 1/13, 17/49, 21/3, 21/4, 22/35, 28/18 [f. N sg.]

þeina[2] 13/29, 21/6 [f. A sg.]

þeinái 21/6 [f. D sg.]

þeináizē 12/19 [m. G pl.]

þeinamma[1] 12/18, 12/21, 19/38 [n. D sg.]

þeinamma[2] 21/6 [m. D sg.

þeinana 15/43 [m. A sg.]

þeinis 7/5 [m. G sg.]

þeins 1/10, 12/19, 12/21, 13/27, 13/30, 13/32, 21/4, 21/6 [m. N sg.]

þis[1] 2/8, 7/11, 8/6, 17/49, 24/40 [G sg. of *sa*[1] 'the,' q.v.]

þis[2] 15/45 [G sg. of *sa*[2] 'this, that, he,' q.v.]

þis[3] 10/17, 16/16, 24/43, 24/46, 25/3 [G sg. of *þata*[3] 'this, that, it,' q.v.] (see also *inuh þis*).

þis dagis afarsabbatē 25/2 [adv. phr.] on the first day of the week

þishvah þei cf. §20.2b [indef. pron., n.] whatsoever

þishvazuh saei cf. §20.2a [indef. pron., m.] whosoever

þiuda 22/35 [f. ⟨*ā*⟩] people, nation (pl. = 'Gentiles')

þiudō 15/46, 21/7 [G pl.]

þiudōs 18/32 [N pl.]

þiudan[1] 2/10, 22/39, 23/12 [A sg. of *þiudans* 'king,' q.v.]

þiudan[2] 23/18 [Voc. sg. of *þiudans* 'king,' q.v.]

þiudanam [D pl. of *þiudans* 'king,' q.v.]

þiudanē [G pl. of *þiudans* 'king,' q.v.]

þiudangardi 1/13, 22/36 [f.⟨*jā*⟩] kingdom

þiudangardja 6/10 [A sg.]

þiudangardjái 14/19, 14/20 [D sg.]

þiudangardjō 6/9, 6/10 [G pl.]

þiudangardjōs[1] 6/9 [A pl.]

þiudangardjōs[2] 24/43 [G sg.]

þiudans 2/7, 2/14, 3/3, 7/8, 22/33,

22/37, 23/26 [m. ⟨*o*⟩] king
þiudan[1] 2/10, 22/39, 23/12 [A sg.]
þiudan[2] 23/18 [Voc. sg.]
þiudanam 3/2 [D pl.]
þiudanē 2/7, 2/13, 2/14 [G pl.]
þiudanis 2/1 [G sg.]
þiudanōs 2/12, 2/14 [N pl.]

þiudinassus 1/10 [m. ⟨*u*⟩] reign, principality

þiudō [G pl. of *þiuda*, q.v.] Gentiles

þiudōs [N pl. of *þiuda*, q.v.] Gentiles

þius* [m. ⟨*wo*⟩] servant
þiwōs 2/13 [N pl.]

þiuþjan [i] bless
þiuþjáiþ 15/44 [2 pl. pres.]

þiwi cf. §6.3 [f. ⟨*a*⟩] handmaid

þizái[1] 6/4, 6/6, 6/11, 8/6, 23/15, 23/20, 25/9 [D sg. of *sō*[1] 'the,' q.v.]

þizái[2] p. xvii, 10/20 [D sg. of *sō*[2] 'this, that, she,' q.v.]

þizáiei (= *þizái* + -*ei*) [G pl. of *sōei* '(she) who, which, that,' q.v.]

þizē[1] 2/13, 14/20, 18/29, 20/8, 20/11, 24/35 [G pl. of *sa*[2] 'this, that, he,' q.v.]

þizē[2] 3/10, 19/37 [G pl. of *þata*[3] 'this, that, it,' q.v.] (see also *ni karist . . .*)

þizei[1] 2/10, 16/12, 17/41 [G sg. of *sa*[2] 'this, that, he,' q.v.]

þizei[2] 21/8 [G sg. of *þata*[3] 'this, that, it,' q.v.] (see also *in þizei*)

þizō[1] 6/10, 14/19 [G pl. of *sō*[1] 'the,' q.v.]

þizō[2] 26/13 [G pl. of *sō*[2] 'this, that, she,' q.v.]

þizōs[1] 17/51, 27/19, 27/30 [G sg. of *sō*[1] 'the,' q.v.]

þizōs[2] 10/19 [G sg. of *sō*[2] 'this, that, she,' q.v.]

þliuhan [II] flee
þlaúhun 3/8 [3 pl. pret.]
þliuh 3/7 [2 sg. imper.]
þliuhiþ[1] 16/12 [3 sg. pres.]
þliuhiþ[2] 5/7 [2 pl. imper.]

þō[1] 6/2, 6/10, 8/9, 8/10, 12/22, 27/24 [A sg. of *sō*[1] 'the,' q.v.]

þō[2] 17/52 [A sg. of *sō*[2] 'this, that, she,' q.v.]

þō[3] 3/6, 7/6, 16/12, 16/15 [A pl. of *þata*[1] 'the,' q.v.]

þō[4] 16/14 [N pl. of *þata*[3] 'this, that, it,' q.v.]

þō[5] 16/12, 16/16 [A pl. of *þata*[3] 'this, that, it,' q.v.]

þōei[1] 16/16 [N pl. of *þatei* 'that, who, which,' q.v.]

þōei[2] 11/16 [A pl. of *þatei* 'that, who, which,' q.v.]

þōs[1] 6/9, 20/12 [A pl. of *sō*[1] 'the,' q.v.]

þōs[2] 26/13 [N pl. of *sō*[1] 'the,' q.v.]

þōs[3] 23/24 [A pl. of *sō*[2] 'this, that, she,' q.v.]

þōzei (= *þōs* + -*ei*) [N pl. of *sōei* '(she) who,' q.v.]

þragjands 12/20, 24/36 [pres. part., m., of *þragjan*, i] rushing, running

þreihan [I] crowd, press upon
þraíhun 17/42 [3 pl. pret.]

þreis* cf. §20.1 [num.] three
þrins 4/6, 4/8 [m. A pl.]

þridjō 23/25 [num., f.] third

þrins [m. A pl. of *þreis* 'three,' q.v.]

þu 1/9, 13/31, 21/6, 22/33, 22/34, 22/37; cf. §13.3 [personal pron.] thou
izwara 18/27, 21/1 [G pl.]
izwis[1] 14/18, 14/20, 15/22, 18/25, 18/29, 19/33, 19/41,

21/2, 21/5, 22/39, 25/7 [D pl.]
izwis[2] 15/44, 15/46, 18/30, 19/40 [A pl.]
jus 15/48, 18/26, 21/8 [N pl.]
þuk 21/3, 22/35 [A sg.]
þus 13/29, 21/2, 21/4, 21/6, 22/34, 28/16, 28/19 [D sg.]

þugkjan cf. §17.2 [i] seem
þugkeiþ 21/7 [3 sg. pres.]

þuk [A sg. of *þu* 'thou,' q.v.]

þulan [iii] endure, bear
þuláiþ 26/7 [3 sg. pres.]

þus [D sg. of *þu* 'thou,' q.v.]

þūsundi [f. ⟨*jā*⟩] thousand
þūsundjōs 20/10 [N pl.]

þuthaúrnjandō 26/1 [pres. part., n., of *þuthaúrnjan*, i] sounding, trumpeting

þwmiama [m.] incense (from Gk. *θυμίαμα*)
þwmiamins 28/10, 28/13 [G sg.]

-u 15/46, 15/47, 18/25, 18/26 (*niu*); 22/34 (*abu*); 22/39 (*wileidu*); 24/36 (*qimáiu*) [interrog. clitic]

ubils cf. §18.1 [m.⟨*o*⟩] evil
ubil 26/5 [A sg.]
ubilans 15/45 [A pl.]
ubilin 1/13 [D sg.]
ubilis 23/14 [G sg.]

ubilwaúrdjan 19/39 [i: + D] speak evil of

uf 27/6 [prep., + D, or + A in other texts] under, below, in the reign of

ufar 18/26, 18/32 [prep., + D] over, above, beyond

ufarassus [m. ⟨*u*⟩] abundance, crowd
ufarassáu 12/17 [D sg.]

ufargaggan [VII] transgress
ufariddja 13/29 [1 sg. pret.]

ufarmēli 23/26 [n. ⟨*jo*⟩] superscription

ufarmēliþ 23/26 [past part., n., of *ufarmēljan*, i] written above

ufarsteigan [I] mount up
ufarstigun 9/7 [3 pl. pret.]

ufblēsan [VII] puff up
ufblēsada 26/4 [3 sg. pass. pres.]

ufbrann [3 sg. pret. of *ufbrinnan* 'scorch,' q.v.]

ufbrikan [IV: + D] reject
ufbrak 7/10 [3 sg. pret.]

ufbrinnan [III] scorch
ufbrann 9/6 [3 sg. pret.]

ufháusjan [i: + D] listen to, obey
ufháuseiþ 18/24 [3 sg. pres.]

ufkunnan [iii] know, recognize
ufkunna 26/12 [1 sg. pres.]
ufkunnada 26/12 [1 sg. pres. pass.]

ufsneiþan [I] slay
ufsnáist 13/30 [2 sg. pret.]
ufsneiþiþ 12/23 [2 pl. pres.]

-uh [clitic] and (in *frahuh*, *ƕarjizuh*, *ƕazuh*, *inuh þis*, *namuh*, *naúhþanuh*, *qaþuh*, *qiþiduh*, *qiþuh*, *saƕazuh saei*, *þanuh*, *þaruh*, *þatuh*, *wáituh*, and *wasuh*)
-uhu (see *anþaruþ-þan*, *bidjandansuþ-þan*, *diz-uh-þan-sat*, *wasuþ-þan*, *wēsunuþþan*)

unbrūks [m. ⟨*i*/*jo*⟩] useless
unbrūkjái 27/4 [N pl.]

und 3/5, 14/18, 24/33 [prep., + A] up to, until

und dalaþ 24/38 [adv. phr.] to the bottm

undgreipan [I] seize
undgripun 23/21 [3 pl. pret.]
undrinnan [III] fall to one's share
undrinnái 11/12 [3 sg. pres. opt.]
unhulþō [f. ⟨*n*⟩] unclean spirit, evil spirit
unhulþōn[1] 8/5 [A sg.]
unhulþōn[2] 8/6 [D sg.]
unhulþōns 8/12, 19/38, 25/9 [A pl.]
unkarja cf. §10.4 [substantive, m. ⟨*n*⟩] careless (one), careless person
unkarjans 10/15 [N pl.]
uns[1] 1/11, 1/12 [D pl. of *ik* 'I,' q.v.]
uns[2] 1/13, 19/38, 27/18 [A pl. of *ik* 'I,' q.v.]
unsar 1/9 [possessive, m.] our, ours
unsarái 27/14 [f. D sg.]
unsaráim 1/12 [m. D pl.]
unsarana 1/11 [m. A sg.]
unsibjis* [m. ⟨*jo*⟩] wicked
unsibjáim 23/28 [D pl.]
unsis[1] 25/3 [D pl. of *ik* 'I,' q.v.]
unsis[2] 19/38 [A pl. of *ik* 'I,' q.v.]
untē 1/13, 2/14, 3/3, 3/6, 3/10, 4/3, 5/6, 6/3, 6/10, 7/3, 9/6, 12/24, 13/27, 13/32, 15/45, 16/13, 17/42, 17/52, 19/38, 19/40, 19/41, 21/5, 24/42, 28/1 [cj.] for, because, until
untē allata waírþiþ 14/18 until everything is fulfilled
untē jabái... aíþþáu 18/24 for either... or
unwāhs [n. ⟨*o*⟩] blameless
unwąha 28/1 [N pl.]
urráis [3 sg. pret. of *urreisan* 'arise,' q.v.]
urráisjan [i] raise, rouse
urráisida 8/10 [3 sg. pret.]
urrann [3 sg. pret. of *urrinnan* 'go forth, spring up, rise, go out,' q.v.]
urrannjan [i] cause to come forth or rise
urranneiþ 15/45 [3 sg. pres.]
urreisan [I] arise
urráis 25/6 [3 sg. pret.]
urreis 17/54 [2 sg. imper.]
urrinnan [III] go forth, spring up, rise, go out
urrann 9/3, 9/5 [3 sg. pret.] (see also *hláuts imma*...)
urrinnandō 9/8 [pres. part., n., of *urrinnan*] going forth, springing up, rising, going out
urrinnandin 9/6, 25/2 [f. D sg.]
us 2/4, 3/7, 3/8, 6/4, 6/11, 8/6, 8/7, 20/13, 22/36, 24/46 [prep., + D] out of, from
us dáilái 26/10, 26/12 [adv. phr.] in part
usbaúhtēdun [3 pl. pret. of *usbugjan* 'buy,' q.v.]
usbeisneiga 26/4 [f. ⟨*o*⟩] long-suffering
usbliggwands 23/15 [pres. part., m., of *usbliggwan*, III] scourging
usbugjan [i] buy
usbaúhtēdun 25/1 [3 pl. pret.]
usbugjands 24/46 [pres. part., m., of *usbugjan*] buying
usdáudjan [i] strive
usdáudedideina 22/36 [3 pl. pret. opt.]
usdreibands 17/54 [pres. part., m., of *usdreiban*, I] putting out, driving out
usdreibandan 19/38 [m.

A sg.]
usfilmei 25/8 [f. ⟨*n*⟩] amazement
usfulljan 14/17 [i] fulfill
usfullnan [iv] be fulfilled
usfullnōda 23/28 [3 sg. pret.]
usgaggan [VII] go out, go forth, go away
usgagg 8/6 [2 sg. imper.]
usiddja 8/7 [3 sg. pret.]
usgaggands 13/28 [pres. part., m., of *usgaggan*] going out, going forth, going away
usgaggandeina 25/8 [f. N pl.]
usgeisnan [iv] be amazed
usgeisnōdēdun 17/56, 25/5 [3 pl. pret.]
usgiban [V] reward, give out, restore
usgibiþ 21/4, 21/6 [3 sg. pres.]
ushafjan [VI] lift up
ushōf 20/5 [3 sg. pret.]
ushramiþs 23/15 [past part., m., of *ushramjan*] crucified
ushramidan 25/6 [A sg.]
ushramjan [i] crucify
ushramei 23/13, 23/14 [2 sg. imper.]
ushramidēdeina 23/20 [3 pl. pret. opt.]
ushramidēdun 23/25, 23/27 [3 pl. pret.]
ushramjandans 23/24 [pres. part., m., of *ushramjan*] crucifying
usiddja [3 sg. pret. of *usgaggan* 'go out, go forth, go away,' q.v.]
usleiþan [I] pass away
usleiþiþ 14/18 [3 sg. pres.]
usliþa [substantive] a paralytic
usliþan 8/12 [m. A sg.]
usluneins* [f. ⟨*i/ā*⟩] redemption
uslunein 27/21 [A sg.]
usniman [IV] take away
usnam 8/12 [3 sg. pret.]
usnimiþ 10/15 [3 sg. pres.]
usnimands 24/46 [pres. part., m., of *usniman*] taking away
usqiman 3/4, 3/5, 3/6, 7/6 [IV] kill
usstandan [VI] rise up
usstandands 3/7, 12/18, 12/20, 25/9 [pres. part., m., of *usstandan*, VI] rising up
usstiuriba 11/13 [adv.] riotously
ustaúhan 26/10 [past part., n., of *ustiuhan*] led out, fulfilled, perfected
ustaúhana 27/24 [f. N sg.]
ustaúhans 4/3 [m. N sg.]
ustiuhan [IIb] lead out, fulfill, perfect
ustaúhun 4/2, 23/30 [3 pl. pret.]
usþriutandans 15/44 [pres. part., m. A pl., of *usþriutan*, II] abusing, troubling
uswaírpan [III] cast out, reject
uswarp 8/12, 25/9 [3 sg. pret.]
uswandjan [i] turn aside, go astray
uswandidēdun 27/3 [3 pl. pret.]
uswindandans 23/17 [pres. part., m. N pl., of *uswindan*, III] plaiting, weaving
ūt 8/6, 8/7, 13/28, 17/54, 22/38 [adv.] out, forth
ūta (or *uta*) 28/10 [adv.] outside
uzanan* [VI] expire
uzōn 24/37, 24/39 [3 sg. pret.]

wahsjan [VI] grow, increase
wahsjand 18/28 [3 pl. pres.]
wahsjandō 9/8 [pres. part., n., of *wahsjan*] growing, increasing
wahstus [m. ⟨*u*⟩] growth, size
wahstu 18/27 [A sg.]
wáidēdja 22/40 [m. ⟨*n*⟩] evil-doer, criminal, robber
wáidēdjans 23/27 [A pl.]
waíhsta [m. ⟨*n*⟩] corner
waíhstam 21/5 [D pl.]
waíht (see *ni waíht*)
waíhtái ni 20/12 [D sg.] nothing (literally "in nothing")]
waíhts 26/2 [f. ⟨*i*/*rt*⟩] thing
waíht 25/8 [A sg.] (see also *ni waíht bōtōs*...)
wáila (?*waíla*) 12/23, 13/32 [adv.] well
wáila táujáiþ 15/44 do good
waír 17/41, 26/11 [m.⟨*o*⟩] man
waírōs 2/10, 20/10 [N pl.]
waírpandans 23/24 [pres. part., m., of *waírpan*, III] throwing, casting
waírþan 8/3, 11/14, 27/26; cf. §§4.2, 24.1 [IIIb] become, be, happen
waírþái 1/10, 6/7 [3 sg. pres. opt.]
waírþáiþ 15/45 [2 pl. pres. opt.]
waírþand 16/16 [3 pl. pres.]
waírþiþ 10/19, 14/20, 28/20 [3 sg. pres.] (see also *skula waírþiþ*, *untē allata*...)
warþ[1] 26/1, 26/11 [1 sg. pret.]
warþ[2] 4/1, 4/3, 4/6, 6/6, 7/1, 9/4, 11/14, 12/24, 13/28, 13/32, 24/33, 25/11, 28/4 [3 sg. pret.] (see also *warþ* ... *in siunai*)
waúrþun 20/12, 27/5 [3 pl. pret.]
waírþs 12/19, 12/21 [m. ⟨*o*⟩] worthy
wáit[1] 26/12 [1 sg. pres. of *witan* 'know, possess knowledge,' q.v.]
wáit[2] 21/8 [3 sg. pres. of *witan* 'know, possess knowledge,' q.v.]
wáitei 22/35 [adv.] perhaps
wáituh (= *wáit* + *uh*) 18/32 and (he) knows
waldufni cf. §3.3 [n. ⟨*jo*⟩] authority
waldufneis 3/5 [G sg.]
waldufnja 8/8 [D sg.]
wann [3 sg. pret. of *winnan* 'sorrow,' q.v.]
warjan [i: + D] forbid
waridēdum 19/38 [1 pl. pret.]
warjit 19/39 [2 pl. imper.]
warþ[1] 26/1, 26/11 [1 sg. pret. of *waírþan* 'become, be, happen,' q.v.]
warþ[2] 4/1, 4/3, 4/6, 6/6, 7/1, 9/4, 11/14, 12/24, 13/28, 13/32, 24/33, 25/11, 28/4 [3 sg. pret. of *waírþan* 'become, be, happen,' q.v.]
warþ ... in siunai 28/11 [verb phr.] appeared, came into sight
was[1] 26/11 [1 sg. pret. of *wisan* 'be,' q.v.]
was[2] 2/14, 3/1, 3/10, 4/5, 4/6, 5/6, 5/8, 5/9, 6/1, 6/3, 6/4, 6/6, 6/8, 6/10, 7/3, 8/1, 8/5, 12/24, 13/32, 17/41, 22/40, 23/26, 23/28, 24/39, 24/40, 24/41, 24/42, 24/43, 24/46, 25/4, 28/2, 28/9 [3 sg. pret. of *wisan* 'be,' q.v.] (see also *ni kara* ..., *wasuh*, *wasuþ-þan*)
was imma 17/42 he had
wasjan [i] clothe, dress

wasjáima 18/31 [1 pl. pres. opt.]
wasjáiþ 18/25 [2 pl. pres. opt.]
wasjiþ 18/30 [3 sg. pres.]
wast [2 sg. pret. of *wisan* 'be,' q.v.]
wasti* [f. ⟨*jā*⟩] garment
wastja 12/22 [A sg.]
wastjái 25/5 [D sg.]
wastjōm 18/25, 23/20 [D pl.]
wastjōs 18/25, 23/24 [A pl.]
wasuh (= *was* + *uh*) 20/10, 23/25 and there was *or* and he was
wasuþ-þan (= *was* + *uh* + *þan*) 13/25 and (he) was . . . then
watō cf. §8.1 [n. ⟨*n*⟩] water
watins 19/41 [G sg.]
waúrd[1] 10/15; cf. §3.1 [n. ⟨*o*⟩] word
waúrd[2] 5/1, 5/3, 10/14, 10/15, 10/16, 10/18, 10/19, 10/20 [A sg.]
waúrda[1] 3/3 [D sg.]
waúrda[2] 5/5, 7/6 [A pl.]
waúrdis 10/17 [G sg.]
waúrkjan cf. §17.2 [i] work, make, prepare, arrange
waúrhta 7/7 [3 sg. pret.]
waúrkeiþ 20/10 [2 pl. imper.] (see also *raíhtōs waúrkeiþ*)
waúrts [f. ⟨*i*⟩] root
waúrtins 9/6, 10/17 [A pl.]
waúrþanamma 24/42 [past part., n. D sg., of *waírþan*] become
waúrþanō 17/56 [past part., n. A sg., of *waírþan*] happened
waúrþun [3 pl. pret. of *waírþan* 'be, become, happen,' q.v.]
weihnan [iv] be hallowed
weihnái 1/9 [3 sg. pres. opt.]
wein [n. ⟨*o*⟩] wine
wein 23/23 [A sg.]
weis [N pl. of *ik* 'I,' q.v.]
weitwōdjan [i] testify
weitwōdjáu 22/37 [1 sg. pres. opt.]
wēnjan [i] hope, expect
wēneiþ 26/7 [3 sg. pres.]
wēns 26/13 [f. ⟨*i*⟩] hope
wēsi [3 sg. pret. opt. of *wisan* 'be,' q.v.]
wēsjáu [1 sg. pret. opt. of *wisan* 'be,' q.v.]
wēsun [3 pl. pret. of *wisan* 'be,' q.v.]
wēsunuþþan (= *wēsun* + *uh* + *þan*) 24/40 and (there) were then
wigs [m. ⟨*o*⟩] way, road, journey
wig 2/10, 4/3, 9/4, 10/15 [A sg.]
wiga 19/33 [D sg.]
wigam 3/10 [D pl.]
wikō [f. ⟨*n*⟩] week
wikōn 28/5 [D sg.]
wilda [3 sg. pret. of *wiljan* 'will, desire,' q.v.]
wildēdi [3 sg. pret. opt. of *wiljan* 'will, desire,' q.v.]
wildēdun [3 pl. pret. opt. of *wiljan* 'will, desire,' q.v.]
wileidu (= *wileiþ* + *u*) 22/39 do you wish?
wileiþ [2 pl. pres. of *wiljan* 'will, desire,' q.v.]
wili [3 sg. pres. of *wiljan* 'will, desire,' q.v.]
wilja 1/10 [m. ⟨*n*⟩] will
wiljan cf. §19.1 will, wish, be willing, desire
wilda 3/4, 3/6, 7/6, 13/28 [3 sg. pret.]
wildēdi [3 sg. pret. opt.] (see *ƕis wildēdi*)
wildēdun 20/11 [3 pl. pret.

opt.]
wileiþ 23/12 [2 pl. pres.] (see also *wileidu*)
wili 19/35 [3 sg. pres.]
wiljands 23/15 [pres. part., m., of *wiljan*] wishing, desiring
winnan [IIIa] sorrow
wann 4/5 [3 sg. pret.]
wunnum 4/8 [1 pl. pret.]
wunnuþ 4/9 [2 pl. pret.]
wintrus [m. ⟨*u*⟩] winter, year (see *twalibwintrus*)
wintriwē 17/42 [G pl.]
wipja [f. ⟨*jā*⟩] crown
wipja 23/17 [A sg.]
wisan 4/3, 4/10, 12/24, 13/32, 19/35; cf. §§13.1, 16.1 [Va] be (homographic with *wisan* [V] 'feast')
im 12/19, 12/21, 16/11, 16/14, 22/35, 22/37, 26/2 [1 sg. pres.]
is[3] 13/32, 22/33 [2 sg. pres.]
ist 1/13, 2/6, 2/7, 5/9, 7/5, 13/31, 15/21, 15/43, 15/48, 16/13, 18/25, 19/39, 19/40, 20/9, 22/37, 22/38, 22/39, 23/16, 23/22, 24/34, 24/42, 25/4, 26/4, 26/10, 27/28, 28/17 [3 sg. pres.] (see also *nist*)
sijái 19/35, 21/4 [3 sg. pres. opt.]
sijáima 1/12 [1 pl. pres. opt.]
sijáiþ 15/48, 21/5 [2 pl. pres. opt.]
sijuþ 18/26, 19/41 [2 pl. pres.]
sind 10/15, 10/16, 10/17, 10/18, 10/20, 16/12, 16/16, 20/7 [3 pl. pres.]
was[1] 26/11 [1 sg. pret.]
was[2] 2/14, 3/1, 3/10, 4/5, 4/6, 5/6, 5/8, 5/9, 6/1, 6/3, 6/4, 6/6, 6/8, 6/10, 7/3, 8/1, 8/5, 12/24, 13/32, 17/41, 22/40, 23/26, 23/28, 24/39, 24/40, 24/41, 24/42, 24/43, 24/46, 25/4, 28/2, 28/9 [3 sg. pret.] (see also *wasuh*, *wasuþ-þan*, *was imma*, *ni kara . . .*)
wast 13/31 [2 sg. pret.]
wēsi 3/3, 5/5, 13/26, 19/34, 22/36, 23/15, 24/47 [3 sg. pret. opt.]
wēsjáu 22/36 [1 sg. pret. opt.]
wēsun 2/3, 3/9, 3/10, 5/3, 6/2, 8/2, 28/3 [3 pl. pret.] (see also *wēsunuþþan*)
wisam 12/23 [1 pl. pres.]
wisands 27/16 [pres. part., m., of *wisan*] being
wisandam [m. D pl.] (see *miþ imma wisandam*)
wisandan 12/20 [m. A sg.]
wisandō 11/13, 18/30 [n. A sg.]
wissa [1 sg. pret. of *witan* 'know,' q.v.]
witan cf. §16.2 [pret. pres.] know, possess knowledge
wáit[1] 26/12 [1 sg. pres.]
wáit[2] 21/8 [3 sg. pres.] (see also *wáituh*)
wissa 20/6 [3 sg. pret.]
witi 21/3 [3 sg. pres. opt.]
witjáu 26/2 [1 sg. pres. opt.]
witōþ cf. §3.1 [n. ⟨*o*⟩] law
witōda 3/5, 4/2, 14/18 [D sg.]
witōdis 4/4 [G sg.]
witōþ 14/17 [A sg.]

wiþra 10/15, 19/40 [prep., + A] against, near, beside, by (see also *andwaírþi wiþra andwaírþi*]
wiþrus 5/9, 27/28 [m. ⟨*u*⟩] lamb
wōpjan [i] call, cry out, crow
  wōpeiþ 24/35 [3 sg. pres.]
  wōpida 17/54, 22/33, 24/34 [3 sg. pret.]
wōpjandins 6/3 [pres. part., m. G sg., of *wōpjan*] of one crying
wrakja 10/17 [f. ⟨*jā*⟩] persecution
wrikandans 15/44 [pres. part., m. A pl., of *wrikan*, V] persecuting
wulfs 16/12 [m. ⟨*o*⟩] wolf
  wulf 16/12 [A sg.]
wulþáu [D sg. of *wulþus* 'splendor, glory,' q.v.]
wulþriza [adj.] (comparative of *wulþrs*) more valuable
  wulþrizans 18/26 [m. N pl.]
wulþus 1/13 [m. ⟨*u*⟩] splendor, glory
  wulþáu 18/29 [D sg.]
wunnum [1 pl. pret. of *winnan* 'sorrow,' q.v.]
wunnuþ [2 pl. pret. of *winnan* 'sorrow,' q.v.]

Xristus 2/6, 5/5 [m. ⟨*u*⟩] Christ
  Xristáus 19/41 [G sg.]

Zakarias 28/14 [m.] Zachariah
  Zakaria 28/26 [Voc. sg.]

SELECT BIBLIOGRAPHY

PHOTOGRAPHS AND REPRODUCTIONS OF MANUSCRIPTS

Bennett, William H. *The Gothic Commentary on the Gospel of John.* New York: Modern Language Association of America, 1960. Cod. E.

Codex Argenteus Upsaliensis Iussu Senatus Universitatis phototypice editus. Upsala, 1927. A penetrating study of the MS containing photographs taken under various light frequencies, especially filtered and unfiltered ultraviolet, with supplementary photographs of less decipherable pages.

Vries, Jan de. *Wulfilae Codices Ambrosiani rescripti epistularum evangelicarum textum goticum exhibentes, phototypice editi.* Florence, 1936. Codd. A-D.

COLLECTIVE EDITION

Streitberg, Wilhelm. *Die gotische Bibel.* Vol. I. 2nd ed. Heidelberg: Winter, 1919. Subsequently reprinted at intervals.

GRAMMARS

Braune, Wilhelm. *Gotische Grammatik.* 19th ed. Rev. Ernst A. Ebbinghaus. Tübingen: Niemeyer, 1981. Primarily descriptive, with an excellent cumulative bibliography.

Guxman, M. M. *Gotskij jazyk.* Moscow, 1958.

Hamel, Anton G. van. *Gotisch Handboek.* 2nd ed. Harlem: Tjeenk Willink, 1931.

Hempel, Heinrich. *Gotisches Elementarbuch.* 4th ed. Berlin: de Gruyter, 1966.

Jellinek, Max H. *Geschichte der gotischen Sprache*. Berlin and Leipzig: de Gruyter, 1926.

Kieckers, Ernst. *Handbuch der vergleichenden gotischen Grammatik*. 2nd ed. Munich: Hueber, 1960.

Krahe, Hans. *Historische Laut- und Formenlehre des Gotischen*. 2nd ed. Rev. Elmar Seebold. Heidelberg: Winter, 1967.

Krause, Wolfgang. *Handbuch des Gotischen*. 3rd ed. Munich: Beck, 1968.

Mossé, Fernand. *Manuel de la langue gotique*. 2nd ed. Paris: Montaigne, 1956.

Streitberg, Wilhelm. *Gotisches Elementarbuch*. 5th-6th ed. Heidelberg: Winter, 1920.

Wright, Joseph. *Grammar of the Gothic Language*. 2nd ed. With a supplement to the grammar by O. L. Sayce. Oxford: Clarendon, 1954.

Especially for syntax:

Balg, Gerhard H. *The First Germanic Bible*. Milwaukee, 1891.

Gabelentz, H. C. von der, and J. Loebe. *Ulfilas* II.2. Leipzig, 1843-46.

Streitberg, Wilhelm. *Gotisches Elementarbuch*. See above.

DICTIONARIES

Balg, Gerhard H. *The First Germanic Bible*. See above.

Streitberg, Wilhelm. *Die gotische Bibel*. Vol. II: *Gotisch-griechisch-deutsches Wörterbuch*. Heidelberg: Winter, 1928. Reprinted at intervals; see Collective Edition, above.

For etymologies:

Feist, Sigmund. *Vergleichendes Wörterbuch der gotischen Sprache*. 3rd ed. Leiden: Brill, 1939. A new edition is planned.

Pokorny, Julius. *Indogermanisches etymologisches Wörterbuch*. 2 vols. Bern and Munich: Francke, 1959 and 1965. Vol. II is Index.

INDICES AND LISTS OF WORDS

Tollenaere, Felicien de, and Randall L. Jones. *Word-Indices and Word-Lists to the Gothic Bible and Minor Fragments*. Leiden: Brill, 1976. Invaluable, correlated with Streitberg's *Gotische Bibel* as a point of reference.

BIBLIOGRAPHY

Mossé, Fernand. "Bibliographia Gotica." *Mediaeval Studies*, 12 (1950), 237-324. First supplement, 15 (1953), 169-83. Second supplement completed by J. W. Marchand, 19 (1957), 174-96. Subsequent supplements by Ernst A.

Ebbinghaus, 29 (1967), 327-43; 36 (1974), 199-214. To be continued at intervals. For interim publications see the annual *MLA International Bibliography*.

GENERAL INFORMATION

Scardigli, Piergiuseppe. *Die Goten: Sprache und Kultur*. Munich: Beck, 1973.

CRIMEAN GOTHIC

Stearns, MacDonald, Jr. *Crimean Gothic*. Saratoga, Calif.: Anma Libri, 1978.

INDEX